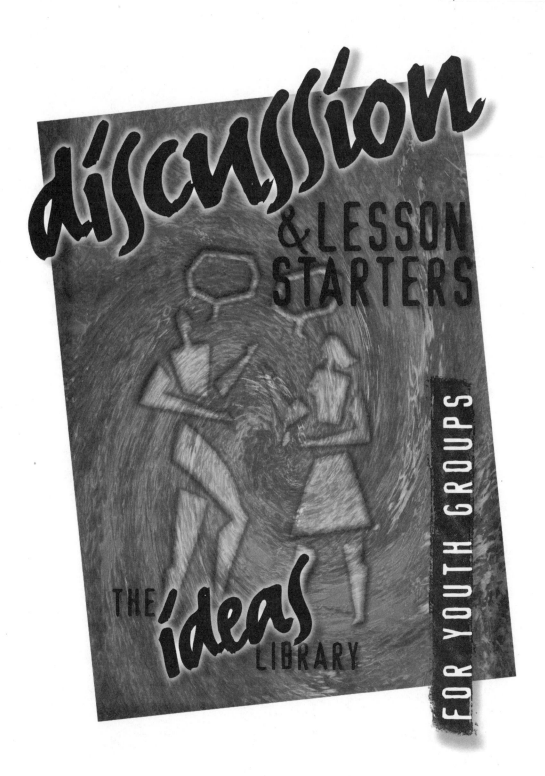

discussion & LESSON STARTERS

THE ideas LIBRARY

FOR YOUTH GROUPS

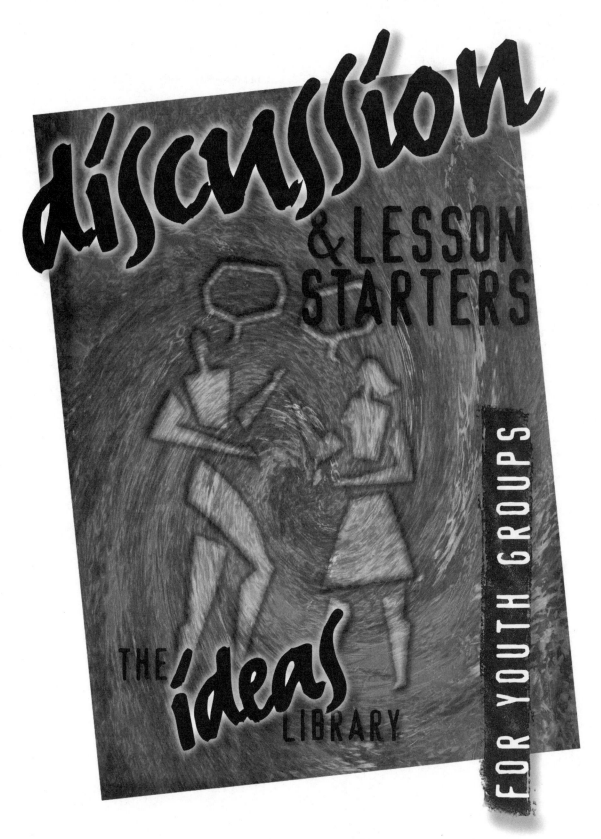

discussion & LESSON STARTERS

THE ideas LIBRARY

FOR YOUTH GROUPS

Youth Specialties

ZondervanPublishingHouse

Grand Rapids, Michigan
A Division of HarperCollinsPublishers

Discussion & Lesson Starters

Youth Specialties Books, 1224 Greenfield Dr., El Cajon, CA 92021, are published by Zondervan Publishing House, 5300 Patterson Ave. S.E., Grand Rapids, MI 49530.

Project editor: Vicki Newby
Cover and interior design: Curt Sell
Art director: Mark Rayburn
0-310-22034-3

CONTENTS

So what meeting starter have you used lately that snared your group's attention or launched furious discussion?

Are your kids still talking about that opener—the one with the live cat, a bag, and a seventh grade volunteer? Youth Specialties pays $25 (and in some cases, more) for unpublished, field-tested ideas that have worked for you.

You've probably been in youth work long enough to realize that sanitary, theoretical, tidy ideas aren't what in-the-trenches youth workers are looking for. They want—*you* want—imagination and take-'em-by-surprise novelty in meetings, parties, and other events. Ideas that have been tested and tempered and improved in the very real, very adolescent world you work in.

So here's what to do:

- Sit down at your computer, get your killer discussion or lesson starter out of your head and onto your hard drive, then e-mail it to ideas@youthspecialties.com. Or print it off and fax it to 619-440-4939 (Attn: Ideas).
- If you need to include diagrams, photos, art, or samples that help explain your idea, stick it all in an envelope and mail it to our street address: Ideas, 1224 Greenfield Dr., El Cajon, CA 92021-3399.
- Be sure to include your name and all your addresses and numbers.
- Let us have about three months to give your idea a thumbs up or down*, and a little longer for your 25 bucks.

*Hey, no offense intended if your idea isn't accepted. It's just that our fussy Ideas Library editor has these *really* meticulous standards. If the discussion or lesson starter isn't creative, original, and just plain fun in an utterly wild or delightful way, she'll reject it, (reluctantly, though, because she has a tender heart.) Sorry. But we figure you deserve only the best ideas.

ALPHABETICAL LIST
OF ALL IDEAS IN DISCUSSION AND LESSON STARTERS

THE IDEAS LIBRARY

Administration, Publicity, & Fundraising
Camps, Retreats, Missions, & Service Ideas
Creative Meetings, Bible Lessons, & Worship Ideas
Crowd Breakers & Mixers
Discussion & Lesson Starters
Discussion & Lesson Starters 2
Drama, Skits, & Sketches
Games
Games 2
Holiday Ideas
Special Events

A Primer on Leading Discussions

A Primer on Leading Discussions

Starting a discussion, and keeping it going...
the importance of confidentiality...asking questions that get responses...
and working with different personalities.

Starting a Discussion—and Keeping It Going

Consider these 10 tips for creating a comfortable small-group atmosphere—a necessary quality if you want all students to enjoy participating.

1. Encourage your students to verbalize their views and feelings, however unorthodox those thoughts may be.

Nothing stifles a discussion faster than when kids don't feel safe to say what they feel. Small groups should be a place where adolescents can be honest about what they're thinking and feeling—no matter what's on their mind. What students discover for themselves remains with them far longer than anything you tell them. Be slow to correct them, but, instead, let them think through their own responses. This is usually a better way for them to make genuine and lasting discoveries about God.

2. Be grateful for every answer.

Yes, every answer. Leaders can also stifle discussion by inadvertently making students feel silly or dumb about their responses and comments. Your job is to create a safe place for kids to say whatever they want—and be appreciated for it. Sure, if you work with seventh grade males, you'll need to gently redirect the tangents that pop up every three minutes. (Hmmm...seventh grade males...did we say gently?) But it's generally better to encourage freedom of speech. Your kids will trust you (and themselves) more.

3. Don't be satisfied with the first response to your question.

Avoid setting a question-answer-question-answer pattern. Here's a better way to start a discussion. Ask for several responses to your question, then provoke the speakers to dialogue with each other. That is, move them from merely answering toward discussing or conversing—with each other, not just with you. Start the ball rolling in this direction by asking "Why do you think that?" and "What do the rest of you think?"

4. Keep the discussion moving.

A Bible study that does not move along at a good pace tends to get dull. Notice when kids are starting to lose interest, then quickly move on to the next question. If you must choose your evils, choose frustrated students who wanted to spend more time resolving an issue—not bored students who have been gradually distancing themselves from the 30-minute discussion between you and one other student. Jesus, you remember, often left questions unanswered. It helps people think for themselves.

5. Be alert to the individuals in your group.

Be aware of what's going on with your kids as they come to your small group. In fact, you may want to reserve the first few minutes of your small group for small talk and sharing. During your Bible study, notice when a student begins speaking, but stops. Look beyond those who are monopolizing the discussion, and deliberately ask other, quieter students for their responses. You'll never stop some personalities from standing out in your group; others will insist on staying in the background. That's okay. Your goal is to make every student feel that he or she is an important member of your group, whether or not that person contributes a lot to the discussion.

6. Don't be afraid of silence.

If your question gets no immediate response from a student, don't feel you have to jump in and answer it yourself. Let the question linger in the air for a while. And let kids know this, too. In fact, silence is often an answer in itself—or can be a necessary prelude to a deeply felt response. Of course, if every question you ask is met with prolonged silence, you may need to take a hard look at the kinds of questions you're asking. (More on asking good questions in "Ask Questions That Get Responses" on page 5.)

7. Turn difficult questions back to the group.

If you're intimidated by a student with a tough question, join the crowd. Yet that very question, tough as it may be, can be give you a chance to get a lively discussion going. Don't think you have to try to answer it—try turning the question back to the group instead: "Whoa, good question. What do the rest of you think?" You may get some wild answers, but the students will be encouraged to think for themselves rather than to look to you for answers. If a question remains unresolved, now and then challenge your small group to find the answer by your next meeting. (A prize can add some motivation here.)

8. Let your group self-correct its tangents.

The technique of turning a question back to the group is also a remedy for wild tangents. Don't just tell the student that he or she is wrong—ask instead, "What do the rest of you think?" Chances are as students give their input, the group will correct itself. This also encourages your students to dialogue with each other instead of directing their dialogue toward you.

9. Stay flexible to the group's needs.

Sooner or later (usually sooner), a student will come to the small-group meeting with a specific, significant, and often immediate concern that needs to be addressed in the context of the small group. It may be an unresolved conflict between group members, a friend (perhaps there that night) who wants to know more about Christ, a recent death, an impending divorce. Now is the time to put aside your agenda and deal with the issue. This shouldn't happen every week, however. Leading a small group requires the judgment to decide when an issue is sufficiently critical that you need to deal with it instead of leading your planned discussion.

10. Be prepared to learn from your group.

This is the sometimes the best part of leading a small group. Your weekly preparation, as well as the students' feedback, can profoundly influence your own spiritual development. Ministry breeds maturity, and your ministry as a small-group leader will nurture your spiritual life as well as the spiritual lives of your students.

THE IMPORTANCE OF CONFIDENTIALITY

If you want kids to feel safe enough to share themselves deeply with others in their small group, then it's up to you to establish trust and confidentiality. Some small-group leaders use a written or verbal agreement, committing signers to the principle that whatever is shared in the group stays in the group. They don't tell their parents or their boyfriends the particulars of what they hear in their small group, and you don't tell your spouse.

If what you hear from a student during a meeting of your small group makes you think that a one-to-one talk would be appreciated or helpful, it is no breach of confidence for you to meet with the student over a hamburger later that week and talk personally.

There are critical exceptions to this rule, of course. If a student confides anything that even hints at physical or sexual abuse, you are required by some state laws to report that information to law-enforcement authorities. Know ahead of time what course of action is required of you by your supervisor, your church, and your state if you hear inklings of self-destructive or addictive behavior from students in your small group. At least you will probably talk to such students privately, recommending professional help with specific names and numbers. Keep an up-to-date list of local referral agencies for this purpose.

If confidence is broken in your group, deal with it immediately so that trust can be re-established. Meet privately with the group members who were involved, either individually or together, depending on circumstances. Your goal is to help kids learn when to share personal information with a third party, and when to keep such information to oneself.

Ask Questions That Get Responses

Whether they're personal questions, topical questions, or Bible study questions, the way you ask them can make the difference between lively small-group discussions and dead ones.

Avoid yes or no questions.

Stay away from questions that begin with "Is there...?", "Are they...?" or "Do you think...?" Instead ask more *why* questions. For starters, run your questions by a friend before your small-group meeting and see if they're dead-end yes-or-no questions, or if they provoke exploration, opinions, and discussion.

Don't ask questions that assume an answer.

Asking "How does Jesus show his anger in this passage?" assumes that a) Jesus is angry, and b) there is a right answer you want your kids to discover. The problem with such questions is that they tell students too much without leaving students room to discover answers and insights themselves. A better question: "What is Jesus feeling in this passage? Why do you think he feels this way?" Get ready for a much more interesting discussion!

Write questions that are relevant to your kids.

Some good questions will spring to your mind during the meeting, but don't rely on those. Instead spend some thinking time before the meeting—about where your kids are, what their maturity level is, what in the study is particularly relevant to your students—and thoughtfully write out most of your questions. Doing a Bible study on David and Bathsheba (2 Samuel 11)? Don't ask "What effect do you think David's sin of adultery had on his life?"—it's not nearly as relevant to kids as "What could David have done to keep from giving in to his lust for Bathsheba?" Kids are more apt to talk if questions clearly reflect issues in their own lives—and what they learn from the ensuing discussions will be more valuable to their spiritual journeys.

Learn how and when to ask direct questions.

Direct questions like "Sue, is Jesus the Lord of your life?" may lead to meaningful dialogue, but only with the right people at the right time. The *wrong* time to ask questions this direct and personal is probably the small group's first meeting. Try the less threatening "How does Jesus become the Lord of your life?" and open it up to the group in general instead of directing the question to an individual. As your small group grows in trust and openness between members, you can gradually use more direct questions to challenge your kids personally.

Ask questions that deal with feelings as well as facts.

Your goal is to engage your students' hearts as well as their minds. It's usually safer to deal with issues objectively ("What sins in St. Paul's list are teenagers at your school particularly inclined to?") rather than personally ("What sins in St. Paul's list should you give up?"). Yet the longer your small group meets, the deeper and more personal your questions can become.

Working with Different Personalities

You know what it's like watching the individual personalities in a small group emerge—even if the small group is a family. Your challenge as a small-group leader is to learn to work with the personalities in your small group and help all your students grow individually even as they learn to function as a group.

Here are six types of student personalities, most of which you'll meet in a typical small group of teenagers. The aim isn't to stereotype students, but to forewarn you of common traits and characteristics you'll encounter in your small group—and then to help you find ways to minister more effectively to them.

The Talker

This is the student in your small group who never stops talking, who always has a comment for everything. You're tempted to apply duct tape, but don't—there are more productive ways to handle this student. First, position the Talker next to you when you begin your group, which reduces eye contact with her when you ask a question—and, when she interrupts someone, lets you reach over and touch her arm (usually a silent but effective cue). If you have a whole group of Talkers, you may want to try the ground rule that stipulates that the small group must circulate an object—a stuffed animal, Nerf Ball, spit wad, whatever—and that a student must possess it before speaking. This will help Talkers wait their turn.

Chances are, the Talker has some natural leadership ability that you should encourage. So let her lead the small group now and then. This can help her appreciate what you endure as a leader, and she just may become more supportive when *you* lead.

If the problem persists, get some time alone with her and talk with her about giving others a chance to answer the questions. Help her feel that she's on your team, and that the two of you need to work together to encourage the other students to respond.

The Thinker

This student is quieter (and usually shier) than the others, with a tendency to get drowned out by the louder personalities in your group. So bring him out more by positioning him across from you, to increase the chances of eye contact with you. You can also use the tried-and-true method of occasionally directing questions to specific students, thereby eliciting responses from the Thinker.

If the Thinker is particularly shy, spend one-on-one time with him to discover what he's interested in—and so you can create the kinds of questions that will bring him into the discussion. Use the positive reinforcement of affirming him on those occasions when he actually *does* respond publicly. And when he lapses back into silence, don't interpret that silence as something that needs to be fixed. Some kids just learn best by listening and watching—and there's a good chance he's one of them.

The Church Kid

This kid has already spent more hours in this church than you probably have. She's progressed from the church nursery to the high school room in the course of her 14 or 15 years there. She consequently knows more about the Bible than any other kid in youth group, not to mention her small group. Of course, her knowledge may or may not indicate spiritual depth.

Church Kids can be the hardest to reach because they've heard it all, and therefore feel they have nothing to learn. One way to challenge them is by not being satisfied with pat answers. Always ask *why*. Or play devil's advocate by countering her squeaky-clean, correct answers with provocative arguments from the "wrong" side of the issue. Such strategies usually force a Church Kid to think more deeply about her answers instead of just rattling them off.

Ask her help you create questions for a Bible study—or even let her lead the small group once in a while. In any case, avoid asking questions that invite a "right" answer. Opt instead for questions that leave room for a variety of valid responses.

The Distracter

This is the student who can't sit still and ends up distracting everyone in your small group—including you. Rather than constantly stifling him, direct his energy toward productive ends: ask him to help you pass out Bibles, set up chairs, serve refreshments. Or (and this is good advice for all small groups, with or without Distracters) do some active-learning experiences with your small group—like object lessons or field trips—instead of just sitting and talking week after week.

You may better understand this student (and where his energy comes from) if you get together with him outside of your small group. Even a Distracter can be good for your small group, if only because he doesn't let you get by with boring Bible studies. (Remember *that* when you're tempted to quit.) Really—your leadership skills will be sharpened as you find ways to engage him as well as the tranquil students in your lesson.

The Debater

She irritates you by challenging every point you (or anyone else) tries to make. Sure, she brings a creative energy to the group sometimes—but she often stifles the other kids by making them feel too threatened to voice their opinions or feelings.

Deal with the Debater by establishing ground rules for your small group, the first (and perhaps the only) being: It's okay to disagree with opinions, but it is inappropriate to attack or put down other small-group members if their opinions differ from yours. A second ground rule may be that only one person may talk at a time. Ground rules like these help make a Debater's criticism less caustic and restrains her from interrupting others in order to make her point.

The good news: once Debaters understand and abide by such rules, their input can actually enliven your discussion. Just remember that your goal is to direct, not stifle, their participation.

The Crisis Producer

This student is in perpetual crisis—and lets your small group know about it every meeting. He's often self-absorbed and therefore unable to participate in the discussion, except when it's focused on him. So get together with him before your small group begins in order to talk through his problems with just you instead of bringing them to the small group. (Lucky you.) Or begin your small-group discussion with the assurance that everyone will have a chance to share problems, prayer requests, etc., at the end of the group. This help members—and especially Crisis Producers—stay focused on your Bible study.

Whatever your strategy with your Crisis Producer, your long goal is to help him see past his crises to some solutions, and then to participate in your small group without having to constantly bring the focus back to himself.

What about a student who raises a legitimate crisis during the discussion? Be flexible enough to postpone your study and deal with the issue at hand.

Adapted from The Youth Worker's Pocket Guide to Leading a Small Group *by Laurie Polich. Copyright 1997 by Youth Specialties.*

35 Creative Ways to Start A Discussion or Lesson on Any Topic

35 Creative Ways to Start a Discussion or Lesson on Any Topic

Here are techniques general enough to fit just about any subject, but still quirky enough to attract adolescent attention.

Groupers

Groupers are unfinished sentences like "I wish I were...." They can be used to stimulate discussion. Through them, young people can express and explore their beliefs and goals. As a result, kids can discover what their values really are.

One way to use Groupers is to follow these steps:

1. Give each participant a pencil and index card.

2. You can read aloud the groupers, write them on the board, or distribute them on index cards. Then have each person complete the groupers.

3. Encourage kids to complete their groupers honestly. No one will be graded or judged right or wrong. Every answer is acceptable. Each person has the right to decline to participate and the right to anonymity.

4. Collect the completed cards, read them aloud, and discuss them.

5. Conclude your discussion by reading your own grouper, and ask for feedback. Or read your grouper with the others so that kids won't know it's yours. Conclude with your own comments about the discussion.

Instead of reading answers for them, have kids read their own responses aloud. This works best if kids know each other well and if there is an atmosphere of freedom and trust among them. Kids can elaborate on their responses and answer group questions or not. All answers are acceptable, and kids can decline to participate.

Here is a sampling of groupers:

I fear most...

I wish I were...

I wish I were not...

I wish I had...

I wish I had not...

I wish I could...

If I were the leader of this country, I would...

The leader of this country should...

The happiest day of my life was...

If I could start this year over, I would...

My favorite place is...

My parents should...

I wish my parents wouldn't...

What hurts me the most is...

If I had $25, I would...

I would like to tell my best friend...

The worst thing a person could do is...

What always makes me mad is...

If I could do anything without being found out, I would...

I always cry when...

I always laugh when...

I hate...

If I were the principal of my school, I would...

If I had a million dollars, I would...

If my parents left me alone, I would...

The most important thing in my life is...

If I had X-ray vision, I would...

The hardest thing for me to do is...

No-Risk Discussion

Many young people are intimidated in church situations when asked to express opinions on controversial issues in front of their peers and/or adult leaders. This approach will allow them to say what they feel without fear of what others might think. Cut up paper strips, about 11 1/2" x 8" long. Give everyone a pencil and a strip of paper. Ask questions that only require short answers and ask them one at a time. Each student writes a number 1 at the top and answers the first question, then folds the paper down to conceal his or her answer. The papers are then passed to the person on the left and question number 2 is answered just below the folded-down portion. With each question, the paper is folded and passed to a new person until all the questions are answered. Collect the papers and redistribute them again and have everyone unfold the paper they received. As you repeat the questions for discussion, each person answers the way their paper reads. Usually the result will lead to further, less inhibited discussion, especially when students discover that their views are probably shared by quite a few others in the group.
Whitey White

Tape Talk

One of the best ways to get discussion going in a youth group is to bring in various points of view on a subject. One way to do this is by interviewing people outside of the youth group on tape or video and playing it for your youth group. For example, if the subject is love, interview a young child, an elderly person, and someone from an urban neighborhood, asking them how they would define love. Edit out the bad or dull ones and this can make an interesting program and a good discussion starter.

Textimony Service

Do you have trouble getting your young people to share their experiences? Try a Textimony Service. On slips of paper write verses of Scripture dealing with some specific promises that the Lord makes to believers for their everyday lives. Then pass out the slips to the group and have them share how the Lord has been keeping that promise in their lives. If you like, you could let them pick their own verse to illustrate something that has been happening in their lives. Perhaps someone hasn't taken full advantage of a promise to which he is entitled; he might share that with the group. Someone else may have a helpful insight for that person. The group could pray for individual needs and needs that the whole group may have. Possible promises can be found in the following verses: Gal. 5:18, Eph. 2:14, John 16:23, John 14:27, John 10:10, Ps. 91:15 *(Reprinted with permission from HISWAY, 1445 Boonville, Springfield, Missouri 65802)*

Yarn-Sharing Experience

In order to get your group to open up and share their inner feelings and Christian experience, try using this technique. Take a ball of yarn (size is determined by the size of the group involved) and explain to the group that you are going to ask them to participate in a little experiment. Tell them that in a moment you are going to throw the ball of yarn (while holding onto the end so the yarn will unwind) to someone in the group. The group should be standing in a circle. When that person catches the ball of yarn, she should share either:

- **What God has done for her**
- **What God has done for someone she knows**
- **What God has done for all of us (Christ's death, given us his Word, etc.)**
- **Something that she is thankful for**

Then after she has shared one of the above, she will throw the ball to someone else in the circle (while holding onto the yarn) and the next person who catches the ball will also share one of the four things above. Keep this going until everyone in the group has had a chance to share at least once (several times is best, but this depends on the size of your group and the time you have).

After you have made a spider web pattern with the yarn and everyone has had a chance to share, stop the ball and begin to ask some questions:

1. What is this yarn doing for us physically? Answers would range around the idea of holding us together. (Before this you could comment that the effect of the sharing has created a somewhat beautiful web between the members of the group.) You could briefly mention that for a beautiful pattern to evolve, everybody had to participate.

2. Have one or two members of the group drop their hold of the yarn. Immediately the center web becomes loose and the effect is for the circle to widen a little. Then ask: "What happens to the group when someone drops their yarn?" It becomes less close—looser knit and it makes something beautiful fall apart and turn ugly. You then could follow up with a brief talk on how the Bible teaches us to bear each other's problems, to share our happiness and sorrows, to be thankful, etc. You could really emphasize that in sharing, a beautiful network of relationships and ties are formed just like what is physically illustrated by the yarn, but that it takes everyone to hold it together. *Jim Munson*

Mystery Gifts

Wrap several mystery gifts, using seasonal paper for wrapping. Vary the size of the boxes. Have several kids come up and select a gift from a box or pile of gifts. They open (before the audience) then give an impromptu parable, thought, lesson, or something with the gift as a theme. If the treasury is able, the participants may keep the gifts. This is a great way to enhance creativity. *W.C. Arnold*

Mystery Guest

Divide the youths into small groups of three or four per group. Then have each group choose a Bible character and research and collect information about him or her for 10 minutes. Each group then takes the stand, and the rest of the youths ask questions of the group to try and discover who the character is. Each question must be answered yes, don't know, or no. If 10 no answers are given before the identity of the Bible character is guessed, the group wins. The game can be played with flip cards similar to the old TV show "What's My Line." *James Brown*

Relay Discussion

Set up two, three, or four chairs (no more) in front of your group. Select a person to sit in each chair and explain that you are going to have a relay discussion. You, as the leader, will read agree-disagree statements that beg debate or discussion. Only the people in the chairs up front can speak, everyone else listens. Once the statement has been read, the leader can turn the discussion over to those people or he can stimulate and encourage by asking each person's opinion. If a person in the front chairs does not want to speak about an issue, she may go out into the audience and tap anyone on the shoulder to take her place. The chosen person then must go up front and join in the discussion. Also, if any person in the audience has something to say at any time, he may run up front and replace any person there. Only the people in the front chairs can speak. Once you see the discussion slowing down, throw out a new statement. Also, to stimulate give and take, people can be assigned one point of view or the other, or certain chairs can be labeled AGREE and DISAGREE. Here are some sample discussion statements:

- **Jesus identified more with the lifestyle of the poor than the rich; therefore, poor people make better Christians.**

- The reason a church runs a youth program is to prove to itself that it is doing something for young people.
- A Christian should obey his government even if it violates the authority of Scripture.
- Abortion should be a decision left to the parents or parent of the fetus.
- Bad language is cultural and is thus not un-Christian.
- Physical violence can be justified by a Christian if it is in self-defense.
- It is wrong for a Christian to drink an alcoholic beverage.
- Christianity is the only religion through which a person can get to heaven.
- Our parents discipline us because they are trying to do what is best for us.

Dick Davis

SPOTLIGHT MEETING

In a darkened room have kids sitting in a large circle. One person—usually the youth director or sponsor—has a spotlight (flashlight) that he shines on someone's face. Only the person the light is shining on may speak. The first round is usually word association or some nonthreatening kind of game just to get kids loosened up and into the spirit of things. In the second round, the person with the spotlight can ask each person he shines the light on one question, which that person is to answer as honestly as possible. The spotlight draws everyone's attention to that one person and can be a very effective way for kids to share with each other. Questions can be as deep or shallow as the leader feels he wants to go without embarrassing anyone, but the questions should be designed to allow kids to honestly express themselves and their faith without fear. Allow anyone to pass if they are unable to answer the question. *Jim Hudson*

WISHING WELL

With the youth group seated in a circle, give each person two or three pennies. In the center, place a tub of water, which becomes your wishing well. Various puns can then be employed, such as "You can put in your two cents worth" or "A penny for your thoughts." Any person in the group who wants to speak—sharing some concern, a wish, something they are thankful for, a special blessing—throws a penny into the well and speaks. Make your well small enough so that it will take a little aim to sink the penny. This adds a little comic relief when some kids miss. Most kids will enjoy the experience and improvise as they go along, sharing pennies, pretending to throw a penny and making a "kerplunk" sound, throwing nickels for "longer thoughts," and so on. Pennies can be saved and used again or given away. *Gregg Selander*

CURING DISCUSSION DOMINATORS

You know the pattern—a couple of kids dominate your discussions, while the rest sit and listen to what degenerates into a conversation between two or three people. Here's a fun and nonthreatening way to break the pattern.

Before beginning your next discussion, hand out two 3x5 cards to each group member. Establish these ground rules:

- Each time students (or sponsors!) want to make a comment, they must give one of their cards to the moderator of the discussion. Use your judgment to permit clarifying questions without losing a card.
- After both their cards are gone, students may make no more comments until all participants have used both their cards.

Two benefits are usually accomplished: the normally talkative kids will do more thinking before they speak, weighing if the comments hanging on their tongues are worth using up a card. And because the normally quieter kids know that they must inevitably venture a comment sometime, they become more mentally involved—and usually make excellent contributions to the discussion. *David Wright*

HUMAN CONTINUUM

When discussing subjects that have many points of view, have the kids arrange themselves (prior to the discussion) in a human continuum from one extreme viewpoint to the opposite extreme. For example, if you are discussing drinking, have the kids line up with all those who are for drinking on one end and those who are against it at the other. Undecideds or moderates would be somewhere in the middle.

Kids may discuss the issue among themselves as they attempt to find the right spot in the line in relationship to each other. After they are settled, further discussion or debate can take place as kids attempt to defend their positions. Anyone may change positions at anytime. *Mike Renquist*

LEGOS GAME

The following experiment can be used with either adult youth sponsors or with kids. When used with sponsors, it can demonstrate to them the advantages of allowing kids to discover truth on their own. With kids, it will help them to see the value in using their heads rather than being fed the information.

First, divide your group into small groups of four or five. Then give each group a box of Legos with instructions to make something that works.Insist that each person has a say in the project.

Kids will have a good time with this, so allow plenty of time. When the masterpieces are completed, ask each group to explain what they have.

Second, line everyone up in a single line. Scatter the Legos evenly throughout the line. Now you are the director and you guide them piece by piece to build a simple structure with the Legos. (For example: "Take the red pieces and fit them together like this...") It doesn't matter what you make but keep it simple. Don't let anyone get ahead of the group. If they put the piece in before you tell them, get mad or call them down. Make them go step by step as you instruct them. When you finish go around the line and have them tell you what they have. Everyone will give a different answer, but you inform them that they can't tell you what they have because you are the one who made it and only you know what it is.

Third, it's time for discussion. Be sensitive to your own group and its special needs as you discuss. The two experiments represent two ways of teaching. The first experiment guides the student to come up with something on his own that works. It is his and he has ownership of it. The second represents cramming your beliefs, prejudices, or opinions down the throat of the student. Ask your people which way they preferred, and have them give reasons why.

Larry Jansen

STRAW PICTURES

For this activity you will need many boxes of ordinary drinking straws. You might try getting some donated by a local fast-food restaurant or a grocery store. Divide the kids into small groups and give each group a couple boxes of straws and a large place (maybe a 15-foot square) on the floor to work.

The leader then gives each group a topic or theme to be illustrated, using only the straws. The kids lay them around, placing them in position so that they eventually become a picture. The straws can be cut or hooked together, but that's all. Set a time limit and when all are finished, have some impartial judges award prizes for the best, most unusual, worst, and so forth. Topics can be just for laughs, or they can be more serious. At Christmas, for example, the group might put together a giant nativity scene, using straws. When it's completed, take some photos. *Marian Trievel*

STUDY BUBBLE

Find two large sheets of plastic, tape them together,

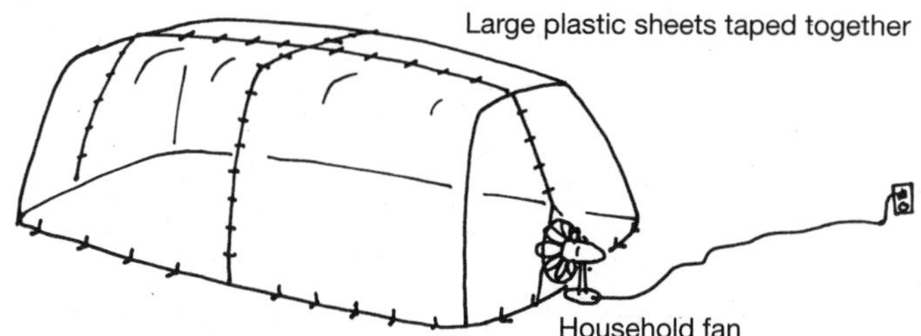

add a fan (an ordinary household fan will suffice), and you've created a great new discussion place. It really works well, kids like it, and you can decorate it.

Geoffrey Koglin

TRUTH OR DARE

Pass out two 3x5 cards and a pencil to each participant. On one set of cards students put questions about the Christian life—one per card—that they would like answered, fold them in half, and mark them with the letter T. These cards are placed in a box marked TRUTH. On the other set of cards they put Christian dares—one thing they dare another student to do for Christ during the next week (dares should be specific and possible). These cards are folded in half, marked with the letter D, and put in the DARE box.

Now, each participant chooses one card at random from the Truth box, answers the question, and tells why she thinks her answer is correct. No one else can speak until the person has answered. Then others can discuss whether they agree or disagree and why.

After the discussion, the participant draws a card from the Dare box, reads it to the group, and keeps the card to remind her to do the dare for Christ that week. Proceed until each person has answered a Truth question and chosen a Dare card. You can usually handle between six and nine questions in an hour, depending on how much discussion is allowed. For larger groups, divide into small groups of five or six.

Truth or Dare has been used successfully with high school youth. It lets you know what the kids are thinking, it gives them a chance to ask questions anonymously, and it challenges them to do something positive that week.

• **Dare Box.** You may want to challenge your kids to find creative ways to put their faith into action with the dares on page 29. Put each dare in a numbered envelope and seal it if you want to add a surprise element.

Then students read their dares, but they must keep them secret from the rest of the group until they've completed their dares. When a dare is completed, students can tell the rest of the group about the experience. If a dare is too intimidating to a student, allow that student to trade for a different one. *Larry Jansen and Leslie Riley*

TALK IT OVER

This is a great discussion starter that provides a good exchange of ideas on a number of topics. Divide into groups of three. Give each group a list of statements like the one below and give each person a stack of 10 cards. Have them number the cards one through 10. Students will choose one of the cards to represent their position on a scale of one through 10 as they discuss topics.

To begin, one person in each group reads a statement from the list. Students decide how strongly they agree or disagree with the statement and choose a number that reflects their position. A 10 indicates total agreement; a one indicates total disagreement. When everyone has chosen a card, students reveal them all at once.

If the numbers shown are all within a range of two, the group doesn't need to discuss the issue—although they can if they want to. If the numbers are further apart than two, they must talk over the issue.

After 30 minutes, have the entire group come back together and share which statements generated the most discussion and which ones had the widest difference of opinion.

A variation is to have the kids use their fingers instead of using cards. For each statement, they would simply show the appropriate number of fingers. Some sample statements:

- I would leave a party shortly after arriving if I were not having a good time.
- I would discuss my personal family problems with friends.
- There are some crimes for which the death penalty should apply.
- If I were offered a less satisfying job at 25 percent increase in salary, I would take it.
- Parents should stay home from a long-awaited party to attend to a sick child.
- I could forgive and forget if my mate were unfaithful.
- I think laundry is woman's work.
- I think any teenager who wants birth control should be allowed to get it with no hassle.
- I would ask a friend to stop smoking around me if the smoke bothered me.
- A parent should immediately defend a child if the other parent is punishing him or her unfairly.
- There should be no secrets between good friends.
- Housework done by the female is usually taken for granted by the male.
- I think there should be sex education in schools starting in kindergarten.
- I think there should be sex education in churches.
- Children should be spanked for some types of misbehavior.
- If a man enjoys housework and a woman enjoys a career, they should pursue these roles.
- It is a parent's duty to attend school functions in which their child is participating.
- I think it is important to remember birthdays of family and friends.
- I think it's okay for a 13-year-old to see an R-rated movie.
- Women with small children should not work unless it's a financial necessity.

Dare Box Dares

1. Ask for a salvation testimony from one of the elders of our church. Be prepared to share parts of it with the class.
2. Read Philippians chapter 1. Write a letter to your parents expressing your thankfulness for their support in your life.
3. Memorize the first chapter of James. Recite it for the class.
4. Select a secret pal from the youth group and do something special for that person every day for one week.
5. Ask for a missions testimony from someone on the missions committee. Share it with the class.
6. Offer to work in the nursery next Sunday in someone's place.
7. Bake a batch of brownies or cookies for one of the leaders in our church, with a note that simply says "Thanks!"
8. Wash your parent's car. Accept no money for doing it.
9. Empty all the trash cans in your house and scrub them all with soap and water.
10. Make a phone call to someone who is not in Sunday school this week but should be.
11. Send a funny card to someone who needs encouraging.
12. Give one of your parents a back rub.
13. Choose a favorite Scripture passage and share it with the class. What does it mean to you?
14. Ask our pianist the following questions: When did you join our church? What was your most moving experience at our church? What do you think have been the three greatest events in the history of this church? What is the funniest thing that ever happened in our church? When you were my age, what was your Sunday school group like?
15. Ask the chairman of the deacon board the following questions: When did you join our church? What was your most moving experience at our church? What do you think have been the three greatest events in the history of this church? What is the funniest thing that ever happened in our church? When you were my age, what was your Sunday school group like?
16. Ask the oldest member of our church the following questions: When did you join our church? What was your most moving experience at our church? What do you think have been the three greatest events in the history of this church? What is the funniest thing that ever happened in our church? When you were my age, what was your Sunday school group like?
17. Watch a movie and answer the following questions: Who do you think is the hero of this movie? Who is the villain? Why? What is the bad or evil thing that could or does happen? How is the evil dealt with? What do you think the producer and director are trying to teach us through this movie? Do you agree with what they are saying? Do you feel this movie will help build up your relationship to God, your family, or your friends? Read Philippians 4:8-9.
18. Watch a music video and answer the following questions: Name the music video and the artist. Did you like this video? Why or why not? Did the visuals have anything to do with the song? What was the song about? What did the person singing the song want to happen? Is this a good thing? Why? Do you think that this is a video a Christian could recommend as good for someone to watch or listen to? Why? Does it fit the qualifications that Paul wrote about in Philippians 4:8-9? How?

- **Marijuana should be legalized.**
- **Kids should not have to account for their allowance.**
- **Parents should regulate how much TV a small child can watch.**
- **School should eliminate the use of grades.**
- **I would say something if I saw a friend littering.**

Syd Schnaars

PHOBIA MONTH

Here's an idea you do not need to be afraid of. Plan a phobia month during which you have lessons in areas your kids are finding difficult. To build interest keep the subject matter of each session a secret except for the name of the related phobia. For example, advertise a discussion on Christmas season depression as Santa Claustrophobia Night. Here are some other possibilities:

Fear of	Condition Name
aloneness	monophobia
crowds	ochlophobia
darkness	nyctophobia
death	thanataphobia
The Devil	demonophobia
failure	kakorrhaphiophobia
God	theophobia
hell	hadephobia
jealousy	zelophobia
being looked at	scopophobia
marriage	gamophobia
pain	algophobia
poverty	peniaphobia
responsibility	hypengyophobia
ridicule	categelophobia
school	schoolphobia
sin	hamartophobia
work	ponophobia

Your kids probably won't have any of these phobias, but they are topics that sometimes can cause fear and concern. This will give you a different approach to some important topics for your youth.

Aaron Bell

HANGMAN LESSONS

If you have a good idea for a lesson but aren't sure how to present it, play Hangman to reveal your outline. For example, four points on a lesson about friendship might be Acquaintance, Casual, Special, and Intimate. Instead of just telling your group these points, have kids guess each word a letter at a time. For every wrong guess, hang a part of the body from the noose. Teens will usually guess the word and will become more involved in the lesson. *John Stumbo*

LIGHTS ON, LIGHTS OFF

This idea can be used as a discussion starter with any topic, or it can be used simply as a fun way to test everyone's power of concentration. You will need some large drawings, photographs, or slides.

Give each person a sheet of paper. Have kids number down the left side of their sheets corresponding to the number of pictures you will show. Have them create three columns across the top of the page (Columns A, B, and C). They should write their answers in each column as they view each picture. Here are the three questions they should answer for each picture:

A. What is the first word that this picture brings to your mind?

B. What feeling did you experience when the picture was revealed?

C. Write a sentence that summarizes the picture.

Turn out the lights and put up the first picture. Flip the lights on for five or 10 seconds and then off again. (If you are using slides, simply show the slide for a few seconds while the lights are off.) Next, remove the picture and put the lights back on just long enough for the kids to write down their responses. Repeat this for each picture.

After viewing all of the pictures, discuss your group's responses, pointing out the differences and the various points of view that arise concerning the pictures. The goal is to help the group learn to appreciate other viewpoints. *John Peters*

WORD PICTURES

Here's an idea that can help your teens do word studies, examine Bible characters, or delve into theological concepts. Pass out worksheets with a word picture diagram printed on them. (See page 32.)

Have your group write the key word (it can be any word or name you suggest) in the center. Then, combining the key word with the guide words on the outside, ask them to write in additional descriptive words. See our sample. It's easiest to write the first thing that comes to mind. When teens have completed this exercise, they will have a better understanding of the key word and will be able to see more of the implications involved in study of Scripture.

Keith Curran

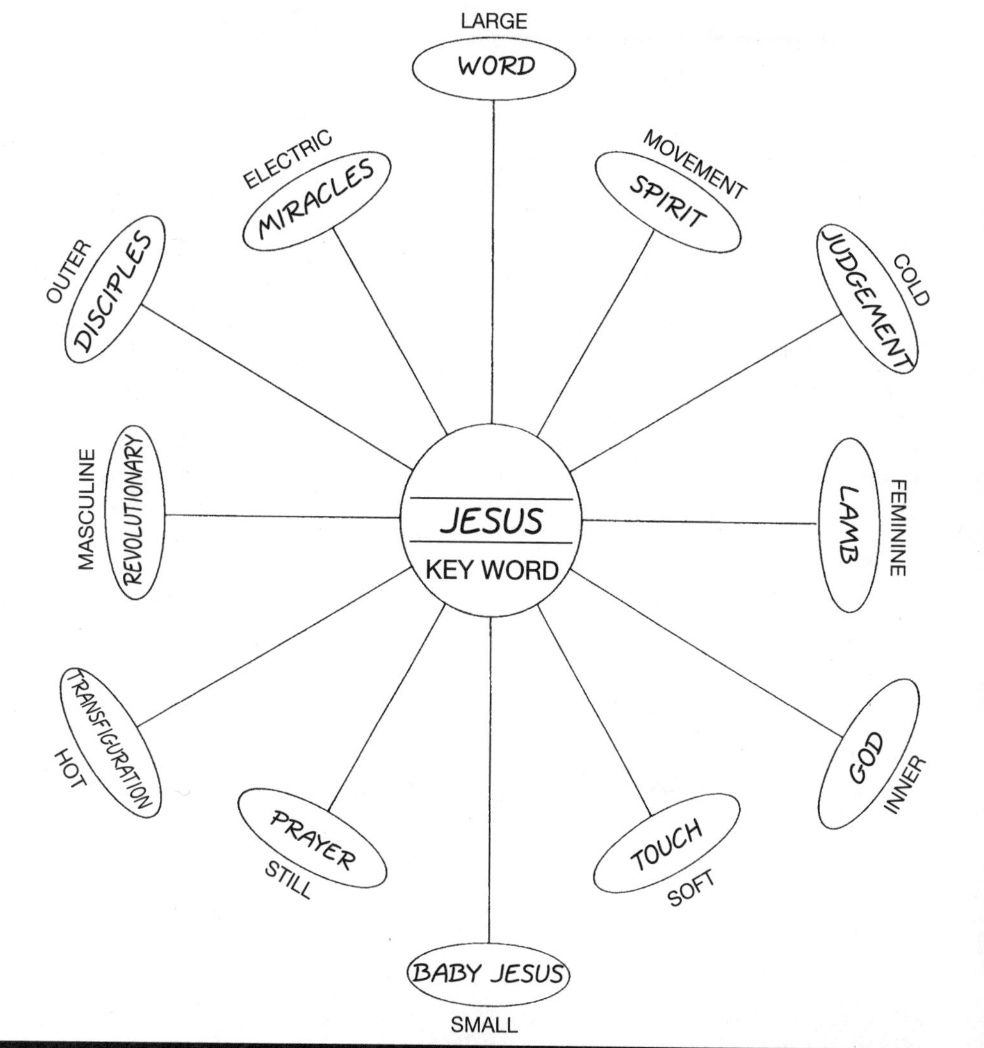

CRISIS RESPONSE

This is a good activity to help your kids develop their abilities to deal with difficult situations quickly and decisively. It stimulates thinking, and it encourages kids to realize that they really can come up with answers to tough issues on their own.

Divide into small groups of three or four. Select a panel of judges (adult sponsors or a group of kids).

Next, present a problem, crisis, or ministry situation to the entire group. Here's an example:

> **You are at school one day, getting something out of your locker, and you accidentally slam your finger in the locker door. Under your breath, you let out a choice swear word. A friend overhears this and says to you, "Hey, I thought Christians didn't say things like that." Now what do you say?**

Give the groups exactly one minute to come up with a response to the situation. Each group has one person (a different person each time) present the group's response.

After this, the panel of judges chooses the best response and explains why. It's a good idea for the judges to affirm the groups whose ideas are not chosen as well.

This approach adds the elements of fun and competition to learning in a very effective way.

Alan Hamilton

RUG DISCUSSION

Here's a great idea to use when you just don't have

Word Picture

This is a worksheet for you to produce a word picture uniquely your own. You will be surprised at the new light you bring to the key word in the center of the picture. You may even be surprised at how creative you really are.

Directions: Write the key word in the center circle. Fill in the smaller circles using the nearby words as guides. You can write down words that are opposites to the guide words if you like. This is your picture of the key word. Have fun.

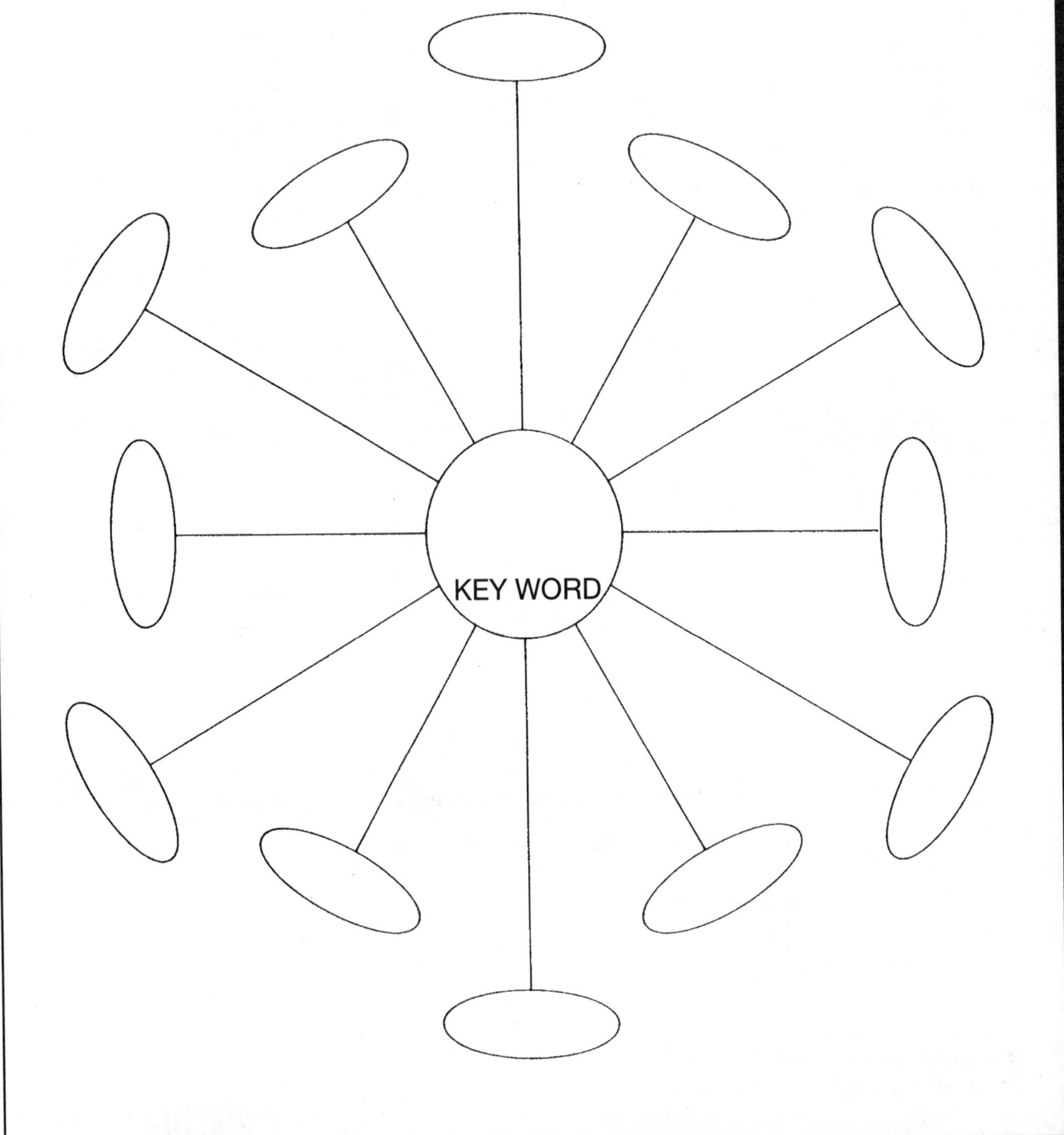

time to plan your usual terrific youth meeting. It's simple and works like a program that you've spent hours working on.

Pass out 3x5 cards to everyone in the room. If you have a topic you were planning to discuss, ask each of the kids to write out a question relating to the theme about something that's been bothering them or that they're struggling with in their lives. If you aren't using a theme, then they can just write out questions they have of any kind. Cards should not be signed.

You will get a great variety of questions. After kids finish writing them, pass a box or container around the room to collect them. Have the leader read the questions, one at a time, and let the kids suggest some answers.

This is a useful approach to questions because kids can often do a great deal to help out their peers and because honest questions can be asked when they're anonymous. To make this a "rug" discussion, have all the finished 3x5 cards thrown on the rug in the center of a discussion circle, mixed up, and then read. Kids love it. *Mark C. Christian*

Spiritual Adventureland

Many games can be used to teach spiritual truths. The following ideas will give you an idea of how you might follow up after games your kids enjoy. Many scriptural principles and applications can be found in the simplest and wildest of games if you look for them. Such an approach is especially good for junior highers and kids who don't enjoy sitting in one place for very long.

• **Line Pull.** Two teams line up on opposite sides of a line and try to pull members of the other team across the line. Once a person is pulled across the line, he becomes a member of the opposing team. After playing by these rules for a while, put everyone on one side of the line except for one strong guy, who is the only one on his team.

Have someone read John 6:40-48. Ask the question, "What does Jesus mean when he says, 'No one can come to me unless the Father who sent me draws him'?" Ask the kids to compare the game they just played with that statement.

• **Sardines.** This game is essentially hide-and-go-seek in reverse. One person—"It"—hides. As other players find "It," they hide with "It." Pretty soon more people are hiding than are looking. The object is to avoid being the last person to find the hidden group.

Ask someone to read Philippians 3:7-16. Divide the kids into groups of four and ask them to design a coat of arms that displays what Paul knew to be the purpose of life. This Scripture centers on Paul's desire to be like Christ and to share in his sufferings.

• **Hares and Hounds.** Have everyone stay in one room for a few minutes while two members of the group go through the church (or wherever you are playing), leaving a trail to another point in the church. The trail can be marked with small pieces of paper, by adjusting the furniture, or whatever. It should be clear, yet only traceable by careful, deliberate observation. The object of the game is to successfully track the two volunteers after they have completed the trail. The challenge is not tracking quickly but simply tracking them successfully.

Have someone read Mark 1:16-20. Ask the kids, "What did it mean to those people to follow Christ? How did the game simulate what you go through as you try to follow Christ?" At this point, you can enter into a discussion of the lordship of Christ, and allow the kids to reflect on how they attempt to follow Christ in their daily lives. *Jim Walton*

Sitcom Discussions

To encourage discussion and creative thinking about any topic, divide into small groups of four or five people. Assign each group a popular TV situation comedy and a topic. Their task is to dramatize the topic, using the characters and format of their particular sitcoms. If the topic is substance abuse, for example, the group would act out a typical scene from the program, playing the show's characters—but in the process communicating tips, warnings, or whatever, about substance abuse.

There are always dozens of sitcoms to choose from—or old

classics can also be used: "I Love Lucy," "Ozzie and Harriet," and "Gilligan's Island."

This activity is not only a lot of fun, but produces some great discussion as you debrief each performance. *Michael W. Capps*

TRIANGULAR TEACHING

Teaching can be enhanced considerably simply by how the room is set up. The following idea is a good setup for teaching about the Trinity, the three loves—agape, philos, and eros—or any other topic that has three or four distinct points.

Set up the chairs in a triangle, so that they face the middle. At each corner of the triangle, place a speaker's stand.

When you get to the part in your lesson about God the Father, for example, you stand in corner A. When you teach about God the Son, you move to corner B—and then finally on to corner C when you teach about God the Holy Spirit.

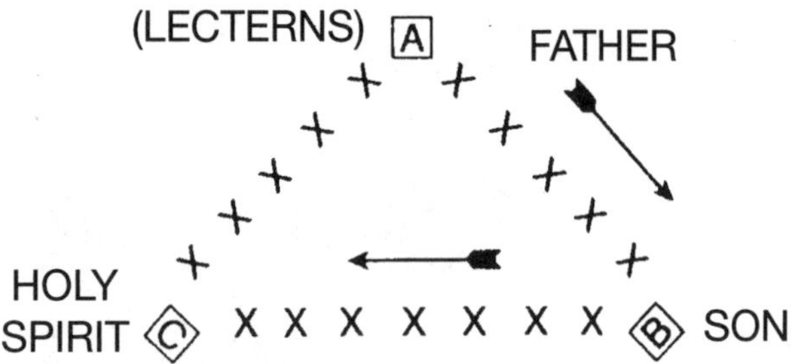

During the discussion after the lesson, follow the same pattern: move from corner to corner, depending on which person of the Trinity you are discussing.

This sort of arrangement offers variety, as well as helping kids to keep things clear in their minds during the lesson. Use any variation of this that fits your facilities or your lesson. *Michael W. Capps*

FISH BOWL

Ease your teens into Scripture reading and sharing by playing Fish Bowl. Arrange chairs in a circle, with one chair in the middle. Whoever sits in the middle is in the fish bowl and does the talking.

Next prepare some devotionals on note cards—a Scripture verse and a brief commentary, with perhaps a question that invites readers to add to the commentary or to share their thoughts.

Here's a sample card:

> **Putting Love in Action (Matt. 5:7)**
>
> Love is not merely a nice feeling. God's love is action in the form of mercy. Before the Sermon on the Mount, Jesus had healed large numbers of suffering people; he had eaten supper with Matthew—a despised, rejected tax collector—as well as the undesirables at Matthew's place—people who had dubious morals, who used coarse language, who drank and ate to excess. His only comment to the Pharisees, who criticized his choice of company, was "Mercy—not sacrifice—is what pleases God."
>
> Love is love only if it is put into action, only if it is given away, only if it looks and focuses on the good in others and their needs. It would have been easy for Jesus to dwell on the negative in others, but he always drew attention to the positive, good qualities that people possessed—even if they were unaware of their good qualities. That is love in action—to be merciful as God is merciful.
>
> What are your thoughts?

Add the note card with the Scripture reading to a stack of blank cards, then deal out the cards at random to the kids. Whoever receives the card with the Scripture reading goes into the fish bowl and reads the Scripture, the commentary, and responds to the question. If a student gets the card more than twice, she has the option to choose someone else to take her place. *David Washburn*

ON THE SPOT

Even in a small group, it is not as easy to initiate an honest dialogue between members on serious, risky topics in a safe, controlled atmosphere. If your group is small, On the Spot will give all participants the full attention of the group, without competition or interruption, as they attempt whatever degree of personal transparency they are comfortable with. The game adapts to your group's needs and is especially appropriate for late-night discussion starters at retreats.

Prepare three stacks of cards—a stack of low-risk questions, a stack of high-risk questions, and a stack of PASS cards. The three types of cards should be three different colors.

Sample low-risk questions:

- **If Jesus visited my school this week, three things he'd want to change immediately are ________, ________, and ________.**
- **To be popular at my school, you must ________.**
- **I think most people spend too much time ________.**

- Most people think Christians are too ________.
- Three facts that most people don't know about Jesus are ________, ________, and ________.

High risk questions:

- If Jesus had been visibly with me today, I would not have said three things I did. They are ________, ________, and ________.
- The man, woman, or child in the Bible most like me is ________.
- I felt farthest from God when ________.
- Two details about myself I like most are ________ and ________.
- One thing that God most wants me to change is ________.

Here's how the game proceeds. Each player is given the same number of PASS cards—usually one or two, depending on how frank players feel like being with each other. One person is chosen to be on the spot. The next player to the right is the dealer, who in this game deals out questions, not cards.

Whoever is on the spot chooses which pile to answer a question from. The dealer takes the top card from that pile and reads it aloud. The on-the-spot player has 30 seconds to answer the question honestly. The dealer then has the option to ask the same player a question of his own. After this second question, the on-the-spot player can choose to either entertain more questions on that topic from anyone in the group or elect not to, in which case play moves clockwise and a new player is on the spot.

A typical round sounds like this:

DEALER: (selecting card from the stack that was chosen and reads) I think most people spend too much money on ________.

ON THE SPOT: Hmm. I think most people spend too much money on clothes.

DEALER: Do you think you spend too much money on clothes?

ON THE SPOT: Yes, I guess so. It's a big priority for me to look nice, but I don't think there's anything especially wrong with that.

PASS cards are played by at any time in order to escape an especially risky or embarrassing question. Play passes immediately clockwise when a PASS card is used. Encourage students to use their PASS cards rather than to be less than completely honest. On the other hand, PASS cards must be used strategically—if a player uses them too quickly, the player must answer the questions.

Control the flow of the game, and permit no interruptions or speaking out of turn. There are no wrong answers, no points are scored, and everyone wins. *Mary Gillett*

VIDEO INTROS

For a fun way to introduce a lesson, say, on God's love, get a video camera and tape the leader asking a question like "How do you know that God really loves you?" Then, as if in response to that question, videotape the answers of some of your kids to the slightly different question, "How do you know your boyfriend/girlfriend really loves you?" Their answers will play back immediately following the original question, making for hilarious results. Make sure the kids you videotape use only the pronoun he or she in their answers, and not proper names or other references. *Todd Hinkie*

CHUTES AND LADDERS

Life is full of ups and downs. Using a Chutes and Ladders game board and rules, play with the following additions: When players land on a ladder, they describe a good experience; when landing on a chute, they describe a bad experience. If players have trouble thinking of specific experiences, use the following questions to prompt them:

- What was the experience?
- Has the experience left a lasting impression on you?
- Would you describe the lesson as a reward or a reprimand?
- How have you grown from this experience?

Conclude the play by discussing the kinds of experiences that individuals apparently have little control over—like the roll of the die. Ask the group how they think God fits into these kinds of experiences. Ask how God is a part of the good and the bad in our lives. *Laurie Delgatto*

HOW DO YOU FEEL?

To help kids express their feelings to each other in creative ways, form small groups in which students express how they are feeling in terms of, say, automobiles: "I feel like a red Porsche" or "I'm just about out of gas right now."

Here are more subjects and images to choose from:

Car	Flower
Song	Number
Toy	Color
Year	Day
Month	Season
Stone	Fruit
Vegetable	Flavor
Holiday	Sandwich
Candy	Road sign
Recipes	Sewing
Book	Clothes
Shoes	Time
Money	Jewelry
Furniture	Animal
Building	Sport
Movie	Cookie
Cake	Beverage
Fabric	Cereal
Ice cream	Feeling word
Temperature	Weather

Sherry Wingert

KIDS ON CAMPUS

Here's a good way to identify different kinds of problems kids deal with. Bring in an assortment of common items to use as object lessons to generate discussion about the characters you describe.

- **Mr. Clean** represents church kids—those who think they have it all together. Though they look good on the outside, there can be a lot of struggles on the inside. How do we relate to kids like that?
- **Cover Girl** make-up represents kids who are preoccupied with their appearance. They want to look good, no matter what it costs. Why do you think some people are obsessed with their looks? What should our attitudes be?
- **Beer cans** symbolize the party guys at school. Their idea of fun is getting wasted, getting in trouble, and acting like jerks. Could their behavior be a smoke screen for a lot of pain on the inside? How can we reach out to guys like this?

- **Chunky** candy bar illustrates overweight kids left out of certain circles or kids who may be loners for other reasons. Their isolation may be obvious, or they may hide it by laughing at themselves, pretending to be jolly and content. Any ideas about sharing Christ with kids like these?
- **Aspirin** portrays Johnny Advil—the kid who gives you a headache. He's obnoxious and seems to go out of his way to irritate you. You wish he'd leave you alone. But what do you think Johnny's real problem is?
- **National Enquirer** represents the person who spreads rumors about everyone. He or she has a tongue of fire and loves to cut people down. How do you feel when people spread rumors about you? What can be done about it?

These are only ideas—add others as you wish; the possibilities are endless. *Tim Freet*

NAME THAT SIN!

This game show activity also makes an easy and entertaining opener for a weekly meeting—especially if your lesson is about one of the sins mentioned in this game.

The emcee (you or a sponsor) runs into the room and in typical Guy Smiley fashion shouts, "It's time to plaaaay...'Name That Sin,' the game where knowing your sins wins you big prizes!" The emcee then divides the group into two teams, or—if the group is large (50 or more)—selects a five-student panel from each team, and the rest of the students cheer for their representatives.

The game itself is simple: the emcee reads the question (see a sample list below; answers follow in parentheses), and the first player to raise a hand has a chance to answer. Remind players that they should respond with the predominant sin, not the related, subtle ones underlying the problem. If the answer is wrong, the other team gets a chance to answer the question—and so on, until there are three wrong answers, and then the question is thrown out. Award a point per correct answer—or three points if the answer is given on the first attempt, two points on the second attempt, and one point on the third attempt.

The emcee can toss a Tootsie Roll (or similar small treat) to players who give correct answers. All members of the winning team get a prize at the end of a round.

- **Your best friend gets a new car and you wish she'd die of a disease and leave the car to you. Name that sin! (covetousness or envy)**
- **Your girlfriend smiles at another guy, and you want to kill him. Name that sin! (jealousy)**
- **Your parents forbid you to see a movie, but your friends talk you into it and you go. Name that sin! (disobedience)**
- **During the prayer-and-share time in Sunday school, you mention your grandparents' $1000 gift and explain how you plan to spend it. Name that sin! (boasting)**
- **You replay the bedroom scene three times in a movie you rented. Name that sin! (lust)**
- **When your friend tells you in confidence that she might be pregnant, you tell a couple of your friends at church—just so they can pray about it. Name that sin! (gossip)**
- **You've just turned 21, you're out to dinner with some younger Christian friends, and to celebrate you order a beer with your meal. They wish they could have one. Name that sin! (causing a weaker brother to stumble)**
- **Your curfew is midnight. You get home at 12:20 a.m. In the morning your parents ask what time you got in, and you answer, "Around 12:00." Name that sin! (lying)**
- **You reject Jesus as Savior and Lord. Name that sin! (unbelief)**
- **Your sister borrows your best sweater without asking you and accidentally ruins it. She's miserable about it, apologizes to you, and even offers to replace the sweater. You don't speak to her. Name that sin! (unforgiveness)**
- **When you get a new car, you spend most nights and weekends either working on it or working at a job for cash to spend on the car. Name that sin! (idol worship)**
- **You figure that as long as you and your girlfriend don't go all the way, it doesn't really matter what else you do. Name that sin! (sexual immorality)**
- **You "accidentally" let a newspaper clipping about your recent football accomplishments fall out of your Bible during Sunday school in front of the girls so they will comment on your achievements. Name that sin! (pride)**
- **You tell your little sister never to touch your things—but when you're out of hair spray, you use hers without asking. Name that sin! (hypocrisy)**
- **You're mad at your little brother, so you purposely leave his hamster cage open so the hamster can escape. Name that sin! (malice)**

Or vary the game's title and questions to match your teaching series—"Name That Old Testament Prophet," "Name That Spiritual Gift," "Name That Prophecy," "Name That Parable," etc.

Lynne Marian

STUMP THE SPEAKER

Here's a youth group version of Stump the Band, a game that's been featured on "The Tonight Show" for many years.

Ask kids to find objects in their pockets, purses, or around the room. Call on students one at a time to give you their objects. You then have 15 seconds to think up a 30-second object lesson, using that item to teach a spiritual truth. If you can't do it, but the student can, the student wins a prize.

This game will get your creative juices flowing—plus, it's a great way to pass the time if you finish your Sunday school lesson early and are waiting for dismissal. As a variation, select a kid to be the speaker. *Michael Frisbie*

THIS BOTHERS ME

Here's an idea that seeks to get kids to air their gripes or hang-ups about whatever topic you want to address. It can be set up like a TV game show entitled "This Bothers Me" or "What's Buggin' You?" The kids are the players and the youth leader is the host. The rules are simple: A kid tells what bothers him most about the topic, and the group members vote for the complaints they agree with the most. Each kid in the group gets a chance to describe what really bugs him or her the most. You can then use the answers the kids give as a springboard for discussion. *Phil Print*

DISCUSSION & LESSON STARTERS

BY TOPIC

DISCUSSION AND LESSON STARTERS

BY TOPIC

What subject are you teaching this week? Look up your subject (they're arranged alphabetically, starting on this page). Then choose the opener that fits your discussion (or lesson) and—most importantly—your group. In fact, with the merest of tweaking, many of these, openers are virtually complete lessons in themselves, with questions, activities, parables, object lessons—all designed to draw opinions, thoughts, and feelings from your students.

APOLOGETICS

CHRISTIANITY QUESTIONNAIRE

The questionnaire on page 42 is excellent for testing your kids' knowledge of basics in the faith. Many of the questions are deliberately antagonistic toward Christianity, but then so is the world, and kids need to have answers. It is suggested that you give this questionnaire to your group one week, let them fill it out at home (or during the meeting if you have time), and then discuss each question. *Jim Grindle*

ATTITUDE

ALL TIED UP

At the beginning of the meeting or lesson time, seat the kids around a table. Tie their hands behind their backs. (Be sure that they are tied securely enough so that they cannot get loose.) Before tying them, give them these instructions:

1. They are being tied for a deliberate reason.
2. They are to try to remember how they felt while tied.
3. They are not to try to untie themselves or get loose until they are told to do so.
4. They must remain seated at all times, with feet flat on the floor.

Then read passages of Scripture that describe people who had positive attitudes in negative situations (examples: Acts 12, 14, 16, etc.). After reading these passages and commenting on positive attitudes in negative circumstances, give the group the task of handing you a dollar bill. Put a dollar on the table with a paper weight on it. Give them a time limit of 30 seconds. If you have tied them securely, it is an impossible job. After they have finished trying, untie the ropes. Collect the ropes if you want their attention during the rest of the time. Ask them how they felt when tied and yet given a job. Make the

CHRISTIANITY QUESTIONNAIRE

1. Why do you believe in God? Don't use the Bible as proof, because I don't believe the Bible is true.
2. If God is so loving, how can he send nonbelievers to hell?
3. If God is so loving, how come he allows so much pain and suffering to go on in the world?
4. Christians say that God is omnipotent. If this is so, could God make a rock that was too heavy for him to pick up?
5. Christians are always talking about the power of prayer. It seems that it's all in their minds, and that it's nothing more than a psychological boost. Also, when prayer does come true, it's probably just a coincidence. Can you show evidence to prove otherwise?
6. Christians believe that God forgives them for their sins if they ask him to. This seems to be just an easy way to clear one's conscience, and is used by Christians to ease their minds. Which explanation is correct?
7. Hasn't science disproved the Bible? For example, evolution clearly eliminates any possibility of creation as Genesis teaches.
8. Considering all the technological advances which have been made recently, it seems that God is no longer needed as an explanation for things being as they are. Why then do Christians continue to believe in God?
9. What is so special about the Bible?
10. Are the right books in the Bible? If so, how do you know?
11. Is the Bible really true, or is it just a book of myths and fairy tales that make people feel good?
12. Why is religion even necessary? Science is the only answer for educated people.
13. Who says Christians are right and all the other religions are wrong?
14. How do you know that Jesus Christ is who he said he was?
15. How can Christians believe in the Resurrection? What evidence is there to support this belief?
16. How do you know Christ is alive today?
17. Christians are always talking about love, kindness, and serving others, but in reality they're all hypocrites. How can you expect anyone to want to join this kind of group?
18. What is so special about having a personal relationship with Jesus Christ? If someone wants to get high, there are always drugs, alcohol, and sex.
19. How can you believe in the Trinity? It's impossible for three people to be one person.
20. If God created man perfectly in the beginning, why did Adam sin?
21. Why does the church spend so much money on big, fancy buildings?
22. Why does the church talk about money so much?

application that negative attitudes tie up God when he wants to do good things for us. Positive attitudes free him to really do great and exciting things in our lives. *Peter Torrey*

BODY OF CHRIST

HANGING FROM THE VINE

When you teach John 15, illustrate how Jesus is the vine by—prior to the meeting—tying a rope across the room, corner to corner and close to the ceiling. Attach to this rope as many lengths of green yarn as there will be kids. Next set up several stations around the room—one where your students will explain their testimonies, another where they'll memorize Scripture, another for praying, another for presenting the Gospel, etc.

When your students arrive, tie them each to one of the green yarns—branches—which are long enough for them to move freely among the several stations. When they complete a task at a station, they are given a piece of fruit—a banana, orange, apple, grape, berry, etc. After 15 minutes or so of this, when you gather them together to start the lesson, they understand more readily how Christians are connected to Jesus, the Vine, and how we bear fruit. *Ron Sylvia*

YELLOW BRICK ROAD

This is a simulation game that teaches the balance between competition and cooperation. To play the game, a map must be made on the playing area that looks like this:

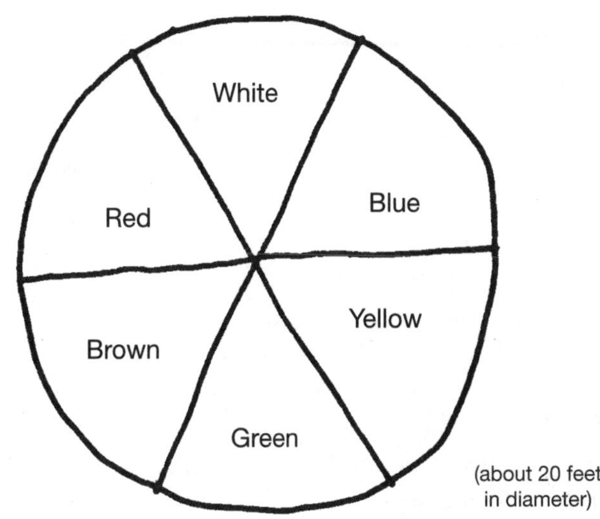

Divide the group into six smaller groups and assign each a color (one of the six on the map). Each group gets a paint brush fastened to a three-foot-long stick and some poster paint the same color as the one assigned them. The following instructions are given to the players:

• The job of your group is to build roads to the outside edge of the map. You build roads by painting

Hanging from the Vine

them on the map in your color. The group with the most roads when the game ends is the winner.

• You can build roads on your own property. To make points, roads will only count if they start at your property and end at the outside edge of the map in another's property.

• You cannot speak to anyone outside your group. Only your leader can talk to the leader of other groups. Your leader must receive permission from a group to enter its property to build a road. This must be done each time you want to build a road or branch. You must ask permission every time you cross another group's road, even in your own property. Your leader must have approval from everyone in your group before giving permission to another group.

• A leader and painter are elected each round. Leaders cannot paint roads. Painters cannot talk to anyone, only follow directions of the leader.

• There is no time limit. The game can end anytime. You must solve your own problems. The only people allowed on the map are the group leader and the group painter. No one else.

Questions for discussion:

• Give each player the chance to express feelings of their experience during the game.

• Have them compare these feelings to real-life situations.

• Is there anything in the game that is like a neighborhood where the players live?

• What does the game say about the nature of man?

• What decisions did you make in the game?

• What would you now do differently in the game?

• What was the degree of competition and cooperation in the game?

• How could the game be played so there is more cooperation rather than competition?

• What should the church's job be? What does your church do in terms of what Jesus said in Luke 4:18?
John E. Washburn

BODY PUZZLE

Have a picture of your church enlarged into poster size. Mount it on a piece of plywood and cut it with a jigsaw into puzzle shapes. This can be used very effectively to bring out the concept of the body, diversity of gifts, and a reminder that each member is part of the church. Pass the pieces to each member and ask them to take one as a constant reminder that they represent the church wherever they go. *William Hicks*

DEPENDENCE MEAL

As a discussion starter, plan a group dinner in which everyone must feed the person to his or her right. No one may feed himself anything. Obviously this works best when everyone is seated around one (or several) big tables.

JIGSAW PUZZLE OBJECT LESSON

For a great crowd breaker that can also be used as an object lesson for a discussion on the body of Christ, get a large jigsaw puzzle and have the kids put it together. The results will be—

• People communicating a great deal, since they have to work together on a common project

• Teamwork developing with certain people looking for edge pieces, others looking for certain colors, etc.

• Young people seeing the body of Christ concept in action

Not only does everyone participate, but the importance of a single puzzle piece is seen, demonstrating that all of us are important to the functioning of the body. *Don Maddox*

BODY LIFE GAME

This game is a good way to demonstrate the need for cooperation and unity within the body of Christ as presented in New Testament Scripture. To set up the game, divide the entire group into five smaller groups, which will symbolize various members or parts of the body. Each group should be named accordingly: EYES, HANDS, EARS, FEET, AND MOUTH.

The object of the game is fairly simple. The five groups, all members of the same body, must work together to perform various tasks before LIFE dies. To symbolize LIFE, something (a helium balloon, for example) can be locked in a trunk or box and a road flare can be lit nearby. When the flare goes out, LIFE will be considered dead. The only way that LIFE can be saved is to complete the tasks that lead to the trunk key that lets LIFE out before the flare burns out. Flares are usually good for about 30 minutes.

Each of the five groups needs to be distinguished some way (different color arm bands or signs hanging around their necks, etc.). In order to complete the tasks, each group may function only in the way it functions in a normal body. In other words, an eye will not be able to hear and an ear won't be able to see. Therefore, everyone except the eyes must be blindfolded.

When the game begins the blindfolds go on, the flare is lit, and the group gets its first task. The instruction for that task is written and presented to the eyes, who whisper it to the ears, who likewise whisper it to the mouths, who then verbalize it to the rest of the body. Whenever the group must go anywhere, the feet must carry the eyes (the only ones who can see) and the remaining members of the body must follow behind in a single file line, holding on to each other's waists. The eyes in that case are allowed to speak, giving directions to the rest of the body.

The tasks may be relatively simple ones. Three or four good ones are enough. Here are a few examples:

- Crackers and juice should be fed to the mouths by the hands while being guided by the eyes. The feet will then carry the ears to the next room followed by the rest of the body in a single file line.
- The ears will be given a number (by the leader) between one and 10. The ears must then hold up that many fingers for the eyes to see, who then tell the mouths, who shout it to the hands and feet. Everyone must then get in smaller groups of that number of people. The eyes can help everyone get together. (This can be repeated.)
- Splints and bandages can be provided that the hands should use to splint one arm and one leg of each of the feet, guided by the eyes.

It is best to work out a few things that your group can do to fit each local situation. The last task should lead to the envelope that contains the key to the trunk. The hands must use the key to open the trunk, again guided by the eyes and carried there by the feet.

The discussion that follows could include the following questions:

- **Talk about the game and how each part of the body did or did not function.**
- **Did all players do their parts?**
- **Why didn't some people get involved?**
- **Relate this to Paul's analogy of the body in 1 Corinthians 12:14-26.**

The game, although reasonably simple, must be thought through carefully by the leader before trying it out. One youth group used three different "bodies" and three different keys on the trunk, representing faith, hope, and love. The possibilities are great with a little creativity. *Bruce Otto*

FOOTBALL STADIUM

This can be a good small group experience designed to help members of the group not only learn more about each other, but to affirm each other's gifts and position in the body of Christ.

Picture the Christian life as a football game. Each person shares with the group where he feels that he fits into the picture and why. For example, one person might consider himself to be "sitting on the bench" and not very active. Someone else might consider himself to be a cheerleader, giving encouragement to the team but not participating.

Others may identify with the coach, the quarterback, or even an empty seat in the stands. Then allow everyone to share where they would like to be in the picture and why.

This can be great way to help kids visualize where they are today and where they want to be in the future. You might want to prepare a photograph or drawing of a football stadium with players, coaches, and spectators for each group to use or perhaps a list of possible participants in a football event to choose from. Close the experience with a round of affirming prayer for each other.

MISFIT

Here's a very practical activity that could help your young people learn how to handle the misfit or newcomer to your group.

During one of your meetings, send one of the young people on a short errand. While he is gone lead the rest of the group in a game that requires total participation of all members so that a latecomer couldn't possibly play. Also, instruct the kids to ignore the errand person when he returns. After the game spend some time discussing with the "misfit" his feelings about being left out. Then, as a group, have the kids reflect on a time when they were newcomers and share a one-word description of what it felt like. You might then read John 8:1-11 about the woman caught in adultery, and discuss Jesus' gentle attitude. Role-play the next day as the adulterous woman runs into two friends. Conclude with the following role-play: A visitor walks into one of your weekly youth programs. Repeat the role-play several times until the kids have a handle on how to treat visitors. *Gerald Morgan*

COMMUNITY

Using Acts 2:44-37 as a model, have the group define what the ideal community living situation would be for our culture today. Divide into small groups and attempt to cover these areas:

1. Living quarters. Should there be separate living quarters for each person? Family unit? Or one large facility shared by everyone?

2. Meals. Will everyone eat together? Separately? What about scheduling?

3. Food. Should it be bought? Grown? Include meat? Vegetables only?

4. Income. Should the group support itself through a cooperative venture or each hold individual jobs and pool money? What about a budget? Allotments or allowances to each member?

5. Location. Should you locate in the city? Suburbs? Woods? Farm? Mountains? Another country?

6. Decisions. Will the group be governed by a leader, committee, the whole group, or elected officials?

7. Rules. Will there be any?

8. Maintenance. Who will be responsible for upkeep, repairs, "dirty work"?

9. Children. How will they be cared for? How many allowed? What about education?

10. Standard of Living. Will you "just get by"? Live in poverty? Live comfortably? Try to do as well as you can?

11. Entrance Requirements. Who will you let into the group? Christians only? Certain age groups? Disabled? Elderly? Teens? Wealthy?

12. Habits. Will smoking, drinking, or drugs be allowed? What about personal hygiene, cleanliness, etc.? People who are sloppy or irresponsible?

13. Religion. Will you all attend the same church? Different churches? Start your own? Attend none?

14. Law. What about marriage? Taxes?

15. Possessions. Will members be able to keep their possessions? Pool them? What about personal items like cars? Stereos? Toothpaste? Clothing?

Have the group compare their models and try to agree on one ideal community living situation. If you can't agree isolate the areas of disagreement and discuss why you were unable to compromise. Discuss your final model in light of the Scripture's model. Some questions for further discussion:

- **Has anyone had any personal experience with or in a community?**
- **What are the advantages (if any) and disadvantages (if any) of community living?**

MY WORLD

Tell the kids that they have the rare opportunity to wield ultimate authority. Have them work alone or in small groups and create their own versions of society. They should list all the people they want to have in their private society, what positions (if any) they would hold, and tell why they want them. This list may include people from the past, but preferably people who are living. Give them approximately 15 minutes to do this, and then ask them to report to the rest of the group what their perfect society looks like. You may want to use questions such as these:

- **Which person did you choose to be in charge of your society? Why?**
- **Give reasons why you chose each of the people in your society.**
- **What values are represented in the individuals you selected?**
- **What was your main concern when you began forming this community?**
- **What concerned you the least?**
- **Would another Christian looking at your society consider it worldly or godly?**

Dan Vaughn

CO-OPERATIVE PLAY CAR RELAY

Here's an activity that is fun, challenging, exciting, and a great discussion starter. The activity involves a relay between two or more teams of five to 10 members each. Each team is given some type of take-apart, put-together toy like Playschool's 45-piece toy car (model no. 483). Each team member is to place one piece of the toy. The teams are placed 10 to 20 feet from the toy, run up, put their piece on, run back, then the next one comes up, and so on. Before the race begins, the captain has a few minutes to inspect the materials and pieces, and plan how to lay them out. Strategy is all important. The captain can give instructions to each team member when they come up to the table, but the captain cannot touch or help the team member. Offer a reward to increase the level of competition.

Following the relay and the award, evaluate what happened. Toss out discussion questions like: Did you want to win? Why? Did anyone cheat? Why? Did they try to help each other? What about the captain? Did the losers blame the captain? Who was responsible for the loss?

This activity usually turns into a very meaningful discussion and the kids really enjoy the activity involved. *Deane H. Johnson*

SIMULATED PLANNING MEETING

This idea works best with a new youth group, or a new group of officers and can be very effective at demonstrating how group dynamics work. Assign different officers or members of the group one of the characters listed below. Give them a sheet with their instructions and give them a few minutes to think through how they are going to act. No one is to know what each other's description says and you must make it very clear that each will be more effective if they do not attempt to overact. This is not a skit. The rest of the group can simply watch and observe while the cast of characters plans an activity, program, or social event.

- **The Enthusiastic Leader.** You are pro-youth group. You are really excited about getting the group going. You see a lot of potential in the group and sincerely want it to go well. You are vocal and take the lead. You try to get everyone to cooperate, discourage negative thinking, keep order, and keep things from getting off the track or being too boring. You try not to reject anyone. You do not try to dominate and only get your ideas across, rather you try to get everyone working together focusing on one goal.
- **The Follower.** Be supportive of anything positive. You are really excited about the youth group and want to see it go. You want to help in any way you can. You have a lot to contribute and try to cooperate.
- **The Negative Influence.** You are not too sure youth group is such a great idea. You ask questions because you are skeptical of anything working with the kids you know. Don't say anything positive. Point out the problems that need to be considered. Try to postpone making decisions; try to delay coming to conclusions or action. Don't be too obvious. Don't overdo it. Say just enough to be effective.
- **The Pathetic Apathetic.** Don't be interested in anything. Don't be positive or negative. Be bored and say so in your own words. Be sarcastic. Treat the entire activity as a waste of time. Be careful and do not over do it!
- **The Reactor.** React to whatever happens in the group. If someone is being too negative, in your opinion, then confront them and ask them why. If someone is messing around and it bothers you or the

group, confront them. If you notice someone is bored or uninterested, then try to get their attention and make them interested. If that doesn't work, ask them what is the problem. You see your role as a peacekeeper, an in-between person who tries to bring out the best in each person in the group.

• **The Goof-Off.** Do what comes naturally. Make jokes, don't take anything seriously. Try to have lots of fun. Be mildly disruptive. Note: do not overdo it. Do just enough to have a good time without arousing hostility.

After 15 to 25 minutes, end the planning meeting and discuss what happened. Did the group accomplish anything? Why? What contributed to the planning meeting? What hindered the planning meeting? Could you identify different roles? What makes a good planning group? *Denise Werkema*

PARABLE OF THE PLANTS

The short story on page 49 is loaded with discussion possibilities. Like most parables, it is most effective when you allow it to make its own point, rather than merely using it to buttress a point you're trying to make. Some open-ended discussion questions are provided.

Suggested questions for discussion:

- **Complete this sentence: "The moral of the story is..."**
- **Which plant in this story do you most identify with?**
- **What kind of person might each plant represent? What attitudes or outlooks on life do you recognize?**
- **Which plants are more "Christian?"**
- **Can you think of any Scripture which might have application to this story?**

Stephen Bly

CORINTHIANS, CANDLES, AND COOPERATION

This game highlights the importance of spiritual gifts (1 Corinthians 12) and will also encourage cooperation and teamwork in your group. You will need nine identical pieces of paper, a flashlight, a candle, and a book of matches. Before the players arrive, you will have to:

- Place the flashlight in a prominent place
- Hide the candle somewhere in the room
- Hide the empty matchbox or match pack
- Hide some matches in the room

Begin by giving each person a folded piece of paper. Tell kids not to read it until you give the signal. This piece of paper identifies each person's role for the game. Be sure to call it a role and not a gift at this point. It is also important that you give each person the paper and not allow kids to draw paper from a hat. If there are more than nine players, split the group up into teams and see who can finish the game the quickest. Only one team may play at a time; the others will have to leave the room.

Distribute the papers and explain these three main rules:

1. Only the speaker can talk unless a player is asked a direct question by the speaker. Players can respond only by giving a direct answer to the question.

2. All players must remain in their chairs except for the Helper and players given certain restricted movements according to their roles.

3. The object of the game is to get some light into the room (other than the flashlight). The game ends when the candle is lit.

Tell players to read their roles silently. As soon as they understand their roles, turn off the lights.

The following are the roles found on the nine pieces of paper:

• You are the speaker. You have the ability to speak but you may not move.

• Only you have the ability to hold candles. You may move but only when you are holding a candle.

• Only you have the ability to hold a strike pad or a match pack. You may move only when holding the match pack.

• There is a match pack hidden (give location).

• You have the ability to strike matches but you may not move out of your chair.

• Only you have the ability to use the flashlight. You may do nothing else. You may move anywhere, but not until someone gives you a flashlight.

• There is a candle located (give location).

• There are some matches hidden (give location).

• You are the Helper. You may move anywhere but you may not speak to anyone (not even the speaker). You may carry objects from one place to another but you may not use them.

PARABLE OF THE PLANTS

One day a boy named Stu happened to be skipping by an orchard near his home and discovered six small plants all in a nice, neat row. He stopped and looked at each one very carefully. How droopy they each looked.

Being a curious and determined little boy, Stu marched up to the first plant and said, "Little plant, what's wrong with you?"

What's wrong with me? Why, nothing! This is the way I'm supposed to look. Surely you can see I'm the same as the others?"

"Well, yes..."

"Right! That's our nature. We have a limp growing habit."

Stu frowned a bit in thought and then walked over to the second plant. "Little plant, what's wrong with you?"

"Let me tell you what's wrong! First of all, this is crummy soil. I need an acid pH soil and this is alkaline. I need a place where I can stick my roots down deep and there's hardpan here. And who can get any sunlight while that big oak tree hogs it? Whoever planted me didn't know what they were doing."

"Hmmm..." said Stu and strolled over to the third plant. "Little plant, what's wrong with you?"

He pointed his longest, droopiest leaf to the others. "It's their fault. I was here first. I was the first to come up. There was plenty of room for me to grow, plenty of room for just one plant. Then they came. I told them by rights the water belonged to me and they disagreed. Sure enough, the water table soon dropped, the summer heat hit us, and it was too late. Now look at us. If they'd only get up and leave my property I know I could make it."

The boy politely thanked him and approached the fourth plant. "Little plant, what's wrong with you?"

But, the plant said nothing.

"Little plant, what's wrong with you? Little plant, what's..." Stu stood quite still. Now he realized the plant was dead. He shook his head and walked over to the next plant. "Please little plant, tell me what's wrong with you."

"Well, it looks tough now, but I know I can do it. If I just get a little water from over there and stretch out a bit in the sunlight and grow at an angle here, I'll have it licked. I can make it all on my own. I don't know about the rest of them, but I'm going to do all it takes to survive. I'll struggle, cut corners, squeeze – no doubt about it, I'll make it!"

"Good for you!" cried Stu. He hummed a snatch of a cheery little tune and then leaned down close to the last little plant. "Now, little plant, what's wrong with you?"

"Water! I need some water. But, there's no way to get it. Young man, would you be so kind as to fetch me some water and pour it around these parched roots? Then I'll firm up and be healthy and strong."

So, the little boy watered the sixth plant and it grew and grew and grew.

The easiest way to begin is for the speaker to address each player and have players reveal their roles. The game will flow naturally from there until the candle is lit.

A discussion on the different talents in the body (see Rom. 12:6-8; Eph. 4:11; 1 Peter 4:9-10; and Matthew 25:14 and following) might be an appropriate conclusion. *Steven Clouser*

THE RECIPROCAL COMMANDS

If community building is a priority for your youth group, then this study of the reciprocal commands (mutual or back and forth) would be an excellent idea. It helps kids to see that community is not just good feelings in a group, but that it requires commitment and responsibility. Here are the reciprocal commands:

Commands Bearing upon Interrelationships

1. Love one another (*John 13:34; 15:12,17; Rom. 12:9-10; 13:18; Gal. 5:14; 1 Thess. 3:11-12; 4:9-10; James 2:8; 1 Peter 1:22; 4:8; 1 John 3:11, 23; 4:7, 11, 12, 21; 2 John 5; Eph. 5:1; Heb. 13:1*).
2. Receive one another (*Rom.15:7*).
3. Greet one another (*Rom. 16:16; 1 Cor. 16:20; 2 Cor. 13:12; 1 Peter 5:14, Rom. 16:3-6*).
4. Have the same care for one another (*1 Cor. 12:24-25*).
5. Submit to one another (*Eph. 4:31-32; 1 Peter 5:5; Heb. 13:17*).
6. Forbear one another (*Eph. 5:18-21*).
7. Confess your sins to one another (*James 5:16*).
8. Forgive one another (*Eph. 4:31-32; Col. 3:12-13; Matt. 18:21-22; Matt. 5:22*).
9. Be members of one another (*Rom. 12:5*).
10. Be of the same mind with one another (*Rom. 15:5; Phil. 2:1-2*).
11. Accept one another (*Rom. 15:7; 14:1*).

The Negative Commands

1. Do not judge one another (*Rom. 14:13*).
2. Do not speak evil of one another (*Jas. 4:11*).
3. Do not murmur against one another (*James 4:11*).
4. Do not bite and devour one another (*Gal. 5:14-15*).
5. Do not provoke one another (*Gal. 5:25-26*).
6. Do not envy one another (*Gal. 5:25-26*).
7. Do not lie to one another (*Col. 3:9-10*).

Commands Bearing upon Mutual Edification

1. Build up one another (*Rom. 14:19; 1 Thess. 5:11*).
2. Teach one another (*Col. 3:16*).
3. Exhort one another (*1 Thess. 5:11; Heb. 3:12-13; Heb. 10:24-25*).
4. Admonish one another (*Rom. 15:14; Col. 3:16*).
5. Speak to one another in psalms, hymns, and spiritual songs (*Eph. 5:18-20; Col. 3:16*).
6. Worship together (*Ps. 133:1*).
7. Take material care of each other (*Deut. 15:7; Rom. 12:13*).
8. Honor one another (*Rom.12:10*).

Commands Bearing upon Mutual Service

1. Be servants of one another (*Gal. 5:13-14; Eph. 5:21; 1 Peter 4:9*).
2. Bear one another's burdens (*Gal. 6:2; Rom. 15:1*).
3. Use hospitality to one another (*1 Peter 4:7-10*).
4. Be kind one to one another (*Eph. 4:21-22*).
5. Pray for one another (*John 5:16; Eph. 6:18-19*).
6. Be patient with one another (*Eph. 4:2*).
7. Discipline each other (*Gal. 6:1-2; Matt. 18:15; 2 Thess. 3:14-15*).
8. Bear with one another (*Eph. 4:2*).

You might begin by having the kids study these commands individually or in pairs. With their Bibles, paper, and pencil, they can work on the following instructions:

- **Study the Scripture verses that deal with each of the commands.**
- **Write out your own definition of each command.**
- **Find a scriptural example, or non-example, for each command.**
- **List the implications or applications of each command for your personal and relational life.**

For group discussion here are some questions that can be discussed by the group after the individual study on the commands:

- **How many of these responsibilities are getting met in our group?**
- **Are there any that surprise you or that you find unreasonable?**
- **Are there any that you find impossible to do? Why?**

- **Are these responsibilities optional or are they to be expected of all Christians?**
- **Is there one you would like to especially see our group work on?**
- **How can we apply these commands to our group and make them work?**

You might want to take several weeks to study these commands—perhaps by taking only one of the four command groups each week. It would certainly be worth the time. Try to find some practical ways for your group to apply the commands, to put them into action, and to see what the results can be. *James Taylor*

APPENDICES, UNITE!

Here is a game that is great for kicking off a discussion on the body of Christ or Christian unity. When the group arrives, give everyone a slip of paper with a part of the body on it, like ear, nose, foot, kneecap, hand, eye, etc. You should try to distribute these so that there will be enough body parts to make up two or more complete bodies. In other words if you have 30 kids, you might want to have three bodies, each with 10 parts.

When the signal to go is given, the kids try to form complete bodies as quickly as possible by getting into groups. The body that gets together first is the winner. A complete body has, of course, only one head, two arms, two legs, and so on. If a body has three legs, then obviously something is wrong.

Once the bodies are formed, you can then proceed with small group discussions or other activities that require those bodies to work together as a team. This simulates how the body of Christ works. An experience like this can help kids to understand passages of Scripture like 1 Corinthians 12 much better. *Larry Michael*

CHRISTIAN LIFE & CHRISTIANITY

MY LIFE, CHRIST'S HOME

This activity is designed to help young people evaluate their lives in light of Christ's call to be totally committed to him. A discussion of Matthew 19:16-30 or Luke 14:25-35 can start off the meeting, highlighting the radical and supreme commitment Jesus requires of his disciples.

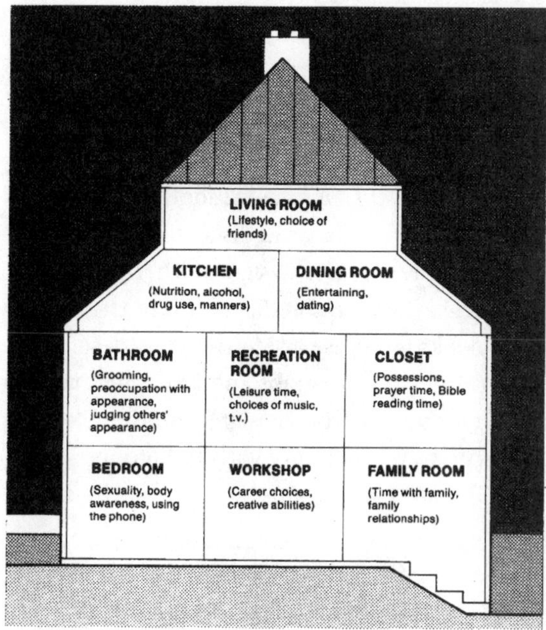

Have kids imagine that their lives are like a mansion with many rooms. Each room represents a different part of their lives. Jesus wants to be allowed into every room to make some changes—redecorate, expand, or close off some parts—and to oversee the use of each room. Without total commitment we may want to control certain rooms ourselves and to shut Christ out of those rooms. Our goal is to examine our lives and to invite Christ into those areas we have kept to ourselves.

Have kids draw diagrams of their lives as if they were a big house, with a number of rooms, and to put their names on the house. The rooms should be labeled according to areas of life that Jesus wants surrendered to him.

After the young people have done this, they can begin by rating each room from one to 10 depending on how much Christ occupies that particular room. For example, a room that is totally under Christ's control would be a 10, and a room that seriously lacks Christ's control would be a one .

Finally, discuss the following questions (or others that come to mind) in small groups or have kids answer them in writing on the backs of their sheets.

- **Which rooms of your house are most occupied by Christ?**

- Which rooms are least occupied by Christ?
- How does your "home-life" need to be remodeled?
- What are some specific actions that you can take to make your house totally Christ's home?

Thomas Cairns

SIGNS OF THE TIMES

This idea uses traffic signs as symbols of faith in Christ and can initiate good discussion. Collect several highway and traffic signs, either packaged or made by the kids themselves, and place these on the walls. Have kids choose a sign that best describes their own lives as Christians and to explain their choices. Discuss each of the signs and their relationship to Christianity with the group.

Here are a few examples:

An ideal time for this discussion would be during summer or Christmas breaks or when the group is about to embark on a trip or retreat. Road signs would then take on new meaning. Other signs include:

Barbara Farish

WHAT IS A CHRISTIAN?

The true/false quiz on page 53 requires students to think through some of their own assumptions about what it means to be a Christian, as well as consider questions that are frequently raised by others. *Eric Lohe*

WHAT KIND OF CHRISTIAN ARE YOU?

This object lesson helps kids evaluate the depth of their Christian commitment.

Begin by telling your kids that you want them to meet several different Christian friends of yours. Each friend has a distinct personality. They will come in one at a time.

Then leave the room and don your first costume. Return, introduce yourself as Chameleon Christian (as described below), perform your impersonation; then slip offstage to change into the next costume and repeat the process.

- **Chameleon Christian.** Remove several layers of clothing of different colors and styles while explaining that you like to change your lifestyle and values from one place to the next, depending upon whom you're with at the time.
- **Colgate Christian.** Enter with a toothbrush and a big phony grin. Introduce yourself as a Christian who always smiles—no matter what. Even though life is sometimes tough and you're really hurting inside, you don't let anybody know—because Christians always smile and pretend that life is continually happy.
- **Foxhole Christian.** Come out with an army uniform. Share the famous quote, "There are no atheists in foxholes." To you, God is someone you turn to in a crisis. The rest of the time you don't need him. But when the going gets rough, you always call on him.
- **Secret Service Christian.** Come out in a trench coat and dark glasses. Explain that you are a secret Christian. In your opinion Christianity is a private matter and should be kept to yourself. You don't want to blow your cover and let anyone else know you're a Christian.
- **Saint Christian.** Come out dressed in a robe and sandals, with a large wooden cross hanging from a chain around your neck. Carry a big Bible and talk in super-spiritual language. Explain that you are a totally committed Christian (as opposed to normal

WHAT IS A CHRISTIAN?

Circle the correct answer.

T F 1. The only thing one must do to be a Christian is to attend church on Sunday.

T F 2. The only thing one must do to be a Christian is to be a member of a church and attend its functions.

T F 3. A person becomes a Christian when he is baptized.

T F 4. A person becomes a Christian when she is confirmed.

T F 5. In order to be a Christian the only thing one must do is believe that Jesus Christ died for your sins.

T F 6. All real Christians are born again.

T F 7. Every member of this church is a Christian.

T F 8. Jesus was a Christian.

T F 9. Only those people who belong to our church or denomination are Christians.

T F 10. Most people in my church only say they are Christians but they really are not Christians.

T F 11. To be a Christian one must read the Bible regularly.

T F 12. Everyone who goes to church is a Christian.

T F 13. All Christians believe the same things.

T F 14. Being a Christian means that I can't do all the fun things that my friends do.

T F 15. One can be a Christian and still believe that drinking alcohol is okay.

T F 16. Once one is a Christian, he never sins again.

T F 17. You can tell that a person is a Christian by the way she acts.

T F 18. Christians do not curse.

T F 19. Christians love everyone.

T F 20. My parents are Christians.

T F 21. As a Christian I must do the right things in order for God to love me.

T F 22. God loves Christians more than he loves non-Christians.

T F 23. God does not allow Christians to get hurt.

T F 24. Most of my friends are Christians.

T F 25. I am a Christian.

Christians), separate from the world, trying to avoid contact with worldly things. Stress that good works and self-denial are the essence of Christianity, and that you are sure that God will give you a special place in heaven because you are such a good person.

Add whatever other Christian family members you can think of. Ask the kids afterward who they thought was the true Christian, who they thought was the biggest phony, who they identified with the most, etc. Discussing the pros and cons of each one will help the kids to examine their own style of Christianity. *Steve Fortosis*

ABC CHRISTIANITY

Your kids have doubtlessly noticed that there are different types of Christians. Here's a small-group activity that allows students to creatively examine the types—and in the process maybe take a hard look at what kind they are.

Divide into groups and assign a letter of the alphabet to each group. Using their assigned letter, the groups then come up with as many words as they can that describe different types of Christians or Christianity. To avoid irrelevant words, require groups to write a short explanation or description of vague words. Some examples are given on this page. *Tom Daniel*

boring
bashful
billboard
(showy, like to attract attention)
baby

faithful
frontier
(bold leaders away from church "frontier area")
financial
(try to buy their Christianity)
future
(party now, live the Christian life later)

dull
dedicated
dependent
(depend on others for their Christianity)
deceiving

CHURCH, LOCAL

TYPICAL-SUNDAY-IN-CHURCH PHOTO

This is a great chance for everyone to be a ham. First have your teens make a list of things people do in church when they are bored—yawning, doodling, touching up one's makeup, or making paper airplanes.

Next, think up ways to act out each idea. Exaggeration is the key to a hilarious picture. Props and costumes might include choir robes, an offering plate, bubble gum, and a large crayon. You'll need volunteers to dress as young children and old folks (find old hats and funky glasses). The following week everyone brings costumes and props for their star roles. Have someone photograph the group sitting in the pews of your church. Everyone poses, hold it, cheese! Develop 4x5 pictures for everyone and an 8x10 picture for the church bulletin board. Really ham it up and you will get plenty of laughs. This could be followed up by a discussion on how church can be made more meaningful, or how we can prevent boredom.

Wayne Deibel

THE LIFE-SAVING STATION

The parable on page 55 is great for discussion or as a simple thought-provoker on the subject of the church and the world. It may be read aloud or printed up and passed out to your group, followed by a discussion, using the questions that are provided. The story was written by Theodore Wedel.

Questions for discussion:

- **When was the life-saving station most effective?**

THE LIFE-SAVING STATION

On a dangerous sea coast where shipwrecks often occur, there was once a crude little life-saving station. The building was just a hut and there was only one boat, but the few devoted members kept a constant watch over the sea. With no thought for themselves, they went out day and night tirelessly searching for the lost. Some of those who were saved, and various others in the surrounding area, wanted to become associated with the station and give their time and money and effort to support its work. New boats were bought and new crews trained. The little life-saving station grew.

Some of the members of the life-saving station were unhappy that the building was so crude and poorly equipped. They felt that a more comfortable place should be provided as the first refuge of those saved from the sea. They replaced the emergency cots with beds and put better furniture in the enlarged building. Now the life-saving station became a popular gathering place for its members, and they decorated it beautifully and furnished it exquisitely, because they used it as a sort of club. Fewer members were now interested in going to sea on life-saving missions, so they hired lifeboat crews to do this work. The life-saving motif still prevailed in this club's decoration, and there was a liturgical lifeboat in the room where the club initiations were held. About this time a large ship was wrecked off the coast, and the hired crews brought in boatloads of cold, wet, and half-drowned people. They were dirty and sick and some of them had black skin and some had yellow skin. The beautiful new club was in chaos. So the property committee immediately had a shower house built outside the club where victims of shipwreck could be cleaned up before coming inside.

At the next meeting, there was a split in the club membership. Most of the members wanted to stop the club's life-saving activities as being unpleasant and a hindrance to the normal social life of the club. Some members insisted upon life-saving as their primary purpose and pointed out that they were still called a life-saving station. But they were finally voted down and told that if they wanted to save lives of all the various kinds of people who were shipwrecked in those waters, they could begin their own life-saving station down the coast. They did.

As the years went by, the new station experienced the same changes that had occurred in the old. It evolved into a club, and yet another life-saving station was founded. History continued to repeat itself, and if you visit that sea coast today, you will find a number of exclusive clubs along that shore. Shipwrecks are frequent in those waters, but most of the people drown.

- **Where did the life-saving station go wrong?**
- **How is the church like a life-saving station? What is the purpose of the church?**
- **Is growth always good or desirable?**
- **Is growth inevitable if needs are being met?**
- **If you don't like the church as it is now, what alternatives do you have?**
- **What should the church do with all its money?**
- **How can the problems that the life-saving station experienced be avoided in the church? What should the life-saving station have done?**
- **Is the church necessary to being a Christian?**
- **What are your chures good points? Bad points?**
- **If you could write a moral that would be added to the end of the story, what would it be?**

PHOENIX GAME

The following is an exercise in establishing priorities in the church and helping young people to determine their own goals and attitudes toward the church. The procedure is as follows:

• Adapt the letter on page 57 to fit your church and place copies in envelopes, with each kid's name on an envelope.

• Distribute the letters.

• Break into small groups and begin planning your new church.

• Regroup at a specified time for sharing of organizational charts and discussion. Ask if the suggestions would really work and whether or not they could be incorporated into the present church structure. *Bill Shepard*

IDEAL CHURCH

Issue five 3x5 cards to each person. Ask each to write one idea on each card with the theme, "The Ideal Church would be one that . . ." Give a few minutes to complete. Then ask each to rank in order of importance, from one (most important) to five (least important).

Mark the rank on the *back* of the card. Then, in a sharing time, trade cards (one for one) with others, that teens might accumulate the five best cards they can for their ideal church. Instruct the group to discard three, keeping the best two. With these two cards, find others with whom you can form a church consisting of several members of the group (perhaps four to five people). Each church group should name their church as they see fit after discussion. Then, each group, if time permits, should design a symbol for their church. The wrap-up would be for each group to present their church to the group, explaining their goals as a church community, in addition to explaining their symbol and meaning. This is great for senior high or adult groups and it really gets some discussion going about what is important in the Ideal Church. *Arthur Homer*

VALUES IN THE CHURCH

The following exercise will help young people—or adults—to set priorities concerning certain values that they have, and also to see the inconsistencies that often exist within the church community, regarding priorities and values. Give one copy of page 58 to each person. Have each person cut the 12 squares apart. Then follow the steps:

1. Rank the concerns in order of importance. Put the most urgent or necessary item on top and the least urgent on the bottom. Now make a list on another sheet from one to 12, showing the order that you decided on. Put the letter of the most important item next to the number one and so on through number 12.

2. Now rank them again, only this time according to the amount of attention they receive in your local church. Put the one receiving the most attention on top, the one receiving the least attention on the bottom. List their letter sequence along side the first list.

3. Now, compare the two lists. How are they different from each other and why are they different? Should they be the same? What changes need to bemade and on which list? Discuss these and other questions you may have with the entire group.

Bob Gleason

THE MAN FROM ICK

The parable on page 59 has many discussion possibilities.

PHOENIX GAME

Dear Church Members,

As an authorized agent of the Naturewide Insurance Company, it is my duty to inform you that at approximately 11:00 p.m. Friday evening, your pastor, Rev. Abernathy called all of the members of your church together for a special prayer meeting. It is my unhappy duty to also inform you that at 11:10 the Air Force accidentally dropped a limited scale atom bomb on the church meeting and completely destroyed the church building and Harry's Bar across the street. Harry wasn't in the bar at the time so he will be able to rebuild his bar but you and the members of your small group will have to make some vital decisions.

You are now the only surviving members of your church and this makes you legally responsible. There is an insurance reimbursement to cover the building and grounds that will be paid to you for approximately two million dollars. However, in order to qualify for this money you must show us your organization of what is now your church. I, for one, will be interested to see if you organize in a traditional manner or in some new way that is unique. I have been told that there are no ministers available from Presbytery so you will have to provide your own.

I wonder whether you will want to hire other people to do the work in the church or whether you will do it yourself. I wonder whether you will pay salaries to yourself. I expect you will build a new building, won't you? What will it look like?

These are all questions that must be answered in the near future, but for now we would ask you to complete these forms so that we can settle your insurance claims as quickly and easily as possible. Thank you and good luck!

1. What will the name of your church be? (Will you keep the name "Memorial Park" or will you change it?)

2. Who are the members of your church and what are their roles and salaries, if any?

NAME	CHURCH	JOB	SALARY

3. On the other side, make an organizational chart of your church.

4. Describe briefly the type of building you plan to construct or your reasons for not having a building (you don't need a building to receive the insurance reimbursement).

5. Describe your new church's type of ministry. What will be your basic purpose?

VALUES IN THE CHURCH

A.
Raising money and spending it

D.
Spiritual Growth of church members enabling them to become mature disciples of Christ

G.
Maintaining or building church attendance

J.
Helping to relieve poverty and/or racial prejudice in the local community

B.
Developing the music program of the church

E.
Winning local people to Christ

H.
Helping to relieve starvation and suffering in the famine-stricken areas of the world

K.
Keeping the existing weekly programs of the church going

C.
Getting workers to fill all the jobs in the church

F.
Building and maintaining larger and more attractive church building

I.
Foreign Missionary Work

L.
Developing a sense of fellowship, love, and mutual concern

The Man From Ick

Once there was a town called Ick. The people of Ick had a problem. They were icky.

For some unexplained reason, everyone who was born in Ick ended up icky. Scientists, doctors, and experts from all over the world had tried to analyze the people of Ick, and although they all agreed that the people of Ick were icky, no one could agree on a cure. In fact, there was no cure.

The scientists, doctors and experts agreed that the only thing they could do would be to give people suggestions on how to cope with their ickyness. But experts or no experts, everyone learned to cope in his own way.

Some pretended they weren't icky. Some tried to keep busy and forget their ickyness. Others decided that being icky was better than not being icky . . . and they got ickier. Some just didn't care. Usually, if you were able to get a person from Ick to be honest, they really didn't like being icky.

Well, you can imagine how many people arrived in Ick with a "cure" for ickyness. And you can imagine how many people were always willing to try each new "cure" that came along. And strangely enough, some of the "cures" seemed to work . . . for a while. But eventually, the cure would stop working and everyone would be icky again.

One day something happened that would radically change the people of Ick.

A long-time resident of Ick began to suggest publicly that he had a cure for ickyness. It was very difficult for the people of Ick to believe that a person who lived in Ick himself could have a real cure for ickyness.

But then something strange happened. One of the ickiest people in all of Ick believed in this cure and was changed. He simply wasn't icky anymore. Everyone thought it was just temporary and waited. But it didn't go away and before long, lots and lots of people started believing the man from Ick...and everyone who believed was cured.

It was incredible and one would think that the people of Ick were overjoyed.

But the people weren't overjoyed and soon a town meeting was called. The fact of the matter was, the business community of Ick had been built around the basic fact of people's ickyness.

And with more and more people losing their ickyness, the economic future of Ick was threatened. After an extremely heated discussion, it was generally agreed that what appeared to be a cure for ickyness was probably like all the other so-called cures and would soon turn out to be a hoax. And since so many people were being misled and since it was possible that many more people could be misled, and since a person who would perpetuate such a hoax on a community like Ick could affect the stability of Ick, the "savior" of Ick was asked to leave.

He refused. He continued to cure people and each day those responsible for the "stability" of Ick became more and more concerned. One day the "savior" of Ick disappeared. It caused quite a commotion and no one to this day knows what happened. Some say he had been done away with. Others said they had actually seen him the day after he disappeared. But what was strange was that even though the "savior" of Ick was gone, people who believed in him and his cure would suddenly find their ickyness gone. And even though the majority of the townspeople agreed that this "savior" was, in fact a hoax, all those who had believed in him were still cured.

The people who had lost their ickyness thought everyone would jump at the chance to be cured. They were sadly disappointed. Very few were even interested. So the ex-icky people did what they could to convince the icky people that their cure was not a hoax and every once in a while someone would believe.

Apparently, and this is only hearsay, a small group of ex-icky people began to worry that if they or their children associated too much with icky people, they might be contaminated or become icky again.

It wasn't long before these people banded together and moved to the top of Ick Hill, an isolated spot on the edge of town. They would work, shop, and go to school in downtown Ick and then return to Ick Hill for their evenings and weekends. But it wasn't long before the people of Ick Hill became so fearful of contamination that they built their own school, market, gas station, and shopping center.

A few more months went by. And one morning the people of Ick woke up to see Ick Hill covered by a large glass bubble. Ick Hill was now a completely self-contained community with everything completely under control.

One particularly cold morning, an icky person in the city of Ick noticed that there was no visible activity going on inside the glass bubble of Ick Hill. A rescue party was sent to see if everything was alright.

After breaking through the glass bubble, they were shocked to find the entire population of Ick Hill dead. Autopsies were ordered and the cause of death was the same for all: suffocation.

Simply read it to the group and provide time to discuss its meaning. Some sample questions are provided, although many others are also possible.

Questions for discussion:

- **Is it a legitimate function of the church to "protect" its people?**
- **What things in the church "suffocate" you? What things in the church are like fresh air?**
- **What do you think of church schools, Christian Yellow Pages, Christian communes?**
- **What does it mean to be "in the world, but not of it"?**
- **Can you separate from the world without being isolated from the world?**

Joe Falkner

CIVIL DISOBEDIENCE

THE BLACK ARM BANDS

Here's a discussion starter on the topic of authority and civil disobedience. After reading the news item on page 61 to your group (which is true, by the way), you might wish to go over the discussion questions and examine other current issues in which protesters use nonviolent expressions of civil disobedience. To wrap up the evening, you might tell the actual fate of the three kids in the story: while their families received hate calls, bomb threats, and a bucket of red paint thrown at their houses, the case of the arm bands was ultimately taken to the United States Supreme Court. The court ruled that peaceful protest in a public school is legal: "School officials do not possess absolute authority over their students. Students in school as well as out of school are 'persons' under our Constitution."

Here are some possible questions for discussion:

- **How do you feel about the three kids and their protest? Would you have joined them? Would you have supported their right to protest?**
- **Do you think the principal did the right thing? What would you have done in his place?**
- **Make a list of authorities you must answer to (such as the principal of your school). Under what circumstances might you have to disobey each of these authorities?**
- **Look up these verses on our relationship to authorities: Romans 13:1-7; Titus 3:1; Peter 2:13-17, Ephesians 6:1-9, and Colossians 3:20. Do these verses rule out civil disobedience?**
- **Now look up these examples of civil disobedience: Exodus 1:15-21; Exodus 2:11; Joshua 2:1-7; 1 Samuel 19:9-17; Matthew 27:64 and 28:2; Acts 4:1-3, 5:17-18, and 12:6-10.**
- **How does one know whether or not to obey or disobey an authority?**

Kraig Klaudt

CLIQUES

FELLOWSHIP GAME

Prepare ahead of time six 3x5 cards with the following instructions:
• Go to the corner of the room and face it. Act as if you are reading your Bible and praying. Do not respond to anyone except your youth leader. (Make one of these.)
• Sit in the center of the circle and lock arms with the three others who will be there with you. Do not let anyone else into your circle. Do not respond to anyone except your youth leader and the three in your group. (Make four of these.)
• Try your hardest to become a part of the group in the center of the circle: try persuasion, begging, crying, acting as if you don't care, force, and any other thing you can think of. If you fail to get in, go to the person in the corner and try to relate to him. (Make one of these.)

To begin the game, have the entire group sit on the floor in a large circle. Give the 3x5 cards to individuals who will feel comfortable doing what the card instructs. Those who do not receive a card simply remain seated and watch. After the exercise, discuss the feelings and responses of each person in relationship to fellowship as represented in 1 John. Allow those who were watching to describe their reaction to what was going on. *Gary Casady*

THE BLACK ARM BANDS

In 1965, during the beginning of United States military involvement in Vietnam, three high school students in Iowa heard of the antiwar protests taking place on college campuses. They decided that they, too, would wear black arm bands to class as a way of saying that war is wrong.

Chris Eckhardt, John Tinker, and his sister, Mary Beth, wrote an article for their school paper explaining why they were about to begin wearing black arm bands. Before the article was printed, however, a copy of it reached their high school principal. He immediately instructed the three that they would not be allowed to stage their protest. The principal explained that such activity would disrupt classes and school spirit.

In spite of their principal's warning, John, Chris, and Mary Beth wore their arm bands anyway, as they felt it was within the rights of students to express their opinions. All three were suspended from school until their arm bands were removed.

THE BLACK ARM BANDS

In 1965, during the beginning of United States military involvement in Vietnam, three high school students in Iowa heard of the antiwar protests taking place on college campuses. They decided that they, too, would wear black arm bands to class as a way of saying that war is wrong.

Chris Eckhardt, John Tinker, and his sister, Mary Beth, wrote an article for their school paper explaining why they were about to begin wearing black arm bands. Before the article was printed, however, a copy of it reached their high school principal. He immediately instructed the three that they would not be allowed to stage their protest. The principal explained that such activity would disrupt classes and school spirit.

In spite of their principal's warning, John, Chris, and Mary Beth wore their arm bands anyway, as they felt it was within the rights of students to express their opinions. All three were suspended from school until their arm bands were removed.

CLIQUES

Do your kids realize how stifling cliques can be? How difficult it is to meet others when you tie yourself exclusively to a single group? Try this—divide your teenagers into small groups of five to 10, then with ropes tie each group together, everyone facing out. Tell them that they must now meet at least 10 people from any of the groups but their own.

When the dust settles and the ropes are untied, talk with your group about why it was so hard, how the activity relates to cliques, how a high schooler feels who's not in a youth group clique, and how God's work is hurt by this. *Michael B. McKay*

SKITS ABOUT CLIQUES

If your group has a tendency to form cliques, try having kids act out some of the negative aspects of cliques. These three discussion starters illustrate both feelings of rejection and of acceptance. Though each one has a definite beginning and end, the mechanics and the outcomes will be as unique as each actor's personality and the group's current situation.

You can assign roles beforehand and have students practice before the performance. This allows them more time to think about what they're doing and usually adds depth to the skit. Or you can assign roles on the spot and have the kids work spontaneously. This usually results in overacting, which can be fun and add more to the discussion; and it allows more people to be involved. If unrehearsed, however, you may want to keep each student's role a secret from the others. In either case, give careful thought to the choice of actors, and tackle the discussion questions immediately after each skit.

Discussion Starter 1: Build a Human Pyramid

The object is to get six people to build a human pyramid.

- **Role 1:**

—You can talk only with the person who has Role 2.
—Your favorite phrases are "No," "Huh," "I don't like this," and "Let's do something else."
—Interfere with the group's efforts by nagging, criticizing, moaning, etc.
—Resist talking to the person with Role 3 at all costs.

- **Role 2:**

—Your best friend is the Role 1 person.
—Your favorite phrases are "No," "Huh," "I don't like this," and "Let's do something else."
—Interfere with the group's efforts by nagging, criticizing, moaning, etc.
—Stay away from the Role 3 person.
—Do not make physical contact with the Role 4 person.

- **Role 3:**

—You really like the idea of building the pyramid.
—Besides building the pyramid, try to get to know the Role 2 person better.
—You want to be at the top of the pyramid.

- **Role 4:**

—You like the idea of building the pyramid.
—Go with the flow of things.

- **Role 5:**

—You like the idea of building the pyramid.
—You want to be at the top of the pyramid.
—You will settle for your place below the top of the pyramid only if three or more people tell you that you can't be on top.

- **Role 6:**

—You are the leader.
—Work toward settling disputes.
—You must be in the second row of the pyramid. Good luck!

Discussion Starter 2: Serious Discussion

You can do this one unannounced if your actors are already selected. That way everyone becomes a part of the skit whether they know it or not. Tell actors that they will be participating in a serious discussion.

- **Role 1:**

—Sit next to the Role 5 person.

—Goof around with the Role 5 person.
—Exchange jokes with the Role 5 person and don't pay much attention to the other things that are going on.
—If you run out of things to do, you may make faces at someone or just walk off.

• **Role 2:**
—You are interested in what's going on and are paying attention.
—Enter into the discussion.

• **Role 3:**
—You will start the discussion.
—Talk about the most important person in your life.
—Tell why he or she is important to you.
—Tell how he or she helped you in your Christian life.

• **Role 4:**
—Listen intently to the Role 3 person.
—Be ready to give your comments, and when the Role 3 person runs out of things to say, you pick up the conversation.
—If you get upset with someone for some reason, you may put that person on the spot.

• **Role 5:**
—Sit next to the Role 1 person.
—You and the Role 1 person are goofing off.
—Tell jokes (whisper) and don't pay much attention.
—If you run out of jokes, you may try to involve someone else in goofing off, but you must remain sitting with the group.
—You may even get involved in the discussion going on, but only as a last resort.

Sample discussion questions for those who weren't acting:

- **Which people liked each other, and which didn't? How could you tell?**
- **Why do you think they behaved as they did?**
- **Which people in the skit did you like the most? the least? Why?**
- **How would you feel and behave in this situation?**

Sample discussion questions for the actors:

- **What was your role?**
- **Why did you behave as you did? What would make a person behave that way?**
- **How did you feel as you acted out that role? Did you like the character?**
- **How would you behave if you really were the person in the role? How would you feel?**

Sample discussion questions for everyone:

- **How can you tell whether or not someone likes you?**
- **How do you let someone know you like him or her?**
- **What should you do if you don't like someone?**

Conclude by reading and discussing Matthew 22:38-39. *Erlan and Jan Leitz*

CLIQUES AND LONERS

This idea gets students talking about the effects of cliques on a youth group. Ahead of time, arrange the chairs of the youth group and let kids know as they come in that the chairs are not to be moved. Here is how the chairs should be set up, and the people they represent:

• A group of chairs in a circle all hooked together: the group of regular teens who attend the youth group.
• A chair in the middle of the circle: the person who wants to be the center of attention.
• A few chairs outside the group: visitors to the youth group who can't seem to break through and be a part of the group in the circle.
• A chair next to the door: a brand new person who has just entered the group.
• A chair outside the door, looking in: someone waiting to enter the youth group who is afraid to come in.
• A chair up on top of the table: a person who criticizes and looks down on everyone else.
• A broken chair or a chair that's different from all the others: a person in the group who may be a little bit different from the rest because of a handicap, a foreign accent, etc.
• A small cluster of three to four chairs off from the large circle: that group of people who stick together and won't let anyone into their group.

You can probably think of some other ways to represent various groupings within a group, and you should try to arrange it so that everyone has a chair, and there are no chairs left over. As the group arrives, give each person a number at random and instruct them to sit in the chair that has the same number. Then during the meeting you can have a discussion on cliques using the questions below. Everyone must stay in the seats that they have been assigned during the entire meeting.

During the meeting you could interview (in front of the group) certain students who are part of the established cliques, and also interview someone who is considered to be a loner. You'll need to be sensitive here. But you could compare the experiences of the youths and try to examine what the problems are, and how they can be solved without destroying relationships or forcing people to do something they cannot do. Here are a few discussion questions that could be tossed out to the group:

- **What is a clique?**
- **What are the advantages or disadvantages of being in a clique?**
- **What are the advantages or disadvantages of being a loner?**
- **What would be the ideal situation in a youth group such as ours?**
- **If Christ were in our group, where would he sit? Would he be in a clique? Or would he be a loner?**
- **Discuss the ways we as Christians can reach out to loners, or how we can develop positive groupings within our youth group.**

Donna McElrath and Carter Hiestand

THE COOLS AND THE NERDS

Here's an idea that will encourage discussion on the topics of conformity, popularity, acceptance, and peer pressure with your kids in a fun and creative way.

First, divide into two groups, the Cools and the Nerds. For obvious reasons, you may want to divide the group, then tell them which of the two groups they are. There should be at least one artistic type in each group, if possible. Give the two groups a drawing pad and some marking pens and have the Cools draw a picture of someone who is really cool—a stereotype of everything that is currently trendy.

The Nerds draw a picture of a real nerd, someone who is totally out of it.

After the pictures are drawn, they can be posted and judged by an impartial jury (sponsors, maybe) for accuracy, humor, creativity, and so on.

List on the blackboard or on poster board some characteristics of a cool person and a nerdy person.

Sample list for a cool person:

- **Doesn't take school work home**
- **Wears Nike sports clothes**
- **Is athletic**
- **Owns a car**
- **Skips classes**
- **Smokes and drinks**
- **Dates**
- **Swears**
- **Eats junk food at lunchtime**

Sample list for a nerd:

- **Carries an umbrella when it rains**
- **Carries a purse (girls)**
- **Carries a briefcase (guys)**
- **Attends church or Sunday school**
- **Takes a sack lunch to school**
- **Gets driven by parents on a date**
- **Spends time with little sisters or brothers**
- **Does well in science class**

Next, discuss questions like these:

- **Do you consider yourself cool or not?**
- **What is the coolest thing you ever did? The un-coolest?**
- **Why are items on the cool list accepted by the crowd and not the other list? What's wrong with the not cool list?**

The People Who Brought You This Book...

— invite you to discover MORE valuable youth-ministry resources. —

Youth Specialties offers an assortment of books, publications, tapes, and events, all designed to encourage and train youth workers and their kids. Just return this card, and we'll send you FREE information on our products and services.

Please send me the FREE Youth Specialties Catalog and information on upcoming Youth Specialties events.

Are you: ☐ An adult youth worker ☐ A youth

Name ______________________________

Church/Org. ______________________________

Address ______________________________

City ____________________ State ____ Zip ____________

Phone Number (______) ______________________________

idst of the chaos that might

lay as many games as you want
f the royal one, dethrone the ruler
questions.

or the ex-ruler:

the center of attention?

ld be an everyday experience?

veryone else felt?

ars and politicians feel?

for the whole group:

nobody?

ttention the ruler was getting?

serve to be treated better than others?

y or friends who seem to be better treated than
feel toward them?

r classes a favorite of your teachers? What do you
on?

r? How did these groups treat him: Family?
? The public? Pharisees and Sadducees? The
God the Father?

nk you stand in God's sight? What about famous

or add to these questions as needed.
ons to lead into more in depth
out popularity, cliques, self-image,
ply Scripture such as 1 Peter 1:9-10, 1
d Ephesians 2:4-7. *Mark Prestridge*

Your Intelligence

Your Talentedship

Kids can be creative with this part of it. As the next game progresses, the ruler can choose to play or not and can banish players from a game or activity at will and pronounce a punishment that must be obeyed ("Race around the perimeter of the gym eight times!" or "Sing 'Santa Claus Is Coming to Town'"). Make sure that leaders are exempt from the royal rule—so that you can keep some semblance of law

COUNSELING

SAYING THE RIGHT THING

It is one thing to know we need to help people, it's quite another to know how to do it. Here is an excellent exercise to give young people some practical options when helping someone in need.

The situations below give different options for a response to a specific problem. Discuss the pros and cons of each response and add whatever other responses you might think are appropriate. There are no right answers, but you should discover that certain responses are more appropriate than others in different situations.

Kid in Trouble

A woman is dying of cancer. She is not an active participant in a church, but does attend worship services. She has three children, ages 12-18. You have been visiting her in the hospital. She has just been sharing concern about her oldest son who's been in some trouble. You have prayed with and for her and are excusing yourself to leave. She begins crying. What do you say or do now? Why?

1. Is there anything you'd like to share with me?
2. I see you have some deep feelings. What are you crying about?
3. It's really difficult being in the hospital when you're concerned about your children, isn't it?
4. Listen, I'll go see your son and try to help.
5. I've got a great book that really will help you with this problem.
6. I'm sorry...Goodbye.
7. I'll send the pastor over.
8. Don't cry...everything will be alright.
9. Listen, don't worry, God will work it all out.

Death of a Dad

You have a good friend (your age) whose father has just died suddenly. Your friend has been out of school for several days and has just returned to school. You see him for the first time since his dad's death. What do you say/do?

1. I hear your father just died. Gee, that's too bad.
2. Boy, I know just how you feel.
3. I'm really sorry about your dad. I don't know what I'd do if my dad died.
4. I'm sorry about your dad, but at least he's in heaven.
5. Hey, how you doin'? Good to see you.
6. Boy, you and your dad were really close, weren't you? It must be tough.
7. What's happening, man? Hey listen, a bunch of us are getting together for a big party this weekend, what are the chances of you coming?

Simmering Sibling

Your brother (or sister) has just had a fight with your mom and dad. It seems that your parents forgot to tell your brother that they had something planned for Saturday, so your brother will have to cancel his plans for Saturday. As a result your brother stomps angrily back to his room and is grumbling about how unfair the situation is. What do you say/do?

1. Boy, did you get the shaft!
2. What are you complaining about, you got to go out last weekend!
3. Let's just forget to tell mom and dad about the next thing we've got planned.
4. What happened?
5. Hey, look, we'll figure something out to do here at home.
6. I think mom and dad are right.
7. Quit acting like a baby!

You might try role-playing each of these situations. They would work very well for stimulating discussion. *Robert Stier*

ROLE REVERSAL

This is a good way to help kids solve some of their problems when they are hesitant to talk about them. Have teens write down their biggest problem on a sheet of paper to be shared aloud. Collect the papers, redistribute them, and have each person assume that the problem on the paper is his. Then each person comes to the front, shares his problem (the one on the paper), and the kids and sponsors try to help him work through the problem by asking questions, suggesting solutions, etc. The person in the group who really has that problem is able to help solve it and gain new insights from others without revealing that the problem is his. *Roger Paige*

HOW CAN I HELP?

Because teenagers naturally spend more time together and talk more to each other than they do to adults, it's a good idea to help kids be better equipped to help each other when a crisis or problem occurs. This idea may encourage better peer ministry among your students.

Several case studies (page 67) can be used to

How Can I Help Case Studies

Read each situation carefully. Consider both what has acutally happened as well as how the person is reacting to what has happened. As a group, rank the responses from best to worst based on what you know about the situation. Discuss together the strengths and weaknesses of each response. Be sure that each member of your group shares in making the decisions.

Situation 1

Fourteen-year-old Susan has been your friend for a long time. You notice that she seems very angry and irritable one day. You ask her what the problem is. Susan pauses for a moment, then blurts out, "Mom and Dad told me last night that they're getting divorced."

Responses:
1. I'm really sorry to hear that, Susan.
2. Why are they doing that, Susan?
3. You can come and stay with me for a while.
4. I know exactly how you feel. My parents fight a lot, too.
5. [Make up your own response.]

Situation 2

Seventeen-year-old Ben is in your calculus class. You've heard through the grapevine that Ben's application to MIT has been rejected. You and Ben aren't great friends, but he has told you that he's looked forward to attending MIT since he was a little kid. During class you notice that his eyes are kind of puffy and red, like he's been crying. You have a chance to talk to him after class.

Responses:
1. Hey, buddy, cheer up! With your grades, there are a dozen other colleges that will be excited to have you!
2. I was sorry to hear that you didn't get into MIT, Ben.
3. Ben, there's going to be a great party tonight. How about going with me?
4. It's too bad about MIT. I guess God must have some other plans for you.
5. You look kind of down today, Ben. What's the matter?
6. [Make up your own response.]

Situation 3

Sixteen-year-old Mary has a locker next to yours. Report cards have come out today. You're feeling a great sense of relief over your geometry grade. Mary, however, appears very upset. She is extremely agitated and is walking back and forth, talking to herself. You ask her what the problem is. "My grades are terrible," she replies. "There is no way I can go home with these grades. I'm really afraid of what my dad might do to me. What am I going to do?"

Responses:
1. Maybe you should just come home with me this afternoon.
2. What are you afraid of, Mary?
3. How bad were your grades?
4. Maybe you could just not tell them about the grades or try to change them on the report card.
5. Come on, Mary. Everyone's parents get upset with grades.
6. [Make up your own response.]

Situation 4

Ted, a junior at your school, has been your best friend for as long as you can remember. He's seemed to be very depressed lately. He's tired all the time. He doesn't want to go out and have fun with you like he used to. You know that things are not going well with his parents, and that his girlfriend broke up with him last week. Until now you've avoided the subject directly, trying instead to encourage him to do fun things and cheer him up. You've just asked him what's been bothering him so much. "I really don't know," he says. "Sometimes things just seem so hopeless. Lately I'm not sure if it's all worth it."

Responses:
1. Everyone gets down sometimes, Ted. I'm sure you'll feel better soon.
2. I'll pray for you, Ted. God understands your feelings and wants to help you.
3. Maybe you just need to get out and do some fun stuff. Let's go to the mall together and get your mind off your problems.
4. What seems so hopeless, Ted?
5. What do you mean, "I'm not sure if it's all worth it"?
6. [Make up your own response.]

help kids think through some of the issues involved in helping a friend or acquaintance through a crisis. Distribute them to the kids and let them respond. Discuss the following questions:

- **Is it best to encourage people to talk about their problems or to try and get their minds off them?**
- **Does it help people to tell them that their problems aren't really so bad, compared to other people's problems?**
- **When is it good to bring God's perspective into the conversation? When isn't it good?**
- **What do you do when someone seems extremely depressed or suicidal?**

If you are not trained as a counselor, you could invite a professional counselor to attend this meeting to help deal with issues like these. *David C. Wright*

DATING

DATING DATA

This idea provides a good opportunity for youths to express their values and opinions about dating in a relaxed and natural way. Place the assignments on pages 69 and 70 around the room, providing blank paper, markers, and resource materials at each station. Ask teens to choose and complete as many assignments as possible in the time allowed. They may work together in small groups or individually. At the end of the period, call for reports and discuss the findings.

Questions for discussion:

- **Why do some people seem to date "below" themselves? (Put up with anger, being used, disrespect, etc.)**
- **Why do some teens find romance earlier than others?**
- **How can we be more comfortable on dates?**
- **Should girls ask guys out?**

Karen Dockrey

DATING ROUND ROBIN

This exercise is a lot of fun and it introduces the subject of dating in a new and helpful way.

Have the group sit in a circle. Go around the circle, giving each person 10 seconds to come up with an idea for a cheap date in their town. If they can't think of one, they are eliminated from the game and you go on to the next person. Continue playing until only one person is left, or until a specified time limit has been reached. In the church where this game was originated, 12 young people came up with 82 ideas! Here are some examples:

Swim	**Visit the zoo**
Get a pizza	**Tend a garden**
Make popcorn	**Listen to a CD**
Walk a dog	**Cook a meal**
Help an elderly person	**Draw or paint**
Talk	**Run errands for someone**
Play tennis	**Play Risk**
Have a pillow fight	**Visit someone in a hospital**
Picnic	**Wash the car**
Shop	**Ride a bus or train**
Attend a ball game	**Go to a movie**

When the game is over, have the group choose the best ideas, or rank the list from most expensive to least expensive, or from best to worst. Follow up with a discussion on dating. Talk about what makes a good date. Your list of ideas can be duplicated and distributed to the group as a resource for future dates.

Karen Dockrey

DATING QUIZZES

On pages 71 and 72 you will find quizzes that will generate a lot of discussion on the subject of dating. After the group has a chance to finish, go over each question and compare answers. *Dan Mutschler and Joe Dorociak*

PERSONS WITH DISABILITIES

Here's a good way to sensitize your young people to the particular needs of handicapped people. Conduct a regular session or banquet. However, as kids arrive,

Dating Data Assignment 1

Write a plan for two people
who like each other to get together.

Dating Data Assignment 2

Devise a foolproof method for deciding the
difference between love and infatuation.

Dating Data Assignment 3

List at least 20 fun things to do on a date.
Each must cost less than 10 dollars.

Dating Data Assignment 4

List five guidelines
for making a date successful.

DATING DATA ASSIGNMENT 5

What advice would you give to a Christian who has a crush on a non-Christian? Include the pros and cons of dating a non-Christian.

DATING DATA ASSIGNMENT 6

Write a plan for breaking up in the least painful and most healthy way.

DATING DATA ASSIGNMENT 7

List the number of people you tell about your dates, and write out 10 pros and cons for talking about your dates.

Dating Quiz

Circle the best answer:

1. As a Christian, I may date...
   a. non-Christians
   b. non-Christians, but only casually
   c. non-Christians only if they are unusually attractive
   d. any Christian
   e. only "strong" Christians
   f. "weak" Christians as a ministry
   g. only unusually attractive Christians

2. It is "more Christian" to...
   a. play the field b. only date one person at a time

3. It is "more Christian" to...
   a. wait for a mate until God brings one into your life b. go out "hunting" for one if one does not appear (even attending a school where prospects look good)

4. It is "more Christian"...
   a. for one's parents to pick his or her mate b. for me to pick my own mate c. to marry someone you meet at a church conference

5. It is "more Christian" to...
   a. date for companionship b. only date someone you might be serious about

Finish the sentences:

6. When you realize that someone you are dating cares much more for you than you do for them, you should ______________________________

____

7. If, as a Christian, you never have any dates and would like some, you should ______________________________

____

8. My pet peeve about dating is ______________________________

____

9. Biblical principles I think I apply to dating are ______________________________

____

10. Some lessons I've learned about dating are ______________________________

____

11. Prevalent dating practices which I feel are basically non-Christian are ______________________________

____

____

Dating Quiz 2

Write the letter of the best answer.

_____ 1. I go on a date because...
a. I like to see the latest movies
b. I enjoy spending my parent's money
c. I like being broke Sunday through Friday
d. it gives me something else to do besides homework

_____ 2. I select a date by...
a. seeing if he is well dressed
b. hearing whether she is a fun date
c. whether or not I want to become romantically involved with him
d. all the above

_____ 3. Where I go on a date is determined by...
a. the amount of money I have, or the amount that I want to spend
b. how far my date will let me go
c. where my parents will let me go
d. where my friends are

_____ 4. I do not like to double date because...
a. I do not like to hear unintelligible noises coming from the back seat
b. we can never agree where to go, so we drive around a lot
c. the other couple always has bad breath
d. one of us has to ride with the other two after one of the dates is dropped off

_____ 5. I do not date people my own age because...
a. we have nothing in common
b. they still suck their thumbs
c. they are all taken
d. it's hard to talk with a gorilla

_____ 6. I only date Christian people because...
a. we both can say "God" without becoming embarrassed
b. she may keep her hands off me longer
c. my parents approve
d. we can pray on our date

_____ 7. I never date the same person twice because...
a. he always goes to the same place
b. I told him that I don't kiss on the first date
c. the weather forecast is the same for this weekend
d. I'm afraid we might get involved

_____ 8. I never spend much money on a date because...
a. I am saving it for college
b. she's not worth it
c. I spent it all on Wednesday night with the boys
d. it has to last me the rest of the month

_____ 9. I do not date because...
a. I have no money
b. nobody has called
c. he might say no if I ask
d. I have a case of terminal zits and donkey breath

____ 10. Dating is fun because...
a. I like to dance
b. I like to get stepped on
c. I get to mess around
d. I get out of the house

True/False

______ 11. You should never hold hands on a date, it may lead to more dangerous things.

______ 12. The boy should ask the parents (preferably the father) for permission to date their daughter.

______ 13. To date someone is to look for a potential marriage partner.

______ 14. You should date only Christian people.

______ 15. I like to date someone because the person has a pleasant personality.

______ 16. It does not matter how much money was spent on the date as long as we had a good time.

______ 17. I could feel closer to her if she did not bring her pet Doberman with her on our date.

______ 18. You should always pray (not prey) on a date.

______ 19. I like having my parents drive us on our date.

have them draw from a box the name of a handicap that will be theirs for the duration of the meeting. For example, one person might draw "poor eyesight" or "blindness"; another might be "deaf," "unable to walk," and so on. The possibilities are, of course, many. Kids must follow through on their handicaps until its time to discuss their feelings and observations about the experience. *Rick Bell*

HANDS

This idea can be used as a icebreaker or as an opening for a worship service. It is most effective with a large group.

Have participants pair off with someone they do not know, and introduce themselves. Then blindfold all participants and explain that there can be no more talking during the course of the game.

The pairs are then directed to face their partners and feel each other's hands—memorizing the feel of them, size, distinguishing features, etc. Once they have had time to do this, mix everyone up. Without making any noise, kids must find their partners by feeling everyone's hands.

Once everyone has paired up, have kids remove the blindfolds to see if they found the correct partner. The game can open up a handful of discussions covering topics such as: handicaps, senses, cooperation, the hands of Christ, and others.

Gaye Lynn Sharp

UNDERSTANDING PERSONS WITH DISABILITIES

A number of simulation exercises can help your kids become more aware of the handicapped members of our society and the challenges they face daily. Try some of these:

1. Have half the kids walk around the buildings and grounds blindfolded while the other half act as their guides. After 15 minutes, switch roles. Then talk about how it felt and what problems they encountered.

2. Blindfold the kids and hang a number of small items on a clothesline. See how many items they can identify by touch.

3. Blindfold the kids and serve them a meal. Suggest that as they serve themselves, they can use a strategy employed by many blind people: They simply imagine their plates to be clock faces as a way of remembering where each food item is located (meat at 12:00; vegetables at 6:00; bread at 3:00; and so on). Or see if the kids can tell what they're eating simply by taste.

4. Have the kids watch TV blindfolded for half an hour, preferably a show they don't normally watch. Then have a discussion to find out how much they understood about what was going on. Watch another program with the sound turned all the way down, and see how well the kids can lip read or otherwise figure out what's happening without the benefit of sound.

5. Have the kids with lace-up shoes take them off. Then see how many of them can tie their shoes blindfolded and with one hand behind their backs.

6. Make a collection of small items such as safety pins, buttons, dimes, paper clips, and sequins. Let kids try to pick them up with rubber gloves on. This will simulate handicaps which restrict use of the hands.

7. Stand a mirror up on a tabletop. Then have the kids try one at a time to write their names on a sheet of paper in front of the mirror so that it reads

correctly in the mirror. They cannot look directly at the paper—only at its reflection in the mirror. This exercise simulates the difficulties encountered by people with cerebral palsy or dyslexia.

8. Find a book at the local library that shows the deaf alphabet. Have your group learn it together, as well as a few common words in sign language. Then try breaking up into pairs and conversing for 10 minutes without any spoken words. Whatever they can't say by word signs or improvised motions they must finger spell.

9. Go for a walk as a group down a street in a business section of town. Note how accessible particular buildings and facilities are to handicapped people. Do they have ramps as well as stairs? Are doorways wide enough for wheelchairs to pass through? Are phone booths and drinking fountains low enough for wheelchairs? Do the bathrooms have facilities for the handicapped? Are there braille floor numbers on elevators?

After each of these experiences, be sure to focus on helping the kids put themselves in the place of a handicapped person, to understand what it would be like. What would be different? What would be the same? How would it feel to be ostracized or ridiculed because of a disability? *Ruth Shuman*

IMAGINE

The following exercise is designed to help young people better identify with the problems and feelings of the handicapped in our society. Instruct the group to read the situation on page 75 and then to complete the questions that follow, answering each one as honestly as they can. Discuss each question with the entire group and try to apply the learning that takes place to your local situation, and to those people who may be handicapped in some way. *Jim Steele*

DISCERNMENT

THE REAL THING

Help young people tell the real thing from a look-alike by providing samples of several brands of cola drinks and letting your kids try to figure out which is Coca-Cola. Let them also try maple syrup and several brands that claim to taste just like it. Finally, have them compare regular milk to two percent, skim, and evaporated milk.

After completing several tastings, lead a discussion about what makes things phony or real. Ask your group to list some things they perceive as phony. Then ask them to list some things that they view as real.

Finally, discuss the reality of God. He really is (Romans 1:18-20), he does what he says (Psalm 119:160), he loves us (John 3:16; Romans 5:8), and he has a plan for us (Jeremiah 29:11; Proverbs 3:5-6). *Mike McKay*

FRIEND OR FOE

This game is designed to illustrate how we are influenced in our lives, and how difficult it is to determine what is good advice and what is bad.

Have a person waiting outside the door while the room is being set up. Place a variety of obstacles, such as pop bottles, around the floor so that one would have to avoid them in order to walk across the room. Then blindfold the person waiting outside and bring the teen in. The object of the game is for the blindfolded person to try to walk from one side of the room to the other without knocking over any of the obstacles.

The blindfolded person must get directions to cross the room (around the obstacles) from others in the room, but he does not know who is a friend and who is a foe. They will both be giving instructions. It is up to the blindfolded person to determine who is giving good advice and who is giving bad advice. Whether or not the

IMAGINE

Imagine that you have been transported to another society in another time and place. People look the same, dress the same, but something very important is different: the way they communicate. All people communicate by telepathy, that is, the direct transfer of thoughts from one person's mind to another. They are carrying on normal lives, enjoying each other, working, playing, going to school, but you have a serious problem—you cannot give or receive telepathic messages. People seem shocked that you are unable to communicate; some avoid you, some even make fun of you. You can communicate if you are able to write messages out, but very few people care to take the time to converse with you in this manner. Unable to find work and support yourself, you go to the local government for help. After waiting in line for an hour and being referred to several different departments, you are finally instructed to apply for admission to a mental institution for the nontelepathic and to begin therapy immediately.

1. How would you feel about the people of this world?

2. How would these experiences make you feel about yourself?

3. How would you feel about the government of this world?

4. Would you go to the institution for therapy or not? If not, what would you do instead?

5. If you came upon a Christian church in this world, how would you expect the people there to respond to your situation?

6. How would you feel about someone who took the time to learn to communicate with you and became your friend?

person can make it through without knocking any obstacles depends upon who he decides to listen to. He may decide to listen to no one at all and simply try to make it on his own.

After that person crosses the room, someone else can try if they think they can do better. (Rearrange the room a different way this time.) Afterward, ask the group questions like these:

- **To the blindfolded people: How did you decide whom to listen to?**
- **To the blindfolded people: How did you feel when you followed a direction and it turned out to be bad advice?**
- **To the friends and foes: What tactics did you use to keep the person on or off the right course?**
- **To the group: How is this situation like the world around us? In what ways does the world try to influence us? How can we learn to stay on course?**

If the group is large, it would be best to only have six or so who are the friends and foes, while the others simply watch the action. This game will provide a lot of laughs, as well as some good learning. *Wayne Peterson*

Truth or Deception

To play this game you'll need a large room to be the mine field, and obstacles such as tables and chairs to be the mines. Set a piece of candy on one of the mines that is out in the mine field, and a cotton ball on another one.

Break up the group into teams of three that play one at a time. One of the three is blindfolded and spun around several times. Write TRUTH on a 3x5 card, and DECEPTION on another; place both in a hat. The two partners who can see each draw a card out of the hat. The player who drew TRUTH tries to get the blindfolded partner to pick up the candy, but the one who picks DECEPTION tries to get the blindfolded partner to pick up the cotton ball. They shout instructions to the blindfolded partner, but they may not touch this partner or follow him around the room. Make a boundary line to prevent them from entering the mine field.

If the candy is picked up within a minute, both the blindfolded player and the truth giver get candy. However, if the cotton ball is picked up, or if the blindfolded person touches three mines during the one-minute period, the deceiver gets candy. After all the groups have played, let them play again until everyone has had a chance to be blindfolded.

Use this activity to discuss the importance of discernment, honesty, or Satan's role as the great deceiver. *Mark L. Thieret*

Let's Pretend

This is a mind trip that involves an imaginary walk with Christ. Tell the young people that you are going to play a game of Let's Pretend. For many of them it will be the first time in years that they have used their imagination (publicly, anyway). Start with a short prayer for God's blessing then ask the young people to lie down on the floor, keep their eyes shut, and get comfortable. Then the suggestions go something like this:

1. **Pretend you are walking down a long dusty road and you are all alone; no one else is in sight. (Give several seconds after each suggestion for them to visualize it.)**
2. **Now, pretend you see Jesus walking on the same road as you. Is he walking toward you or away from you?**
3. **Now pretend that he walks with you for awhile. What do you say to him? He to you?**
4. **Suppose he says, "I'll give you absolutely anything your heart desires." What do you ask for and why that?**
5. **Suppose he asks what is your most troublesome problem? What do you say? Why is that a problem for you?**
6. **Pretend now that you meet your very best friend. Do you introduce your friend to Jesus? If so how? Suppose your friend asks Jesus what you are really like inside and Jesus explains honestly how it is with you? How do you feel? What do you say?**
7. **Now you come to a fork in the road and your paths must part; what does Jesus say to you as he leaves? What do you say?**

Allow a few minutes for each person to wrap things up mentally. Tell the kids to open their eyes when they are through with their walk. Usually you take five to 10 minutes for the walk and about 30 minutes for the discussion. Have the kids describe how they felt and what happened on their walk.

Usually the discussion becomes very interesting and must be cut off at its peak. *Ken Garland*

WORD GAME

Here's a simple discussion starter that can be very effective. Give each group member a blank 3x5 card and a pencil. On one side of the card have the kids write the most important word in their lives. On the other side have them write the most important word in their faith or religion. Then, using Luke 10:25-28 and Romans 12:1-2 and the cards, discuss the relationship between one's faith and one's life. Ask the group to compare the responses on both sides of the cards. *Donald Musser*

THE GOSPEL ACCORDING TO ME

Pass around to your youth group sheets of paper or cards with these words printed at the top THE GOSPEL ACCORDING TO__________. Have teens fill in their names and write their versions of the story of Jesus. They should include their own beliefs about Jesus as well as any doubts they may have. They can be as lengthy as they want. *Bill Boggs*

ROLE BOWL

Copy page 78, cut apart the cards, and put them in a bowl. Let each person in a small group pick one out and think about it. Ask the kids to share their solutions to the situation. (The more verbal kids will obviously share first. But don't force anyone to share.) After each person finishes allow others in the group to comment or to add their own thoughts. *Bob Stier*

ROUTINE AND HUMDRUM

Read the parable on page 79 to your group and then discuss it.

Here are some suggestions for questions to get you started in your discussion:

- **Shouldn't life be exciting for the Christian?**
- **Isn't routine and stability the opposite of creativity and growth?**
- **Is there anything wrong with not working?**
- **Is it wrong to want excitement?**
- **What does it mean to be faithful?**
- **If our church is boring and unfulfilling, should we stick it out or look for a church that is more fulfilling?**

UNFAIR

The following is a role-play that involves five people. The background can be given to the whole group and the instructions to the characters only. Follow up with a discussion on the issues that are raised.

Characters:

Boy 1, Girl 1, Frank (who are brothers and sister); Boy 2 and Girl 2 (who are brother and sister). Frank is a freshman in college; the other four are seniors in high school.

Background:

The five of you have been close friends for about 10 years. You grew up in the same neighborhood, living only two houses apart. As your parents were friends, you often spent time at each other's homes, always staying with your friends when your parents went out of town. You were the nucleus of the neighborhood gang. You walked to and from school together; in high school, when Frank got a car, the five of you always rode together.

You, then, have done just about everything together. When you are with a person that much, you wind up being able to talk to each other pretty well. As best friends you've shared a lot of problems and hurts with each other. That has made you even closer. Really, the only area that you haven't been a group is the area of religion. Boy 2 and girl 2 have always gone to the Methodist church and Sunday school every Sunday. Boy 1 and girl 1 never got interested in the church thing, though Frank would go every once in a while.

Last fall when Frank came home from college for a weekend, he seemed a little different. When the five of you went out for a pizza, he all of a sudden started talking about becoming a Christian. He seemed a little embarrassed about the whole thing, and you at first thought he had gone off the deep end and was going to start witnessing or something. But he didn't. He just said that he had become a Christian, that his relationship with God meant a lot to him now, and that he felt that he was a lot better person for it.

ROLE BOWL

I don't get it. If Christianity is true, how come there are so many religions that call themselves Christian? I mean, what's the difference between Baptists, Presbyterians, etc.?

If God is God, then how come you can't see him or it? Why don't you prove that God exists? Go ahead...prove it to me.

If you ask me, the Christian religion makes you a doormat. Always loving and turning the other cheek stuff.

The Bible has some nice little stories in it, but everyone knows it's full of contradictions, errors, and just plain myths. How can you believe it?

What if I lived like hell for 80 years and then became a Christian on my deathbed? Would Billy Graham and I go to the same place?

I know a bunch of people that go to your church and they are supposed to be Christians, but I also know what they do during the week and at parties that I go to. They are phonies. If Christianity is so great, how come there are so many phonies?

I have been reading through the Old Testament for English class. How come God ordered his people to kill everybody – even women and children – when they conquered a land? What kind of a God is that?

My little brother died of leukemia and I prayed like crazy. Don't tell me there is a God who loves us. How come he didn't help my brother?

Your mother and I do not believe in all this Jesus stuff and we think you spend too much time in church. So we want you to stay away from church for a while.

Look, I know I am overweight and even though it hurts me to say it, I'm ugly. And I started coming to your church because I thought the kids in your youth group would treat me differently than the kids do at school. Wrong! They ignore me and make fun of me just like everyone else. How come?

A Parable

There landed on my doorstep a damsel. And ere I could greet her, she spake unto me, "Is not life so exciting." For she had been travelling here and there, stopping only to visit with other believers.

Musing, I enquired of the damsel, "How doth the excitement of life manifest itself?" Then did she beam. "There are so many new people to meet. And the Lord doth supply all my need."

"How doth he so?" I wondered, "Seeing thou dost remain in one place not so long as to obtain regular employment."

Again she spake in glowing terms. "Do not believers everywhere take me in? For that is the way with Christians. Yea, and I am helpful and do exciting things."

And I bethought me of life and of those who are the faithful in the church. Yea, and especially of those elders who every day for 20 years and more go five days a week to the same job. Yet they give attention to the care of the flock, day after day, year after year.

"But what of those," I asked, "who must each day care for a home and children regularly and continually?" And her reply was, "Oh, that is so humdrum."

Then did I take note that life is for most of us routine. Indeed, chaos would result if we demanded excitement. Even would the church itself fall apart. For order and comfort depend upon routine and stability. It was Solomon who had tried all novelty, who said, "Behold, what I have seen to be good and to be fitting is to eat and drink and find enjoyment in all the toil with which one toils under the sun and the few days of his life which God has given him."

So to the damsel I spake these words in parting, "Thou has not yet grown up."

Frank came home about every other weekend, and you really started to notice a change in his behavior. He really was easier to get along with; he didn't get angry when Boy 1 accidently backed his car into a tree; he seemed to listen more closely to what you said, to care more openly about you. This was strange at first, but you came to like the changed Frank. Sometimes big brothers can be a real pain; Frank was turning out to be a real neat person. When you finally asked him about all this, he just said that he was trying hard to be a Christian, and that with God's help, he felt that he could be different.

Frank was coming home for Christmas on Christmas Eve, as he had to work at his job at school all day. It was a snowy night, and about 50 miles south of home Frank's car was hit by a semi-trailer which jackknifed on the expressway. Frank was killed instantly. You found out later that the truck driver was drunk.

It was a rough time for both your families. The four of you, especially, felt a deep sense of loss. Somehow you couldn't talk about it the way you used to, maybe it just hurt too much right now. But you still held together as a group; you cared about each other.

Instructions to Boy 1 and Girl 1:

Frank's loss has been really rough on you. You are emotionally worn out. The hurt will never be gone, but you have learned to live with it. But you are angry now. The new Frank was a neat person, and you were almost starting to believe what he was saying about God and all that. But how can a God who is supposed to be love allow someone to be killed like Frank was. It was the other guy who was drunk! It simply isn't fair. Frank was young, with a lot to do in his life, and he was a Christian! What kind of God is it that can let someone like Frank die, and the drunken truck driver live?

Finally in desperation, you have decided to talk to Boy 2 and Girl 2. They have gone to church for some reason, maybe they understand what is going on. (Take it from there.) *Ken Potts*

THE CRUTCH WALKERS

The parable on page 81 is based on the idea that to some people Christianity is only a crutch. Read it to the group and then discuss the questions that follow.

Questions for discussion:

- **If you were one of the people in the story, would you have tried the crutches? Why or why not?**
- **Why do you think some people did not want to try the crutches, and put other people down who did?**
- **Do you feel that Christianity is only a crutch? If so, in what way? Is this good or bad?**
- **How would you respond to a person who rejected Christianity because she thought that it was only a crutch?**

You might wrap up with some thoughts on the importance of realizing that we are in fact handicapped without Christ, and that it is only when we admit that we are crippled that we are able to walk. Some applicable Scripture might include 2 Corinthians 12:10, Numbers 21:4-9, John 3:14-16, and John 1:9-12. *Bill and Sheila Goodwin*

FAITH INVENTORY

A helpful way for young people to clarify and evaluate their beliefs is to take a faith inventory now and then. The process is fairly simple. Copy the faith statements on page 82 and give a copy to each person. Next to each statement is a continuum with one representing total unbelief and 10 representing total belief. The kids are to read each statement and decide just how much or how little they believe it and circle the appropriate number.

Kids should be assured that they can be honest and not feel any less a Christian just because they express some doubts. Most everyone has doubts about certain things, and it is through those doubts that growth takes place. They need to be assured that God loves them even though they can't give every statement of faith a 10. This exercise can be useful to determine where kids need a little more guidance. Discuss each statement with the entire group, allowing kids to share on a volunteer basis how they rated each one and why. This can be used many times with excellent results. *Mary McKemy*

PICTURE TESTIMONIES

Most kids need a little encouragement to reveal to the group what the Lord means to them. To give them some direction without providing a canned

THE CRUTCH WALKERS

There existed a planet on which all the inhabitants were unable to walk. They crawled through life not knowing the pleasure of viewing life upright with the easy mobility of walking. History said that many years before, the descendants had been able to use their legs effectively and walk upright without crawling or pulling their bodies with their hands as they did now.

One day a person came among them who showed great love and compassion toward them. He told them that not only had their ancestors walked on their legs, but that this was possible for them, too. He offered crutches for those who believed him, with the promise that someday, if they trusted him, by using their crutches they would be able to walk upright even without them.

Some of the people decided to try the crutches. Once they were upright, they found how much larger their world became because of this new ease in mobility. They encouraged everyone to join them in this newfound freedom.

Others doubted the crutch walkers would ever be free of their crutches and be able to walk alone. They scoffed at them and said, "We are satisfied with life as we see it. We don't need the assistance of a crutch to experience in life. Only the weak need the aid of crutches to get around!"

THE CRUTCH WALKERS

There existed a planet on which all the inhabitants were unable to walk. They crawled through life not knowing the pleasure of viewing life upright with the easy mobility of walking. History said that many years before, the descendants had been able to use their legs effectively and walk upright without crawling or pulling their bodies with their hands as they did now.

One day a person came among them who showed great love and compassion toward them. He told them that not only had their ancestors walked on their legs, but that this was possible for them, too. He offered crutches for those who believed him, with the promise that someday, if they trusted him, by using their crutches they would be able to walk upright even without them.

Some of the people decided to try the crutches. Once they were upright, they found how much larger their world became because of this new ease in mobility. They encouraged everyone to join them in this newfound freedom.

Others doubted the crutch walkers would ever be free of their crutches and be able to walk alone. They scoffed at them and said, "We are satisfied with life as we see it. We don't need the assistance of a crutch to experience in life. Only the weak need the aid of crutches to get around!"

FAITH INVENTORY

1.	I believe in God.	1	2	3	4	5	6	7	8	9	10
2.	God loves me.	1	2	3	4	5	6	7	8	9	10
3.	I love God.	1	2	3	4	5	6	7	8	9	10
4.	Jesus is God.	1	2	3	4	5	6	7	8	9	10
5.	God forgives me for my sins.	1	2	3	4	5	6	7	8	9	10
6.	God hears my prayer.	1	2	3	4	5	6	7	8	9	10
7.	God answers my prayers.	1	2	3	4	5	6	7	8	9	10
8.	I believe in life after death.	1	2	3	4	5	6	7	8	9	10
9.	I believe the Bible is true.	1	2	3	4	5	6	7	8	9	10
10.	I do what the Bible says.	1	2	3	4	5	6	7	8	9	10

FAITH INVENTORY

1.	I believe in God.	1	2	3	4	5	6	7	8	9	10
2.	God loves me.	1	2	3	4	5	6	7	8	9	10
3.	I love God.	1	2	3	4	5	6	7	8	9	10
4.	Jesus is God.	1	2	3	4	5	6	7	8	9	10
5.	God forgives me for my sins.	1	2	3	4	5	6	7	8	9	10
6.	God hears my prayer.	1	2	3	4	5	6	7	8	9	10
7.	God answers my prayers.	1	2	3	4	5	6	7	8	9	10
8.	I believe in life after death.	1	2	3	4	5	6	7	8	9	10
9.	I believe the Bible is true.	1	2	3	4	5	6	7	8	9	10
10.	I do what the Bible says.	1	2	3	4	5	6	7	8	9	10

testimony formula, ask your Sunday school superintendent if you can borrow some of the teaching pictures of Jesus usually found on the walls of classrooms for younger children. Hang a variety of these pictures around your meeting area, such as "Jesus calming the storm," "Jesus feeding the multitudes," "Jesus in the garden," or whatever. Then have each young person select one picture that means the most to him or her, and share that picture with the group, telling why it's meaningful. Encourage them to relate the picture to some specific area of their own lives. To set the pace you can take your turn first. *Del McKinney*

FAMILY

FAMILY CROSSWORD

The crossword puzzle on page 84 can be used to preface a discussion on the family. Divide the groups into teams of less than five and see which group can complete the puzzle correctly within the time limit. Afterward discuss the correct answers. *Mark Senter*

PERFECT PAIR

For a good discussion on the family, and as a way to discover the values of kids in the group, try this. Simply tell kids that they are to find the world's most perfect couple, that is, the man and woman best suited to create the ideal home and family, and most likely to be happy. Divide into small groups and have them describe their perfect couple. Things to consider:

1. The people themselves
    - a. background
    - b. age
    - c. education
    - d. religious affiliation
    - e. race
    - f. political views
2. Their lifestyle
    - a. jobs (employment)
    - b. hobbies
    - c. sex life
    - d. leisure time
    - e. entertainment
    - f. habits
    - g. friends and associations
3. Their possessions
    - a. money
    - b. furniture
    - c. house and neighborhood
    - d. books, magazines
    - e. appliances
    - f. recreational needs
    - g. auto(s)
4. Philosophy on child-rearing
    - a. discipline
    - b. education
    - c. manners
    - d. dress
    - e. independence

The items listed are only suggestions, and kids should not be limited to them. After a 20- or 30-minute period of working in their groups, have each group describe their perfect couple. Make lists on the blackboard or on an overhead projector. Compare each group's description of their couple. Discuss the differences and similarities and ask why certain characteristics were selected. Talk about prejudices and relate to Scripture. How does God describe his perfect family? What matters and what doesn't? Also discuss the interaction that took place in each small group. The disputes, differences of opinion, prejudices, etc. You can get hours of healthy discussion out of this exercise. *Arthur Mees*

FAITH SCULPTING

If you have students who don't mind being candid about their relationships to those close to them—family, teammates, neighbors, friends—this exercise can be a poignant one.

FAMILIES

Across

2. What most family members think they are.
   Babies are especially this.

4. We think we have it
   When we come of age.
   But we learn how to use it
   Before we leave the cage.

6. Mom and Dad
   Are as different as can be
   and from them we learn
   How one plus one equals three.

7. Wear my school colors
   To express this you see.
   Take up for my sister
   'Cause she's part of me.

8. Players don't do it;
   Cheerleaders do.
   When "hero's" home,
   He may do it, too.

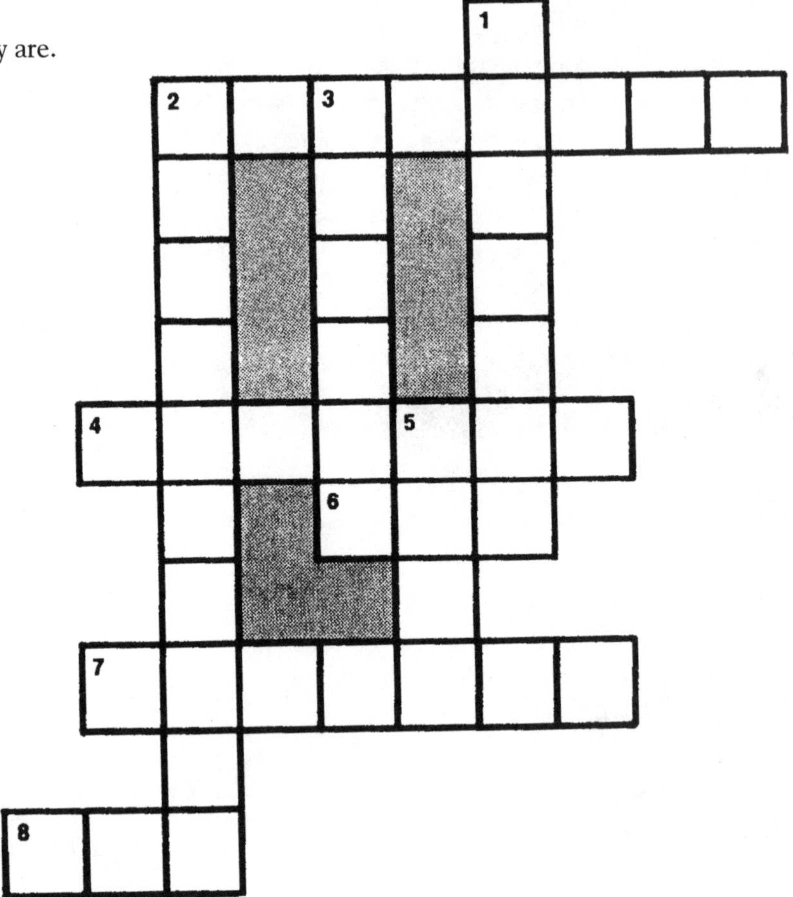

Down

1. When I feel happy and sad at the same time,
   my parents think that I'm a ________.

2. At school we have one
   for chemistry.
   The family is one also
   So we learn how to be.

3. Parents have standards
   Of good and bad.
   Teens develop their systems
   In response to Dad.

5. When thinking of their family, some teens
   think they got a bad one.

Answers:
A2: Lovable; A4: Freedom; A6: Sex;
A7: Loyalty; A8: Cry; D1: Paradox;
D2: Laboratory; D3: Values; D5: Deal

Say that a volunteer student chooses to "faith-sculpt" his family. He selects others from the group to represent God, parents, siblings, and any other family member that lives with him or near him. The volunteer places God in a central part of the room, then arranges the others in such a way as to represent their relationship to God—one family member, for example, who the volunteer perceives to have a very close walk with God, would be placed right next to God, perhaps even touching him. Another family member might be farther away, with her back to God (actively refusing God). Another may be out of the room altogether (does not know God), another laying down (spiritually lazy), others distant but reaching out toward God. Proximity to God and posture are important in this activity.

When the volunteer is finished, ask him to explain his sculpture. The entire group will learn much about how its members perceive their families.
Mark Christian

FAMILY CHOICES

Use this game (reminiscent of the board game Life) to launch your lessons about family life—family choices, dynamics, and communication skills. Your kids will get to know each other a little better, and may even learn some negotiation skills that will benefit their *own* family lives.

Divide your students into families of four, preferably two boys and two girls; at the least, one girl in a family of boys or one boy in a family of girls. Use an arbitrary way to select two parents for each group—choosing a number between one and four, etc. A group's only male or only female is automatically one of the parents.

Supply each family with the materials to make the simple, throw-away spinners (page 87), or make enough spinners yourself beforehand. Then pass out copies of the Family Choices worksheet on page 86 for families to fill in. When everyone's finished ask each family to share its answers with the group.

Finally, take Polaroids of each family and display them in your youth room. *Rob Marin*

DEAR AMY LETTERS

The letters on page 88 are great for starting group discussion on a number of sensitive topics. These letters can be used with kids or parents. They can be answered individually or in small groups. The object is to offer the best possible advice for each problem.
Anne Hughes

PARENT OPINIONS

Give kids a question of the week to take home and get answered by their parents, such as:
- What is the most important objective (goal) in your life?
- What gives you the greatest satisfaction in life?
- If marijuana were legalized, would it still be wrong to smoke it?

Have the kids bring their parents' answers and discuss them, comparing the parental answers with their own.

PARENT BLUNDERS, TEEN GOOFS

Give each kid a sheet of paper that contains two columns of yes and no answers, 10 to each column. Then give the following questions to them orally and have them circle their response after each question. The kids should be as honest as they possibly can, and they need not put their names on their answer sheets.

In column one they answer questions relating to their parents' attitudes toward them, and in column two, questions about their attitudes towards their parents. The total number of yes and no answers in each column can be totaled after the quiz and may then be used as a basis for discussion. Normally whenever the parents score a high number of no answers, so do the kids (and vice versa). For example, if a kid says his parents do not act like they trust him, he will undoubtedly answer no to the questions about trying to earn and keep his parents' trust. The answers should show that both parents and teens have an equal share of the responsibility for their problems.

Parental blunders:

1. **Do your parents listen to you when you have a family discussion?**
2. **Do your parents act like they trust you?**
3. **Do your parents treat your friends nicely and make them feel welcome?**

FAMILY CHOICES

1. Rename the cereal Froot Loops.
2. Figure out a last name for your family.
3. Write down the country or state you want to live in.
4. Write down the kind and number of pets you have.
5. Write down your favorite homecooked meal and fast food place.
6. Choose your favorite amusement park.
7. If your family were a planet, which planet would you be?

Now use your spinner to determine—

8. Number of children your family will ultimately have: ________
9. The make of car you'll drive: ________________________
10. What you'll live in: ________________________________

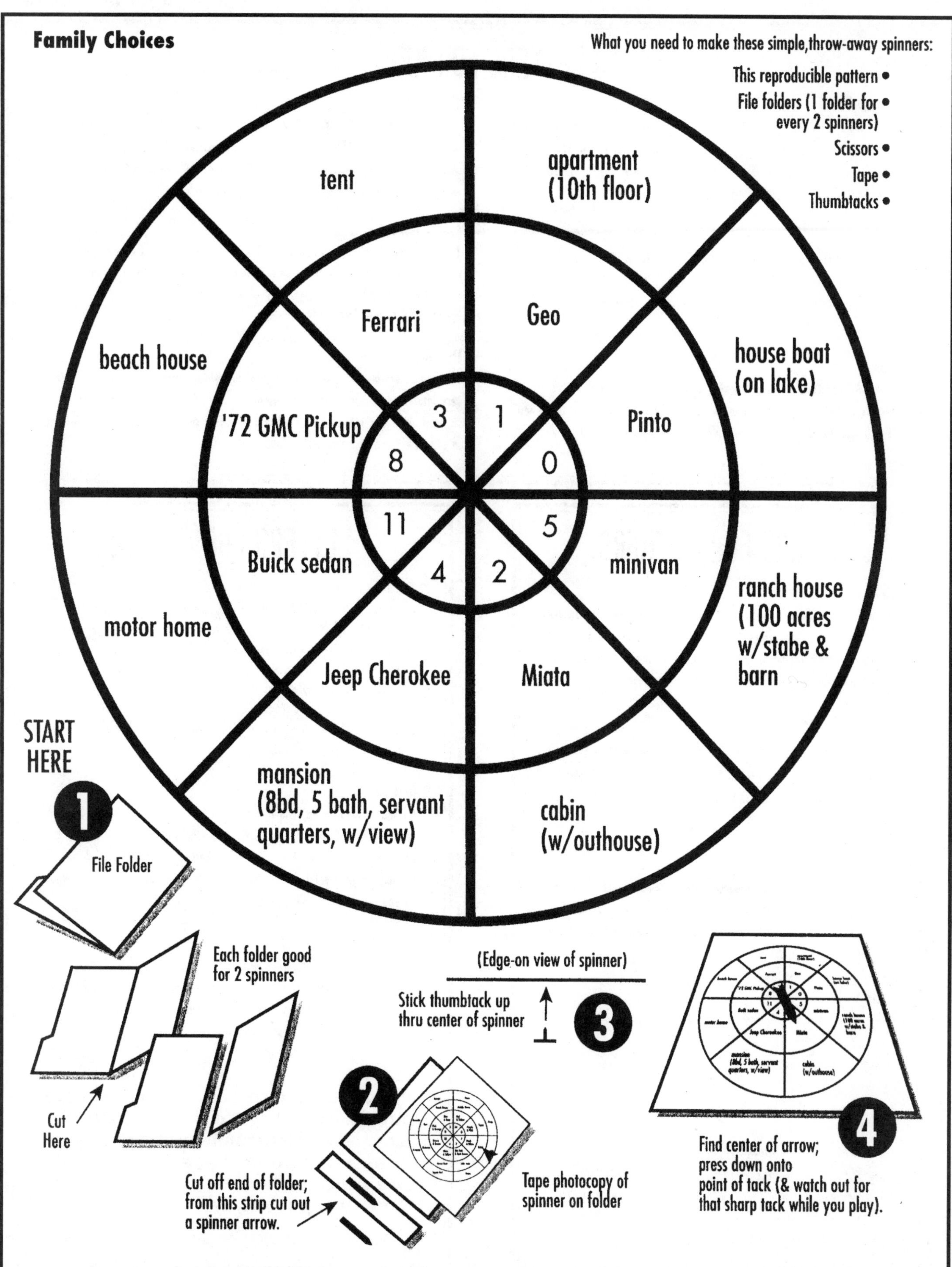
Family Choices
What you need to make these simple,throw-away spinners:
This reproducible pattern •
File folders (1 folder for • every 2 spinners)
Scissors •
Tape •
Thumbtacks •
tent
apartment (10th floor)
beach house
house boat (on lake)
motor home
ranch house (100 acres w/stabe & barn
mansion (8bd, 5 bath, servant quarters, w/view)
cabin (w/outhouse)
Ferrari
Geo
'72 GMC Pickup
Pinto
Buick sedan
minivan
Jeep Cherokee
Miata
3
1
8
0
11
5
4
2
START HERE
1
File Folder
Each folder good for 2 spinners
Cut Here
2
Cut off end of folder; from this strip cut out a spinner arrow.
Tape photocopy of spinner on folder
(Edge-on view of spinner)
Stick thumbtack up thru center of spinner
3
4
Find center of arrow; press down onto point of tack (& watch out for that sharp tack while you play).

LETTERS FOR KIDS

Dear Amy,
My parents always want me to go places with them but I would rather be with my friends. I've had it with this togetherness bit. How can I convince them that I don't enjoy family outings anymore. - Olda Nuff

Dear Amy,
My mother insists that I go to church every Sunday, but my dad never goes, so why should I? Now that I'm older I think I should be allowed to make up my own mind about God, church, and all that stuff. - Tired of Sunday School

Dear Amy,
Our Bible School teacher says every family should study the Bible and pray together, but our family never seems to have the time for that. Isn't going to church together good enough? - Busy Betsy

Dear Amy,
My parents don't like my friends. Whenever I want to go places with my friends, Mom and Dad ask me all kinds of questions. I don't think they trust me either! How can I persuade them to let me go out with whom I want to? - Ina Cage

Dear Amy,
I try to talk to my parents about some of my problems but when I do I usually just get a lecture. How can I make them see that sometimes I just need to talk and do not want their advice? - Lecture Hater

Dear Amy,
My parents are always talking to me about being a minister or a missionary. I am very interested in mathematics and would like to study engineering. How can I talk to them about this without hurting their feelings? I think I can be a good Christian in whatever vocation I choose. - Undecided

LETTERS FOR MOTHERS

Dear Amy,
My husband and I became Christians as adults, but we want our children to let Christ be their guide during their teen years. Our daughter says we're trying to cram religion down her throat. How can we help her understand that she needs Christ now? - Worried Parents

Dear Amy,
I try to spend time with my son and talk to him but when I ask him questions about school, friends, etc. he just clams up. How can I get him to talk over his daily activities as well as his problems? - Clam's Mother

Dear Amy,
My husband and I try to have open communication with our daughter. However, it seems that lately she comes to me with her problems but refuses to talk with her father. He resents this and thinks I'm encouraging her in this direction. Please help. - Caught in the Middle

Dear Amy,
My husband and I come from very different backgrounds and our ideas on child rearing are very different. We seem to be always at odds on rules for the children, punishments, etc. How can we change this? Our children are confused and so are we. — Nita Solution

Dear Amy,
I try to establish good communication with my family by listening to them, asking questions, and encouraging my children to talk about school, etc., and my husband to talk about his work. But nobody listens to me. I want to talk about my activities, too, but no one seems interested. Please advise me. - Wanda Talk Too

LETTERS FOR FATHERS

Dear Amy,
I am bewildered by the way things in the world have changed! When I was a kid life was simple and parents' word was the law. Kids today seem to be living fast and furious. My children think my standards are old-fashioned and impossible to live by in today's society. How can we get together on standards for our family to live by? - Old-Fashioned Dad

Dear Amy,
I'd like to spend more time with my kids but I have a demanding job that requires a lot of overtime. I also try to participate in community affairs and do as much as possible for the church. There simply aren't enough hours in the day for me, yet I realize that my children are growing up fast. What do you suggest? - Full-Schedule Dad

Dear Amy,
My wife and I cannot agree on how to deal with our son. I think she is too soft on him and too sympathetic. He's never going to learn to take it out in the world if we're too easy on him at home. How can I convince her of this? — Ex-Marine Dad

Dear Amy,
My daughter and I used to be very close. We talked a lot and did a lot of things together. But now she's in high school and she seems to have changed completely. She seldom talks to me anymore and seems to spend more and more time away from home. What can I do? - Losing the Apple of My Eye

4. Do your parents admit their mistakes when they have been wrong?
5. Do your parents openly express and show their affection for you?
6. Do your parents avoid comparing you to brothers or sisters or other youths?
7. Do your parents keep the promises that they make to you?
8. Do your parents show their appreciation and give you credit when you do something good?
9. Do your parents set a good example for you in their personal honesty?
10. Do your parents use the kind of language in front of you that they told you to use?

Teen goofs:

1. Do you listen to your parents when they want to share an idea or advice with you?
2. When your parents say no to your plans, do you accept that answer without complaining?
3. Do you try to understand the pressures and problems that sometimes make parents grumpy and hard to live with?
4. Do you say "Thank you" for everything that your parents do for you?
5. Do you try to plan something nice that you can do for your parents occasionally?
6. Do you say "I'm sorry" when you know you have been out of line or have said or done something you shouldn't?
7. Do you try to earn and keep your parents trust by doing what they expect of you?
8. Do you play fair with them and discuss things honestly, without covering up for yourself?
9. Do you ask your parents' advice about decisions that you have to make?
10. Do you try to avoid problems and arguments by doing what you're supposed to before you have to be told?

Bill O'Connor

How to Raise Your Parents

Some good questions for a discussion about parents are on page 90. For best results print them up and pass them out to each person. Give the kids time to answer all the questions individually, then discuss them one at a time with the entire group. *Bill Curry*

Parent-Teen Eye-Opener

Here's an idea that helps young people see that the struggle they may be having with their parents isn't all their parents' fault. It can be a real eye-opener for the kids, and can prove to be a good peacemaker in the midst of family strife.

Pass out a 3x5 card to each person. Then have them draw a line down the middle of the card and write MOM above one column and DAD above the other. Tell the kids that they will be asked 10 questions, and they are to answer them separately for the mothers and fathers. They must grade their parents on a scale of 1 to 10, with one being the lowest or worst possible grade and 10 being the highest or best. Here are the questions:

1. Do your parents show you affection?
2. Do your parents listen to you?
3. Do your parents talk with you about schoolwork? Your interests? Your boy/girlfriend?
4. Do your parents trust you?
5. Do your parents respect you?
6. Do your parents initiate leisure activities that involve you (shopping, camping tennis, walks)?
7. Do your parents treat your friends the way you want them to be treated?
8. Do your parents always have a settled opinion about things? (a one indicates they do, a 10 means they don't)
9. Do your parents respect your privacy?
10. Do your parents treat you the way you want to be treated?

After both parents have been graded on these points, you will want to discuss the kids' answers on a few random questions. What usually follows is a discussion of all the things parents do wrong. But the real key to this exercise is the next step. After the discussion have the kids turn their cards over, and again make two columns with the headings MOM and DAD. But this time they are to grade themselves, using the same questions turned around. (For example: Do you show your mom affection? Your dad?) In this way they can think about their relationships to both their mothers and fathers. The young people will likely see that, in many cases, their attitudes toward their parents are very similar to their parents' attitudes toward them. Close the discussion by having the kids think of ways they can improve the relationships they have with their parents. *Chris and Liz Rhodes*

How to Raise Your Parents

1. How would your rate your relationship with your parent(s)? Poor 1 — 2 — Average 3 — 4 — Great 5

2. What are some of the problems in your relationship with your parent(s)?

3. What are some of the good points of your relationship with your parent(s)?

4. What would help improve the relationship?

5. What do the following verses teach about relationships with parents?
   Col. 3:20
   Prov. 3:1-4
   Ex. 20:3

6. Rate yourself in the following areas:

	Almost Never				Almost Always
a. I obey my parents in all things.	1	2	3	4	5
b. I am patient with my parents' weaknesses.	1	2	3	4	5
c. I apologize to my parents when I hurt them.	1	2	3	4	5
d. I trust God to change my parents if they are wrong.	1	2	3	4	5
e. I do more than my parents ask of me.	1	2	3	4	5
f. I try to see life from my parents' point of view.	1	2	3	4	5
g. I ask my parents for their advice.	1	2	3	4	5
h. I thank my parents for all they do for me.	1	2	3	4	5
i. I pray for my parents.	1	2	3	4	5
j. I show my parents I love them.	1	2	3	4	5
k. I tell my parents I love them.	1	2	3	4	5
l. I live the kind of life my parents can be proud of.	1	2	3	4	5

7. The area which I most need to improve is ______________________________

8. Check any of the following ideas you'd like to commit yourself to do in the next 48 hours:
   ___ Buy my mother flowers.
   ___ Ask my parents to pray with me.
   ___ Take my parents out to eat.
   ___ Ask my parents for some advice.
   ___ Give my parents a hug or kiss.
   ___ Tell my parents I love them.
   ___ Write a note of appreciation to my parents.
   ___ Do some chores without being told.
   ___ Wash the car.

The Parenting Game

Give your teens an idea of what it's like to be a parent. Form families of three—one person plays the role of the father, one the mother, and one the child. The object is for each pair of parents to lead their blindfolded child home (a designated spot), directing the child by verbal guidance only.

But you tell the children and the parents two different things. Take the children to a separate room to blindfold them. Before they return to play the game, tell them that they must attempt to get home and that their parents will attempt to mislead them—even lie to them—about the directions to home.

Tell the parents, however, that this game is a race and that the first child to reach home wins for the team.

Now bring the two groups together to the starting place. After disorienting the blindfolded children by spinning them, say "Go!" Parents may then shout directions to their child. What happens next allows your group to experience some of the frustrations parents often feel.

What you'll see:

- Parents screaming for their child to listen to them.
- Children frustrated by their parents' pushiness to go fast and win.
- Some parents may simply stop giving guidance altogether.
- Perhaps one-half of a parental pair may get sufficiently frustrated with yelling directions that he or she gives up—leaving the other partner as a single parent.

Follow the game with a forum on parent-teenager relationships. *Mike Couvion*

Rotating Fear

Divide your group into eight small groups with one leader in each small group. (If your youth group is too small for eight groups, then just eliminate some of the discussion statements.) Prepare eight rooms by putting in each a stack of eight 3x5 cards with a discussion statement written on each. Each room has a different statement in it. The groups will start out with one group in each room. Each group is to pick a card off the top of the pile, read it, and discuss its implications. The group spends five minutes discussing the validity of the statement and votes whether to agree or disagree with the statement and records the vote in the appropriate spot on the card. When the five minutes is up (ring a bell), each group rotates to the next room and repeats the procedure.

After each group has been through all eight rooms, bring them back together in the large group. Total the votes for each question and share the findings. Discuss each statement further. It can be a very interesting discussion on fear.

Room 1. You're riding on Space Mountain at Disney World. You find yourself screaming at the top of your lungs in fear. This fear is stupid. You should try your best to ignore or repress it.

Room 2. You've read a Stephen King novel or *The Exorcist*. Demonic possession scares you. As portrayed in the book it sounds horrible and frightening. Actually, you shouldn't be afraid.

Room 3. You were just caught skipping class. You face a chance of being suspended. You're scared. You ought to be.

Room 4. You've just returned from a tent revival meeting. The preacher talked about hell and its horrors. The talk scared you. You don't want to go to hell. You shouldn't be afraid.

Room 5. "There is no fear in love: But perfect love casts out fear, because fear involves punishment. And the one who fears is not perfected in love."—1 John 4:18.

Room 6. You have just seen a horror movie. Later, you begin to become terribly afraid. This fear is childish. You should try to ignore or repress your fear.

Room 7. "The Lord is my light and my salvation: Whom shall I fear?"—Psalm 27:1 According to this, Christians should fear nothing.

Room 8. Fear is good.

Ben Sharpton

Freedom for All

Here's a fun way to open a discussion on the topic of

freedom. Divide the group into smaller groups and have each group come up with a short skit that would show what they would do if they were completely free to do their own thing, with no restrictions. Then have them present the skits to the group. Most will be very funny, showing such things as telling off their parents, teachers, etc., dropping out of school, living it up, traveling, and so on. Surprisingly enough, these skits actually help the kids to see the chaos and futility of "complete freedom." The following questions can then be used for an in-depth discussion of the topic:

- **What does the word freedom mean to you?**
- **If you were "completely free," what would you do?**
- **If everyone were "completely free," and did their own thing, what would be the result?**
- **Discuss Romans 6:16-23 and Paul's concept of man as a slave.**
- **Discuss Romans 7:21-25. What was Paul's problem and where did he find freedom from it?**
- **How does Christ define freedom? (See John 8:31-34.)**
- **Discuss freedom vs. responsibility. (See Galatians 5:13.)**

Wayne Renning

REALIZING OUR NEED FOR GOD

As each person comes into class, have their hands taped together with athletic adhesive tape. Have some activities in which they must use their hands and it is inconvenient for them (arranging chairs for discussion groups, reading Scripture, etc.). Read the story of the cripple at the pool of Bethesda in John 5. Tell them that if they can draw a parallel between their situation and the cripple's, they will be set free. Have one person with a tape cutter. The correct answer would be that he was trapped or hindered and needed help outside himself to set him free, as do they. Some will want to know if they can tell others the correct answer. You tell them, "It's up to you."

When everyone is set free, relate a modern day story of someone trapped in a certain situation, possibly drugs, sex, hypocrisy at church, etc., and how they were set free by Jesus Christ.

Draw the analogy now that everyone is bound by something and needs to be set free. There is only one who can set men free (the tape cutter). Christians have the answer that will set men free, but will we share the solution with others? (It's up to you.) *Steven E. Robinson*

FUTURE

FUTURE WORLD

The purpose of this exercise is to help teenagers see how their future is related to the preparation they make now, and how the church can help them prepare for the future. It will also encourage them to evaluate their preparation for the future.

First, divide the youths into small groups of three or four. Give each group three large sheets of paper and some markers. Then read the questions below one at a time, and let them brainstorm about answers. Each group should record its ideas on large sheets of paper, then report back to the large group. Have a separate reporting time for each question.

The questions:

1. **List some characteristics of the world as you think it will be in 10 years.**
2. **List some characteristics of a person who will best be able to deal with the world as it will exist 10 years from now.**
3. **List five goals the church should adopt in order to prepare youth for handling the world of the future.**

After all the answers have been presented and discussed, ask the teens what they are doing now to prepare themselves spiritually for the future. In responding to this last question, many students will realize that the church is already attempting to prepare young people for the future, but they aren't taking advantage of all the opportunities offered. Youth workers may also discover some needs of their youths presently being overlooked. *Del McKinney*

FUTURE FANTASY

Pass out index cards and pencils, and have the group list three or four clues about a vocation they believe they might pursue in the next five or 10 years. The vocational possibilities listed should be serious. Make sure each person keeps his or her vocation and clues a secret. Once the cards are completed, collect and shuffle them thoroughly. (Clue example: Doctor—caring for others, writing messy.)

Next, pass out blank sheets of paper. Count out how many people are playing, and have them number on the paper from one up to that total. While they're numbering their papers, number the cards you've collected. When all the papers and cards are ready, read aloud the clues on the first card, and have everyone write down a guess about who that person is. Remind teens not to comment aloud on any of the cards or their responses. After you've read through all the clue cards, repeat any as needed for clarification.

Now go through the cards again with the person who wrote each one revealing him or herself. The results will be both fun and surprising.

Use the following questions, plus others of your own, for discussion:

- **What do you look forward to in the future?**
- **What do you fear most about the future?**
- **Read Matthew 6:25-34. Do you think God wants you to worry about the future? Why or why not?**
- **What hope does God offer for your future?**
- **What can you do to make your dreams come true?**

Close with a prayer that your students' futures will be centered on God and his Word. *Tommy Baker*

LOOKING AHEAD TO HIGH SCHOOL

Here's an idea for a junior high meeting if you have separate junior and senior high youth groups.

Invite several of your high school students to attend a meeting of the junior high group in order to answer the younger kids' questions and to speak about the high school experience. It's best if your junior highers are in small groups, with one or two high schoolers in each group. Prep the high schoolers to ask the junior highers for their feelings about the following questions:

- **What comes to mind when you think of high school?**
- **What fears do you have about high school?**
- **What are your hopes for high school?**

Next, gather the high schoolers into a panel that discusses their answers to these questions:

- **What did you fear about high school when you were in junior high? What actually happened?**
- **What is the best thing that has happened to you so far in high school?**

Follow the panel discussion with Scripture readings (1 Cor. 10:13; Phil. 4:12-13; etc.) and allow some of the kids to share how the passages apply to their lives in high school. Let some of them share how their faith has grown in high school. Point out to the junior highers that their high school youth group can help them make their high school years the best they can be. *Bob Stebe*

TABLOID PROPHECIES

Want to introduce a discussion about biblical prophecies in a new way? On your way through the check-out line during some late-December grocery shopping, buy copies of National Enquirer and its kin that carry the new-year predictions of psychics. You know, "Elizabeth Taylor Will Receive Scalp Transplant from Elvis Clone," "Scientists Will Discover That Space Aliens Dictate Scripts for TV Evangelists," and that sort of thing.

When the group has laughed its way through them, then bring up discussion questions like these:

- **Which of these prophecies are likely to come true? Why?**
- **Do you think psychics really prophesied these, or that the tabloid editors simply fabricated the prophecies?**
- **What kind of a success rate do these psychics claim? How does that compare with the required success rate for prophets of God?**
- **What accounts for the popularity of such tabloids, and especially their published prophecies? Why do you think people are curious about the future?**

You may want to mention, read, or study any of the biblical accounts of prophesying whether illegitimate (the Endorian seer whom the doomed King Saul consulted, the fortune-telling slave girl in Acts 16) or legitimate (the book of Revelation). Save the tabloids for a follow-up lesson a year later—how close were the psychics' predictions? *Jeff Callen*

GAZING INTO THE FUTURE

The following exercise is designed to help young people think in the future tense and to explore the values of a rapidly changing world. Across the top of a blackboard, write three dates. In the middle column write the current year; to left of it write the date for 20 years ago (year only) and to the right of the current year, write the date for 20 years from now (year only). Then, down the side of the blackboard, write these categories: MUSIC, ECONOMICS, FASHION, ENVIRONMENT, CRIME, EDUCATION, MORALS, TRANSPORTATION, ENTERTAINMENT, and RELIGION (change these or add to them as you want). Through group discussion, fill in the chart by going across the board in each category. Try to come up with a realistic prognosis for the future by looking at the past and present. (Facilitate the discussion by including a moderator who was around 40 or 50 years ago.)

After you have filled everything in, take a look at the future column. You can draw attention to the fact that most of the kids will be approaching middle age then and that this is the world that they might have to live in. How does it look to them? Optimistic? Negative? Are they looking forward to it?

	1963	1983	2003
MUSIC			
ECONOMICS			
FASHION			
ENVIRONMENT			
CRIME			
EDUCATION			
MORALS			
TRANSPORTATION			
ENTERTAINMENT			
RELIGION			

Here are some other possible discussion questions:

- **How do you feel about change? What causes things to change so rapidly in our world?**
- **What things do you think people will collect and reminisce about 20 years from now?**
- **Of the predictions made for 20 years from now, which ones would you want to change? How would you go about changing them?**
- **What kinds of problems will your teenage children encounter 20 years from now? What kind of parent do you hope you'll be?**
- **How accurately could a person 20 years ago have predicted what the world is like now?**

Craig Moulton

FANTASY REUNION

How will your students' priorities now affect their futures? Find out by holding an impossibly early youth group reunion.

Have everyone come dressed as if it were 40 years in the future and they are returning to a youth group reunion. They should come prepared to talk about their husbands and wives, their children, careers, accomplishments, ministries, and so on. Get everyone role-playing as soon as they walk in the door. Start with refreshments and mingling so they get right into their parts. Mingle yourself, too, keeping your ears open for some of the more imaginative "life histories."

After the mingling and refreshments, call everyone together and ask some of those you overheard—as well as any others—to tell the group at large about what's happened with them during the past 40 years. The results are usually hilarious—and afterward you can have a more serious discussion about the lasting value of current priorities. *Marti Lambert*

WIN, LOSE, OR NO!

In your teaching series on covetousness, money, and wealth, do you need a discussion starter for a lesson on gambling? Ask you students to rank the following from 1 to 10 (least wrong to most wrong), as they see it:

1. Placing a five dollar bet on a horse race at the track.
2. Pitching pennies before school with some school friends.
3. Buying a raffle ticket on a car for a football booster-club fundraiser.
4. Playing the slot machines in a Las Vegas casino.
5. Playing poker for pennies with three of your church friends.

6. Playing poker for several dollars with three school friends.

7. Playing games of chance at an amusement park.

8. Entering your name for a free drawing for 200 dollars worth of groceries at the supermarket.

9. Betting your week's salary on the World Series or the Super Bowl.

10. Betting on pool games at the church or community recreation center.

11. Buying several tickets for the state lottery.

Amend these or add to them, depending on your church, your young people, and your situation. Ask students to relate their answers to these and similar passages: Exodus 16:15-21; Matthew 6:19-34; Mark 11:24-25; Luke 12:13-34; 1 Timothy 6:6-10, 17-19. *Tom Daniel*

GODHEAD (FATHER, SON, HOLY SPIRIT)

MODERN DAY JESUS

Here's an exercise that will not only provide you with a good index of your youth group's perception of Jesus Christ, but will also provide clues to their understanding of the implications of being a Christian today. Ask the group to respond to the list of questions below as if they were Jesus Christ here and now. Stress the fact that there are no right or wrong answers to this exercise. The main thing is that each person respond based on how they think Christ would respond if he were alive today.

1. **What kind of clothes do you wear? Do you identify with any particular class of people (poor, middle or upper class, minority groups, etc.)?**
2. **Describe your family relationships (to your mother, father, brothers, sisters). Do you have a girlfriend? Will you marry?**
3. **What kind of people do you hang around with? What do you talk about?**
4. **What do you look like?**
5. **Where do you spend most of your time? What is your favorite hang-out?**
6. **Are you a controversial figure? Why or why not?**
7. **How do you feel about the church today? How do you get along with the religious leaders today?**
8. **How do you feel about the way things are in this country?**
9. **What are your goals for the next 10 years?**
10. **How would you get your message out to as many people as possible? (Think this one through carefully. Is mass media the best way to get your message across?)**
11. **What are you politically? Are you a member of a specific party? What would you consider the important political issues?**

After everyone has answered the questions individually, then discuss them with the entire group. To move the discussion from the hypothetical to the actual, ask whether or not we as Christians should respond to those questions in the same manner as our imagined, modern Christ. Aren't we to follow Christ and to pattern our lives after his example? *Van Edington*

NAME THAT JESUS

Many of us have our conception of Jesus Christ influenced heavily by pictures we have seen of Christ. Ask your young people to write down a description of what they think Christ looked like. Follow that with a comparison of each person's description and a discussion of the physical appearance of Jesus.

Then bring before the group as many different pictures of Jesus as you can find. Discuss each picture and attempt to write a description of the group's response to the picture. (For example, Hook's famous picture of Christ could be described by "strong, masculine, compassionate, determined, intense, healthy, handsome, etc.") You could also discuss different movies or plays in which Christ was portrayed and compare each of those.

As a finale to this lengthy discussion, take different scriptural passages dealing with Jesus and attempt to formulate, as a group, what you think Jesus looked like and why. (Don't be limited to New Testament references to Christ. Include Isaiah 53:1-3 and Psalms 22:6-8.) *Michael McDowell*

DESCRIBE THE COUNSELOR

Illustrate the accuracy of the Gospels' description of Jesus, using your teens' own powers of observation. This works best with at least five groups with three members each.

Pick a well-known adult volunteer or youth leader (someone with a healthy self-image) who is absent from your meeting. Divide into groups, assigning someone who can draw to each group.

Ask the group members to come up with seven things about "Bill" that characterize him. The first four things can be nonphysical descriptions (he's our youth pastor, he's married to Andrea, he drives a red Mustang, he lives in Utica). The next three things should describe his character or specific events about him that stick out as memorable (he does impressions, he always runs late, he built an igloo at the retreat). The group members must agree on each of the descriptions. The goal is to match as many descriptions as possible with the other groups.

Next, have each group's artist draw a picture of Bill from memory only.

Bring the groups together to compare descriptions and pictures. Find the things all the groups had in common (usually there are two or three things all groups agree on). Make the point to your students that many people who know one person can come up with a pretty accurate description of that person. The Gospel writers had some basic common descriptions of Jesus and the things he did, so the post-resurrection appearances of Christ could not have been hallucinations. *Bill Fry*

MATTHEW ONE

Here's how to generate interest among kids in the genealogy of Jesus as described in Matthew 1. An annotated version of Matthew 1:1-16 (that is, it has some material added that explains who a few of the people were) is on page 97. The annotations reveal to the group what otherwise might be evident only to those who are well educated in the Old Testament. The reading also allows for the group's response to many of the people in Jesus' family tree.

Here's how it works: As you read the genealogy aloud, helpers hold up cue cards so that the group can respond as directed by the card. Cue cards should read APPLAUSE, BOO, CHEER, HISS, MOAN, or HUH? (The HUH? cue card is displayed when you read the names of people in the genealogy who are unknown even to biblical scholars or who did little or nothing of consequence.) Briefly rehearse the cue card bit to get kids in the spirit of the activity.

To get the appropriate response, pause as indicated by the parentheses.

A good way to use this for more than just laughs is to point out that Jesus' ancestors were not just good people but that many were evil—prostitutes, murderers, bigamists, and more. Yet Jesus turned out great. So, maybe this means there is hope for us and for our children. We may not be able to blame the way we are on our parents or anyone else. Discuss how we are all responsible before God for who we are. This reading is appropriate for use at Advent or in a Bible study as a way of beginning the book of Matthew. *By Doug Adams; reprinted by permission from* Modern Liturgy *magazine*

YOUR GOD IS TOO SMALL

First, try a word association test with the group. Have the kids give back to you the first word that comes into their minds when you say a word. You might have them write their word associations down on paper. Then you can read them back. Example: cat, boy, movie, red, home, sex, God (always end up with God—pointing out the different responses)

Next, discuss descriptions of God with the kids. Possible questions:

- **What does it mean that we are created "in his image?" Does he look like us?**

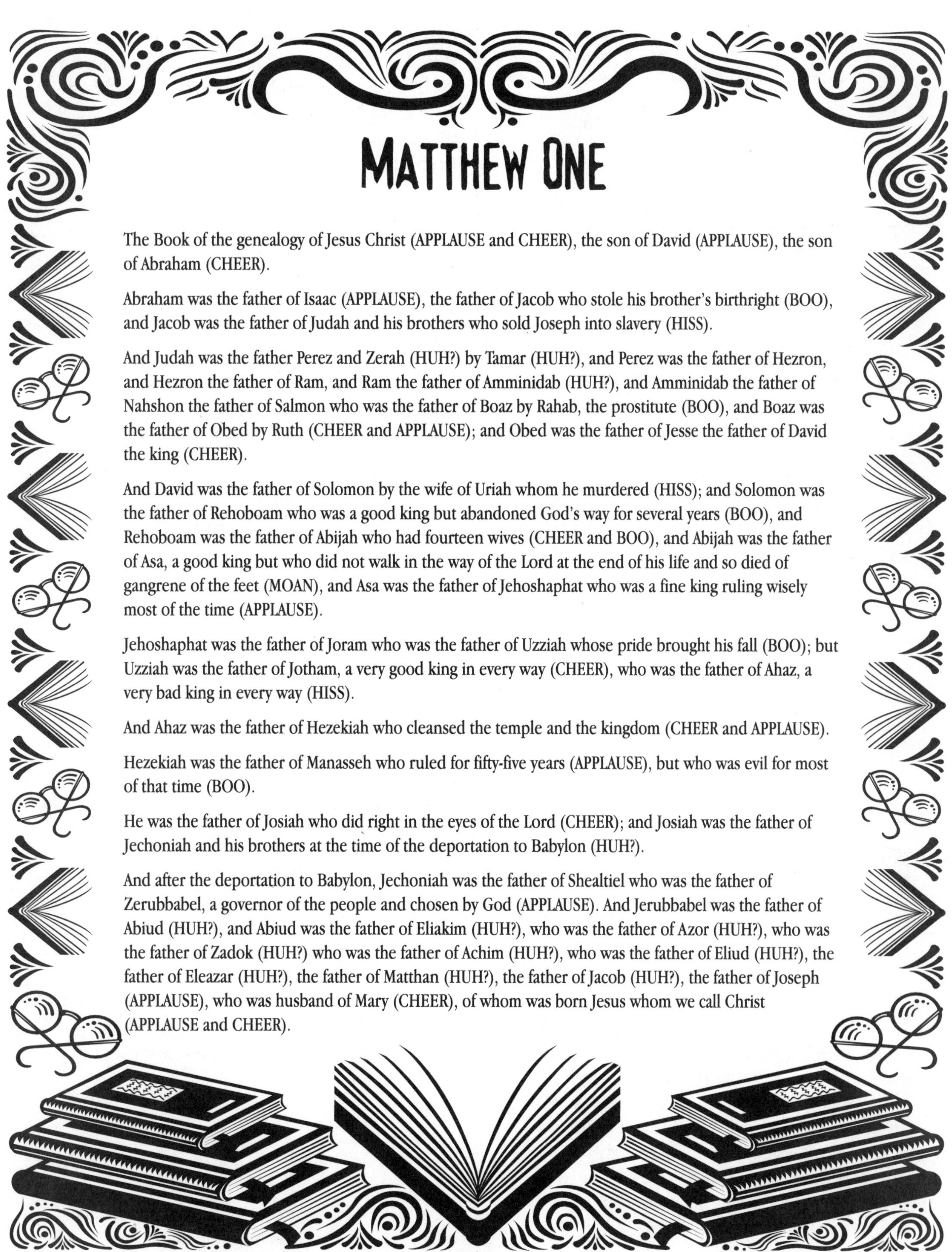

MATTHEW ONE

The Book of the genealogy of Jesus Christ (APPLAUSE and CHEER), the son of David (APPLAUSE), the son of Abraham (CHEER).

Abraham was the father of Isaac (APPLAUSE), the father of Jacob who stole his brother's birthright (BOO), and Jacob was the father of Judah and his brothers who sold Joseph into slavery (HISS).

And Judah was the father Perez and Zerah (HUH?) by Tamar (HUH?), and Perez was the father of Hezron, and Hezron the father of Ram, and Ram the father of Amminidab (HUH?), and Amminidab the father of Nahshon the father of Salmon who was the father of Boaz by Rahab, the prostitute (BOO), and Boaz was the father of Obed by Ruth (CHEER and APPLAUSE); and Obed was the father of Jesse the father of David the king (CHEER).

And David was the father of Solomon by the wife of Uriah whom he murdered (HISS); and Solomon was the father of Rehoboam who was a good king but abandoned God's way for several years (BOO), and Rehoboam was the father of Abijah who had fourteen wives (CHEER and BOO), and Abijah was the father of Asa, a good king but who did not walk in the way of the Lord at the end of his life and so died of gangrene of the feet (MOAN), and Asa was the father of Jehoshaphat who was a fine king ruling wisely most of the time (APPLAUSE).

Jehoshaphat was the father of Joram who was the father of Uzziah whose pride brought his fall (BOO); but Uzziah was the father of Jotham, a very good king in every way (CHEER), who was the father of Ahaz, a very bad king in every way (HISS).

And Ahaz was the father of Hezekiah who cleansed the temple and the kingdom (CHEER and APPLAUSE).

Hezekiah was the father of Manasseh who ruled for fifty-five years (APPLAUSE), but who was evil for most of that time (BOO).

He was the father of Josiah who did right in the eyes of the Lord (CHEER); and Josiah was the father of Jechoniah and his brothers at the time of the deportation to Babylon (HUH?).

And after the deportation to Babylon, Jechoniah was the father of Shealtiel who was the father of Zerubbabel, a governor of the people and chosen by God (APPLAUSE). And Jerubbabel was the father of Abiud (HUH?), and Abiud was the father of Eliakim (HUH?), who was the father of Azor (HUH?), who was the father of Zadok (HUH?) who was the father of Achim (HUH?), who was the father of Eliud (HUH?), the father of Eleazar (HUH?), the father of Matthan (HUH?), the father of Jacob (HUH?), the father of Joseph (APPLAUSE), who was husband of Mary (CHEER), of whom was born Jesus whom we call Christ (APPLAUSE and CHEER).

- **What does God do all day long?**
- **What might he look like if he appeared to us in the flesh?**
- **Does God have a sense of humor?**
- **What would you do if you were God?**
- **Why doesn't God fix the world's problems?**

As a wrap-up to the discussion, respond to the following stereotypes of God with appropriate Scripture. First show what God isn't.

• Is your God an "heirloom?" (Second hand—just assumed? Conscience—environmentally conditioned? Parent image or Santa Claus image?)
• Is he a "lovely old man?" (The bearded Ancient of Days? Old hymns, old-time religion, 14th Century God?)
• Is your God a disappointment? (Someone to blame things on?)
• Is your God a Baptist? (Or Presbyterian, Nazarene, etc.)

Finally, define what God is:

• He is all powerful—the Creator of the universe.
• He is all loving—interested in the individual.
• He accepts you as you are.
• He is contemporary; he understands our modern problems.
• He is perfect justice, yet he is fair.
• He is "not willing that any should perish." This upsets him.
• He is present now and is active in the world.
• He offers life to you when you accept his plan for your life.

Arthur Jenkins

INVENT

Divide your youth group into smaller groups of eight to 10. Describe the situation below and give each group 20 minutes to finish their task. At the end of the allotted time, have the group all meet together and compare their responses.

You find yourself in a new civilization in which everything is the same as our world is now, but there is no Bible, no God, no religion, no church, no religious history. You have been selected by your government to create a God that will have the proper attributes that will cause people to worship. This God should represent everything that you think will be attractive and yet as the same time, explain things like natural disasters (flood, earthquake, etc.), sickness, suffering, and evil.

Questions to help you as you invent God: What is its name, if any? Where does it live? Is it visible? Will your God make any demands on people? How do you worship it? Any rewards or punishments? What does it look like? Is there more than one? Does it have any bad attributes? Just let your imaginations run wild and attempt to invent the perfect God that will attract the most people.

The discussion should then compare the invented God with the God of the Bible. The following questions could be included in the discussion:

- **Why is God so mysterious?**
- **Why did God leave so many unanswered questions?**
- **Why doesn't God make himself visible?**
- **What are the most difficult things about God to believe?**
- **What things would you change about God if you could?**

Timothy Quill

LONG-DISTANCE ROLE PLAY

Here's an interesting role play using simulated telephone conversations. Give each person a card with one of the following situations written on it. The teen must act out only one side of the conversation, and the rest of the group then tries to guess what is going on.

• You have just called heaven to complain about the way things are going and after you have listed all you complaints, you find you were talking to God personally.
• God has just called you to suggest that you break up with your boyfriend/girlfriend, and you are trying to convince him otherwise.
• God has just called to explain that he wants you to be a missionary. You don't want to be so you're trying to convince him that you do, but not right now.
• God called and wants you to give an account of how you have spent the last three days.
• You have just experienced a personal tragedy and you call God to ask why. He answers the phone, listens to what you have to say, and then hangs up without a word.

Marja L. Coons

CREATION, GOD, AND YOU

This exercise and discussion is great for camps and retreats, but it can be used almost anywhere. Begin by giving each person a piece of paper and pencil. Take them outside and have them list all the things they notice about nature—the things it does or is like. (For example, the great variety of colors, the intricacy of plant structure, the sun that heats the earth, enabling life to exist, and so on.)

When the time is up, have the group return and share their results with the rest of the group. After this, ask them to describe the most scenic spot they have ever visited or where they think the most beautiful place in the world is, or what it is about creation that amazes them the most. Use this as a take-off to find out what Scripture has to say about God who created it all.

Have different people read the following passages:

Genesis 1:4, 1:26, 2:7

Romans 1:19-20, 8:21-23

Hebrews 11:3

Revelation 4:1

After each passage have someone briefly state what the basic idea of the passage was.

Lead the group in discussion, using the following questions as a way of getting at God's character expressed through his creation. Tell the group to use the Scripture just read and other Scripture as a basis from which to think about and answer the questions.

• What are some things we know about God upon observing his creation? Can you list some of his attributes?
• Is creation an extension of God or is creation something separate from God?
• In the beginning God looked at creation and said it was good. Is it still good? Did the Fall make it bad?
• What is the purpose of creation?
• Is creation still going on? Is God still involved in his creation? Explain.
• How does creation speak to us in a personal way? Can you name some things that would be relevant to your own personal situation? How does our knowledge of God through creation help us to trust him?

Anna Hobbs

GOD IS LIKE...

If someone asked you to describe God, what would you say? Traditionally, God has been described as the man upstairs, a heavenly father, a mighty judge, a mother hen, and so on. So begin this exercise by listing some commonly known descriptions of God.

In small groups (or individually) have kids list on paper more creative, current descriptions of God beginning with this statement: "God is like...." You could base some of the ideas on advertising slogans such as "God is like Coke...he's the real thing," or "God is like Allstate...you're in good hands with him," or "God is like a good student...he spreads his work over six days instead of pulling an all-nighter." After 10 minutes have each group read its description and contrast and compare results. Eliminate similar slogans or descriptions and vote on the most creative one. Close by discussing the various images of God presented and come to a consensus on the best four or five. *Kathy Horton*

GRAVEN IMAGES

The second commandment, forbidding worship of graven images (Ex. 20:4), can apply to any false concept of God that takes the place of our true Creator. To help your kids identify some of the idols common today which are distortions of God's real character, have them write down one thing they would change about God if they could. Then give them the list of gods on page 100, and ask them to identify the ones they struggle with.

Now that you've considered these graven images, take a look at how the Bible describes the true nature of God:

Unchanging—Ps. 93:2; Ex. 3:14

Majestic—Ps. 145:5; 2 Pet. 1:16

Wise—Ps. 119:99-100; Job 12:13

Loving—Titus 3:6

Gracious—Rom. 9:16; 2 Thess. 2:12-14

Just—Heb. 12:23; Ps. 75:7

Wrathful—Nah. 1:2-8; Luke 21:22-24; Rom. 11:22

Jealous—James 4:5; Ex. 20:5

Tom Westing

NO GRAVEN IMAGE

1. Heirloom God

This is a secondhand god, one you inherited from your parents. You never really discovered this god for yourself; you just believed in him because of what others told you.

2. Cultural God

This god represents the dominant values of the society. He wants us to be beautiful, rich, and successful.

3. Killjoy God

This god is in your conscience, always reminding you not to have too much fun. He has no sense of humor and is always saying "no."

4. Enforcer God

This god is always punishing you for your sins even though they're forgiven. You can never relax because you know he's looking over your shoulder, waiting to nail you.

5. Jellyfish God

This god is helpless in the face of injustice. He allows sin in the world because he's not strong enough to do anything about it. This god promises to answer your prayers, but never comes through.

6. Traditional God

This god is carefully defined by your particular church or denomination, which has him all figured out. You can never challenge the group's view from Scripture, because there's nothing new to learn about him—he's utterly comfortable and predictable.

7. Absentee God

This god may have created the world and might be returning some day, but nobody can really know him today.

8. Cosmic Bellhop God

This one is also called the Santa Claus god. You call him up on the hot line and give him your list of requests. He exists just to serve you, and can be ignored whenever you don't need anything.

Attribute Ads

Here's an exercise that will encourage some creative thinking about God. Divide your group into small groups and give each one an object of some kind—like a lightbulb, for example, or a coat hanger, a roll of tape, a bar of soap, etc. Then have each group compose a one-line slogan (such as "I'm a big kid now" for Pull-Ups Training Pants or "Just for the taste of it—Diet Coke!). The one-liner should describe how God is like the object that each group has been given.

If the object is a lightbulb, for example, a group might come up with "God lights up the darkness!" Or if a group has a roll of tape, it could say that "God holds the world together!" Have groups display their items as they reveal their slogans.

Discuss the various ways that groups described God and how we need to look for God in everyday things. Point out that Jesus often used common things to describe spiritual truths—"The kingdom of God is like a wheat field..." *James Lutes*

Canned Illustration

Many Christian young people find it hard to believe that they have a wealth of untapped power within them provided by the Holy Spirit. A good illustration of this truth can be had by emptying a can of shaving cream on a table top which demonstrates how a small can can actually contain an enormous amount of soap. If a person can do this with shaving cream, how much more can the Holy Spirit fill a person with overflowing power and love?

Egg in a Bottle

Here's an object lesson that is good around Easter or after an evening with an egg theme.

Start with several games using eggs. Use your creativity or consult the *Ideas* Library for a variety of egg games (egg toss, egg roll relay, and so on). After the games, describe how an egg is a lot like God. An egg can be compared to the Holy Trinity in that each has three parts. The shell is the part we see or Christ. The Holy Spirit is the white and God the father is the center or the yolk.

Hard-boil an egg and cut it to show the kids the three distinct parts. Describe how when you take any one of these three parts away, you don't have a complete egg.

In order for a hard-boiled egg to enter a milk bottle (the milk bottle is a person), the shell or the part we see must be broken. This symbolizes the breaking of Christ's body. Take a match or two. Light them and throw them in the bottle and immediately put the shelled egg on top of the bottle. The matches will burn up the oxygen in the bottle and the egg will be sucked into the bottle intact. Draw the analogy that in order for God to come into our lives, the shell must be sacrificed and there must be a tiny spark or opening of our will to allow him to come in.

Discussion questions:

- **How is the bottle like people who need to let God in?**
- **What did it take for the egg to be drawn in?**
- **Can the egg come back out?**
- **What kind of fire within a person does it take to let God in?**

Matt Boyers

To Tell the (Holy Spirit) Truth

Divide the group into small teams. Choose two students to be readers of the text on page 103. One reads the Holy Spirit statement in the left column; the other, the corresponding statement in the right column. After each pair of statements is read, the teams must decide among themselves which of the two statements is correct. Warn them to be cautious: *both* statements in some pairs may be correct.

The correct statements are those with Scripture references. *Mark C. Christian*

Heaven

Heavenly Trip

The imagination is one of God's greatest gifts. This exercise gives young people a chance to really let their imaginations run wild and learn something from the experience at the same time. Have everyone in the group lie down on the floor and get in as comfortable a position as possible. The room should be darkened, although total darkness is not required, since the kids will be instructed to close their eyes. Move through the instructions below slowly. Take your time, speak softly, and allow the kids to develop each idea in their heads before moving on to the next. When you finish, discuss with the kids how they felt and what their experience was like. You can then relate the discussion to a scriptural view of heaven and eternal life.

The instructions:

1. Close your eyes (after you find a comfortable place, not too close to anyone else). Forget about the others in the room. Say nothing so you don't distract others who are doing their own thing. Let your imagination run wild...
2. Get in touch with your senses. Slip off your shoes and silently stamp your feet... Drum with your fingers on the floor or table... Sit or lay perfectly still and try to tune into the signals your nerves all over your body are sending.
   a. Start with your feet...your toes...the arch of your feet...your ankles.
   b. Your legs...your calves...knees...thighs.
   c. Your torso...stomach muscles...back...chest.
   d. Your hands...fingertips...fingers, palms, wrists.
   e. Your arms...forearms...elbows...biceps.
   f. Your neck...your head...jaw muscles...eye muscles.
3. Keep your eyes closed while I suggest some ideas that you may associate with. Put yourself into it and let your imagination go where it will.
   a. You are riding on a roller coaster (the climbs, over the top, curves, dips...).
   b. You are standing inside the observation window of a tall building (you see all the smaller buildings, tiny cars, and people below you...).
   c. You are overlooking the Grand Canyon.
   d. You are standing up on top of one of the two uprights of the Golden Gate Bridge on a foggy, windy day (you can feel the bridge sway beneath you).
4. Go back in your memory. It is one of those summers when you had enough time to do the thing you enjoy most of all...
   a. Experience doing it again.
   b. See yourself doing it.
   c. Feel it.
   d. Smell the smells that go along with it.
   e. Taste it, if there were associated tastes.
5. You find yourself in a strange place...You didn't come here on purpose...You don't know what to expect...
   a. You are alone.
   b. The room is warm, but not too warm.
   c. The colors of the walls and carpets are soft.
   d. You see a face—it's your best friend coming into the room, too. You greet each other, share your confusion, talk about other experiences you've been through together...
   e. Other friends and people you like join you one-by-one, some you haven't seen for years...
   f. Jesus enters the room. He greets everyone personally. You meet him. Then he announces, "Inasmuch as you accepted my gift for life...made me first in your life...and spent your life seeking first to provide for the well being of others...you may spend eternity with those who are your best friends, or are willingly indebted to you. Every personal need will become a source of maximum enjoyment with your friends. Every point of conflict will be

To Tell the (Holy Spirit) Truth

1. The Holy Spirit came after Jesus. (John 16:7)
2. The Holy Spirit is like a gentle mother.
3. It's easy to see and know the Holy Spirit.
4. The Holy Spirit came like wind. (Acts 2:2)
5. The Spirit helps to keep you from sinning. (Rom. 8:9)
6. The Holy Spirit prays to God for us. (Rom. 8:28)
7. The Holy Spirit teaches us about God. (John 14:26)
8. The Holy Spirit is an external force only.
9. The Holy Spirit is called the Spirit of Knowledge.
10. Okay, then how about the Spirit of Promise? (Eph. 1:13)
11. The Holy Spirit is the Spirit of God. (1 Cor. 3:16)
12. The worse sin of all is murder.
13. A Christian is one who is born in God's Spirit. (John 3:5)
14. The word *spirit* means breath. (This is correct)
15. One of the results of the Holy Spirit in my life is I'm full of joy. (Gal. 5:22)
16. The fruits of the Spirit include love, peace, kindness, and faithfulness. (Gal. 5:22)
17. God's Spirit gives me power to be just a bit better than others.
18. The Holy Spirit keeps bad things from happening to me.
19. Sin will kill us. (Rom. 8:13)

1. The Holy Spirit was here before Jesus.
2. The Holy Spirit is more like a Counselor. (John 14:16)
3. No way! You can't know him or see him. (John 14:16)
4. Better than that, he came like fire. (Acts 2:3)
5. No way! Nothing can keep you from sinning.
6. No one prays to God for me but me alone!
7. Better than that, he guides us in life. (John 14:13)
8. The Holy Spirit lives inside every Christian. (1 Cor. 3:16)
9. Nope. The Holy Spirit is called the Spirit of Truth. (John 16:13)
10. Nope again. He's the Spirit of Dreams.
11. Dream on. He's the Spirit of Christ. (Rom. 8:9)
12. Not so. The worst sin is swearing at the Holy Spirit. (Matt. 12:31)
13. A Christian is one who attends church and does good.
14. With breath like yours, a better definition is wind. (This is also correct)
15. The Holy Spirit makes me more competitive and determined.
16. You forgot gentleness, self control, and kindness, didn't you? (Gal. 5:22)
17. God's Spirit gives me power to share my faith. (Acts 1:8)
18. The Holy Spirit shows me the things I am doing that are bad. (John 16:8-11)
19. The Holy Spirit helps destroy our sin and gives us life. (Rom. 8:13)

happily resolved to everyone's satisfaction. You will experience dimensions of peace never before imagined..."

6. Welcome back to Earth! It was only a dream.

Jerry Boutelle

HUMILITY

LAMED VOVNIK CONVENTION

There is a charming Jewish legend that states that the world exists due to the presence of only 36 righteous people. The Jewish name for these people is lamed vov (pronounced "lah-med vov"), which indicates 36. These people may be of any station in life, poor or mighty, men or women, hermits or public figures. The only thing we know about them is that they are alive and that they do not know that they are lamed vovniks. If they claim to be, then they cannot be.

To conduct a Lamed Vovnik Convention, divide your group into as many small groups as you wish, and have each group nominate several individuals whom they think might qualify as a "lamed vovnik." They should be righteous, selfless, and the kind of persons on whom the welfare of the world might rest. Each group should take 10 to 15 minutes for this. Set a maximum number of people that each group may nominate.

When the groups have finished, have a nominating convention. Each group announces its choices and explains why they nominated who they did. A list can be kept on a blackboard, and a final vote can be taken to arrive at the entire group's guesses at who the 36 lamed vovniks are.

Many famous people will undoubtedly be nominated, but the beauty of the exercise is that many ordinary people, not well-known, will undoubtedly be favorites. At one Lamed Vovnik Convention a man named David Rapaport was elected, when a persuasive young man nominated him with the words, "Most of you wouldn't know him, but when I need help or advice, he's always there to help me or steer me through times of trouble." Another notable nominee was an anonymous man on an immigrant ship who helped the father of one of the young people who said, "He gave dad some food and a little money, and did the same for many others on the boat. But no one remembers his name..." Perhaps the best thing about the activity is the shift of emphasis from fame to humility. True models begin to emerge and kids begin to put some handles on what righteousness is all about. *Stephen E. Breuer*

JUDGING OTHERS

LETHAL LABELS

Labels can be wildly misleading. Here's a chance to teach kids to look inside for a true identity before judging someone quickly on appearances. This devotional offers a choice of two object lessons, a brief reading, and some relevant Scripture passages to explore with your students.

• **Object Lesson1.** Buy three kinds of dry breakfast cereal. One of them should be a kid's cereal—outlandish name, shapes, and colors (of cereal as well as of box). The other two should be the kind of cereal that, considering packaging and cereal name, just *look* and *sound* healthy—except that these two are actually *less* nutritious than the kid's cereal, according to the nutritional information on the sides of the boxes (especially fat content and calories per serving).

Show your group all three boxes and ask them to choose the healthiest cereal. (If a student asks you to read the nutritional information, just say you want to test their instinctive responses.) Discuss what makes a food healthy, making sure that *someone* mentions both fat content and calories.

Arrange the cereal boxes according to your students' judgment of least to most healthy. (They'll invariably rate the kid's cereal least healthy.) Now ask someone to read and compare the nutritional data—in particular, the fat content and calories—while you watch their jaws drop.

• **Object Lesson 2.** Before your youth meeting remove the label from a can of soup, and carefully glue on a sauerkraut label. As you begin your devotional, hold up the can and ask, "Who here just *loves* sauerkraut?" After the groaning and gagging, ask them for one-word definitions of sauerkraut; you'll probably hear *gross, nauseating, sick, disgusting,* etc.

Then say something like, "How do you know this is sauerkraut? Do you always go by first impressions, or by how something appears on the surface?" Open the can as proof, explaining that we too easily label others solely because of how they look on the outside.

• **The Reading.** Tell this story, or a similar one of your own:

> **On the first day of school, Jennifer saw a cute new boy. When she found out his name was Britt, she decided to try out the name when she saw him later in the hall.**
>
> **"Hi, Britt," said Jennifer.**
>
> **He didn't even turn around. At lunch she tried again—and got ignored again. Jennifer got steamed. She vowed she'd never talk to him again. Not leaving it at that, all that afternoon she told her friends what a snob Britt was.**
>
> **The next morning in the parking lot, she saw a woman she assumed was Britt's mom conversing with him—in sign language. She realized that Britt had never heard a word she said to him yesterday. And since he had never faced her and seen her lips, he didn't have a clue that she was talking to him.**

• **Scripture Passages.** Discuss Romans 14, verses 4 and 10-13. Notice the context—although this chapter's emphasis is making moral judgments about others, the passage also speaks about judging others falsely or prematurely.

Matthew 7:1 and 1 Samuel 16:7 speak clearly about examining the contents carefully if you want to know the truth.

There is possible parental application here, too. Parents may reevaluate their estimation of some teenagers if they become conscious of how they label kids as rebellious, untrustworthy, or lazy. They may recognize that kids frequently live down to those expectations. *Steve Fortosis and Mike McKay*

LEGALISM

NEW RULES

Why are there rules and laws? What makes them good or bad? What do rules have to do with the grace of God?

Presumably, your group has some rules or established procedures already. Privately draw up a new set of rules that are much stricter than what you already have—almost to the point of being ridiculous. Print enough copies for everyone. At the next meeting announce that you and your staff have noticed that people have been taking the rules lightly, not respecting others, etc. Carry on a while like this. There are undoubtedly some recent examples you can use to make your point. Then get to the point—after careful consideration, the adult leaders decided to make some changes in the rules. Then pass out the new rules. You'll get various reactions, from stunned silence to loud protest—but it will get the kids' attention. Use these sample rules, or make up your own:

• Recreation time will be a half-hour shorter than it has been; lesson time, a half-hour longer.
• You must bring a Bible to every meeting. If you don't have one, we will get you one.
• You must raise your hand to speak.
• You are expected to memorize one new Bible verse every two weeks and to recite it before the group.
• Because of basketball-related injuries during recreation time, basketball will no longer be allowed anywhere on church property.
• Everyone is required to participate in group games.
• No boom boxes are permitted at any group activity.
• You must strictly obey all adult sponsors at all times.
• Anyone breaking any of these rules is forbidden to attend the next retreat.

Before revealing the hoax, allow kids to respond to the new rules. Find out which rules disturb them most and why. When you feel the time is right, repeal the new rules and admit that it was purely a discussion starter.

Follow up by discussing the purpose of rules. Use the Ten Commandments, or study Mark 2:23—3:7, the story of the disciples breaking a rule by eating on the Sabbath. Discuss why God gave us his law and how Christianity is more than a list of do's and don'ts. Talk about what happens when we lose sight of the spirit of a law and look only at the letter of the law. Ask if there are times when a rule should be broken. This topic may be particularly appropriate if you've been having discipline problems lately.

Discuss, too, the relief kids felt when the new rules were repealed. Point out that this is similar to the concept of living under God's grace—there's great relief in knowing that Christ has set us free from the law. The Christian life is governed by the ethic of love, following the example of Christ, rather than obedience to a set of rules and regulations. *Jeff Callen*

LEGALISM STROLL

This is a good exercise to help young people understand that a legalist approach to the Christian life is not feasible. It can be used to compare and contrast righteousness under the law and righteousness under grace.

The basic idea is for kids to follow a strip of tape through the church (or whatever you have available), walking on the tape with both feet, being careful not to leave the straight and narrow path. Stationed along the line at various points are numerous temptations (set up by the youth sponsors) that are designed to get the kids to leave the line. Some of these can be pleasurable things designed to lure them away, and other things can incorporate the use of scare tactics. Students are told at the outset that their task is to stay on the tape, and if they do (without ever stepping off of it), there will be a reward for them at the end of the tape.

Temptations along the way can include the following:

- Someone shooting at them with a squirt gun at a certain point, making them mad or uncomfortable.
- The youth director can sit in a chair about 12 feet away from the line, and there can be a pile of water balloons just out of arms' reach of the students. The youth director dares anyone to try and hit him with a water balloon. (But they have to leave the line in order to do it.)
- At one point, you can try to persuade kids that you need their help to lure someone else off the line.
- Someone dressed as a monster can jump out and scare them off the line.
- Place cookies, punch, candy, etc. on the table just out of reach of the line. Leave the table unattended, but have someone watching from a hidden position.
- At one point, students can be told by a youth sponsor that the game has been terminated, that they don't need to follow the line anymore. The whole thing was just a joke and there isn't really a reward for them.

You can think of other ideas for temptations or tactics designed to get them to stray from the straight and narrow. Some of them will work and some of them won't. There will undoubtedly be some kids who proceed right along the line without leaving it, but many will succumb to temptation somewhere along the way. This will lead into an excellent discussion on the topics previously described. Try to relate the various temptations to actual or real temptations that we face all the time. For example, when they are told the game is over (when it wasn't), they will cry foul because they were lied to, but this can be tied in with the idea that Satan is a liar. Wrap up with a discussion on the impossibility of living a perfect life (or staying on the line forever), and how Christ provided us with another, better way. *Les Palich*

MARRIAGE

DATING AND MARRIAGE

Here's an idea for a two-week program that will help group members of the opposite sex get to know each other a bit better. This one is best with high school or college-age students.

The first week, divide into two groups—the guys in one and the girls in the other. If you have a lot of people, then divide into lots of groups, but they should not be coed. Each group then works on preparing a list of things that they would want in a wife or a husband. After they get a list of 10 or so items, then they should order these from most important to least important. Then have all the groups come back together again and share these with each other. Some discussion can be included in this.

At the end of this first meeting, have the groups get back together again, and prepare another list of questions that they would like to ask members of the opposite sex (and get a straight answer). The questions can be submitted by secret ballot.

The second week, the groups meet again and receive the questions that were submitted the week before. They should work on coming up with satisfactory answers to them. Try to get a group consensus. Then have the groups meet back together again and share the questions and the answers. The results are usually fun and informative. You might want to follow up the whole thing with a speaker, a film, or a panel of some kind on the third week.
Bob Griffin

To Marry or Not to Marry

The questionnaire on page 108 is very helpful as a discussion starter on the subject of marriage. Print it up and give the group enough time to think through their answers. Then discuss each question and try to come up with a group consensus. Encourage each person to answer the questions honestly, as they think they should be answered, rather than answering them the way the church, or their parents, or tradition would want them to answer. *Bob Pickerall*

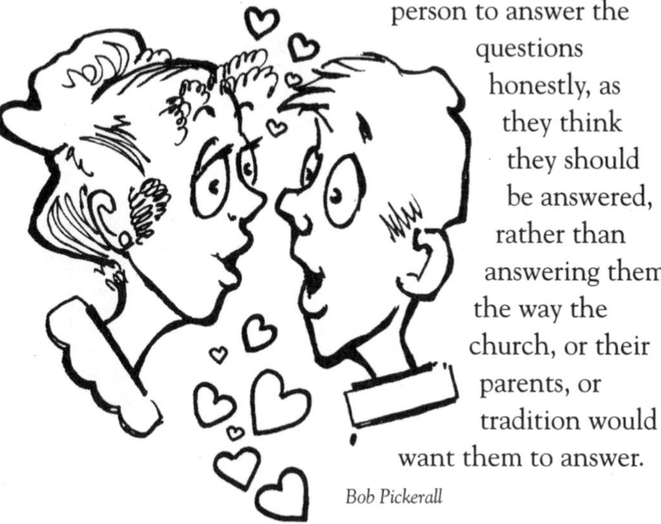

Twenty-Five Cent Mate

Give each person the questionnaire on page 109 and give them enough time to fill it out completely. Then go around the group and discuss each person's answers and why they answered as they did.

Birthday List

Pass out paper and pencils and ask the group to write down what they'd like for their birthdays (or Christmas). Allow five to 10 minutes to complete the list; then have kids reveal one or two of the most important items on their lists.

Next have the group make a list of the blessings, fruit of the Spirit, or spiritual gifts given them by God. Again, allow five to 10 minutes, then have everyone tell one or two of the most important items from the list.

Questions for discussion:

- **Was it easier to compile the birthday list or the blessings/gifts list?**
- **What benefit will you derive from the items on the birthday list?**
- **What benefit will you derive from the items on the blessing list?**
- **Compare the benefits derived from the two lists. Do you think we spend too much time wishing for material benefits? Do we spend enough time seeking God for appropriate blessings?**
- **What are some ways to fulfill our responsibility to use our material gifts and God's blessings wisely?**

These Bible verses can help shape your discussion: Psalm 67 (a good devotion for the beginning of the study); 1 Corinthians 12:4-6; 14:1; Matthew 19:23-24; Luke 6:20-26; John 3:16. *Erlan and Jan Leitz*

The Wealth We Wear

To get your teenagers to understand how rich we are in this country, try this idea. Have the kids total the dollar value of everything on their bodies at the moment (assessed at what the items would cost to replace). You may want to use yourself as an example. Calculate your own "worth" on the chalkboard or overhead projector.

Shirt	$ 15
Jeans	40
Sweater	50
Socks, underwear	15
Shoes	30
Wallet	20
Watch	80
Glasses	125
Wedding ring	400
TOTAL	$823

Teenagers dressed just casually for youth meeting will likely come up with figures over $200. Some will have much higher totals when you consider things like contact lenses and braces.

When everyone has arrived at their totals, mention that the average annual income in many third-world nations is between $200 and $400—which means that most of us are walking around with more wealth on our bodies than many millions of people earn in a year. Ask your students to then imagine trying to convince these third worlders that they aren't really rich.

Your kids will leave with a new perspective of their lifestyle. *Howard B. Chapman*

THINKING ABOUT MARRIAGE

1. I think everyone ought to get married (put an "x" on the continuum).

Definitely Yes ____ Definitely No

2. If a person decides for the option of marriage, I think generally the best age for marriage would be: (circle the best answer)

Girls – 16 17 18 19 20 21 22 23 24 25 26 27 28 29 30 Over 30

Guys – 16 17 18 19 20 21 22 23 24 25 26 27 28 29 30 Over 30

3. When you are married, are you considered an adult, regardless of age? (Circle one) Yes No

4. What do you think of the following statement:
"God has made one special person in the world for you to marry." (Put an "x" on the continuum.)

Strongly Agree ____ Strongly Disagree

5. Marriage is: (Rank these from 1 to 5)
____A legal statement ____A social custom ____God ordained ____A religious ceremony ____A parent pleaser

6. Most people get married because: (Rank these from 1 to 5)
____They have to ____They want to have kids ____They love each other ____Tax benefits ____Sex

7. Our concept of marriage is most influenced by: (Pick top three)
____Friends ____Television ____Movies ____Other adults ____Parents ____Church ____Books ____Celebrities ____Tradition

8. What are the top priorities in marriage? (Rank from 1 to 10)
____Children ____Sex ____Communication ____Mutual trust/confidence in the other person ____Religion/faith
____Mutual interests ____Finances/security ____In-law relationships ____Faithfulness ____Romantic love

9. Divorce is wrong (choose the best answer or answers):
____Always (no exceptions) ____Except when adultery is involved ____Except when both are incompatible
____Except when you don't love each other any more

10. Divorce is (choose the best answer or answers):
____Better than living together when you hate each other ____A necessary evil ____A possibility for any one of us ____A cop out
____Never okay when children are involved ____Sin

11. Living together (not married) is (put an "x" on the continuum):

Wrong (always) ____ Okay (always)

12. Living together (not married) is (choose best answer or answers):
____Better than traditional custom of dating ____The best way to determine if marriage will last ____Is not the same as marriage
____Is more acceptable than marriage ____Is the best alternative to marriage ____None of the above

TWENTY-FIVE CENT MATE

Name ______________________________

You may spend 25 cents to buy a mate. Select all the qualities you wish from below but do not spend over 25 cents. Put the amount in blank at the right. In the center column, spend 25 cents on yourself being the kind of person you wish to be.

Each of this group cost 6 cents:

A good-looking face	____________	____________
Very popular	____________	____________
Quite intelligent	____________	____________
A great Christian	____________	____________
Very kind	____________	____________

Each of these cost 5 cents:

A well-built figure and body	____________	____________
A good conversationalist	____________	____________
Tactful and considerate	____________	____________
Happy and good sense of humor	____________	____________

Each of this grouping costs 4 cents:

Large chest or bust	____________	____________
Likes sports	____________	____________
Attends church—is religious	____________	____________
Honest—doesn't lie or cheat	____________	____________

Each of this group costs 3 cents:

Nicely dressed and well groomed	____________	____________
Likes drama, art, and music	____________	____________
Well mannered—comes from nice home	____________	____________
Ambitious and hard-working	____________	____________

Each of this group costs 2 cents:

The right height	____________	____________
Gets good grades	____________	____________
Likes kids (children)	____________	____________
Brave—stands up for rights	____________	____________

Each of this group costs 1 cent:

Choice of color in eyes and hair	____________	____________
Owns a car	____________	____________
Wealthy—or moderately wealthy	____________	____________
Sincere and serious	____________	____________

20th-Century Talents

As an object lesson on the parable of the talents, give each person a dollar bill and one month to make it grow. They may invest it in something, spend it, save it, or whatever they want, but at the end of the month they must account for their $1 "talent." A discussion on stewardship and using our gifts will follow. This can also become a good fundraiser. Use larger amounts of money at your own risk.

Unfair Money Practice

Hide small amounts of money around a room that can be made totally dark. Announce that you are going to turn the group loose in the dark room to find the money. Before the meeting, however, clue in one or two of the kids and give them a small flashlight that they can use for the money search. Watch what happens when the kids discover that someone has a flashlight. This is excellent as a discussion starter on relationships, selfishness, jealousy, anger, etc.

R. Woody Woodcock, Jr.

Shopping Spree

For a creative look at money and how people spend it, try this simple simulation. Buy or print several million dollars in play money. Then, divide it into random amounts ($3,000 to $450,000) placed in plain envelopes. Give one envelope to each person or small group.

Now for the shopping spree. Set up a table or bulletin board with a wide assortment of full-page advertisements for things such as cars, mansions, computers, vacations, food, savings accounts, and Christian relief efforts. Each person or group receives an order blank to "buy" any items they wish, as long as they can pay for their order individually or by pooling their money. Give them 10 minutes to fill in their order blanks.

Gather all of the order blanks or compile a blackboard list of everything ordered. Discuss the values expressed, feelings about unequal distribution of the cash, and the Christian's responsibility to care for the needy. *Bob King*

The Game of Life

To stimulate some thinking about priorities and values, have your kids play Milton-Bradley's The Game of Life. You'll have about 10 players and one banker (an advisor) for every board, so figure the number of games you need according to the size of your group. Have the kids choose partners—preferably someone they don't know well.

Before the game, display the prizes to go to the winning team. These will appear to be top CD albums, but will actually be only empty CD cases. Then explain the game, noting that it claims to be "true to life." Point out that to win you must end up either as a millionaire tycoon or else as a resident of Millionaire Acres. Each team should start out with only one person in their little car, because in The Game of Life everyone has to get married.

If they move quickly they should be able to play the game in just over half an hour. If you must, stop play after a certain time limit, and call everyone together to award the prizes.

Make a big deal over who won and who had the most money in each group. Then hand out the prizes in front of everyone. Most of the winners will protest immediately that the prizes weren't what they appeared to be. So make pious declarations about how you never promised that they would get CDs; they got exactly what you showed them, and if they assumed that the cases had CDs inside, that's their problem.

Before they have much time to fume, discuss these questions:

- **What did you think of the prizes? Were they what you expected them to be?**
- **What was the object of the game? Does having the most money make you a winner in real life?**
- **Was the game "true to life" as it claims to be?**
- **The prizes were hollow. Do you think that at the end of life, people who have gone after money will feel that their "prize" is hollow?**

Finally, discuss briefly any one of the following passages in which Jesus talks about money and priorities:

- Mark 1:16-20
- Matt. 6:19-20; 7:24-29
- Luke 18:18-30

Ask if they think anyone lives according to Christ's words today. Does his view of success agree with our society's view of success? *Dave Carver and Carrie Wolukis*

Music

American Bandstand

For an effective program on the good and bad of popular music, have an "American Bandstand" night. Bring in a selection of current CDs or cassettes, and have the youth vote on the ones they like best, according to certain standards. You might find it worthwhile to get the words to the songs so that your kids will be able to follow along while listening. Then play the albums and have the students judge them using judging sheets with the following criteria:

- **Lyrics.** What is the message of the song? Does it support or contradict Christian values and the Word of God?
- **The Artist.** What is he or she like as a person? Are the artists good role models for Christian young people? Do they avoid behavior that offends those who follow Christ?
- **Overall Effect of the Song.** Does this song make you feel more positive about your faith or about life? Or more negative? Does it strengthen you as a Christian or weaken you? Or is it neutral?

Before the kids rate the songs, you should discuss each of the three criteria so they fully understand. Also, you will probably want to discuss each song individually. You may want to add another category as well: The Music. In this category students decide whether or not the record would be considered "good music" or not.

After the kids have rated all the songs, take your results and come up with your own youth group "Top 10" or "Top Five." The whole experience can really help students have a better sensitivity to what they listen to. *Randy Wheeler*

Rock Music Council

This idea deals with rock music and its effect upon young people. Very often the trend in churches is to either forbid rock music or to ignore the whole issue. Probably the more sane approach is to allow kids the chance to evaluate the music and make a decision for themselves.

Get a few volunteers in your youth group to form a rock music council that evaluates some of the latest popular music once a month. The council should rate the songs in areas such as: musical appeal, word content, values of the song (compared to Christian values), hidden meanings (if any), and so on. The results can be shared with the whole group, and the kids can decide how to respond. You can get a lot of mileage out of something like this in terms of discussion and interest. *Mike Murray*

Musical Blanks

Here's a fun way to use music in your group. It will not only help kids listen well, it will encourage them to evaluate the type of music they hear.

Choose some contemporary songs (Christian or secular) that have a meaningful message and which have lyrics that are reasonably easy to hear. Duplicate the words on a handout, leaving a blank in place of some key words in each phrase.

Pass out the lyric sheets and some pencils to the group. Play the music, instructing your kids to fill in the blanks with what they hear. Then review the lyrics and give a prize for the one with the most correct answers. Discuss the message of the song. You might want to try and change the message by inserting your own lyrics in the blanks. Finally, play the songs again, for enjoyment and for a better understanding of the meaning. *John Peters*

Music in the Bible

The next time you run a series on rock music, get your young people involved in a study of music in the Bible. Buy some old Bibles at a local thrift store, and give them to your kids with scissors, rubber cement, and a couple of concordances, topical Bibles, or Bible dictionaries. Have them look up and cut out every reference to music they can find that they consider significant and glue the verses to a large sheet of paper. Using the finished product as a basis for discussion, consider these questions:

- **What kinds of musical instruments were used in ancient times? (A Bible dictionary would be helpful here.)**

- How do you think the music of the Bible sounded? Would you have enjoyed it? Does it matter whether or not you would have enjoyed it?
- Why did people make music in ancient times? Name the various functions of music in the Bible (praise, exorcism, battle signals, idol worship).
- Is music always used rightly today?
- Does the Bible have anything to say about how music should be played, or the place of music in the life of the believer?
- What are the implications of these commands for our use of music today?

Steve Perisho

The Music of the Gospel

This idea makes good use of music as a teaching tool. Distribute to the kids a list of popular song titles that most of them will recognize. These can be songs from the current pop or rock charts, or old standards. Then ask the kids to choose from the list one song that best describes their walk with Christ right now. Allow the kids to share their choices with each other and to explain their choices.

Next, ask the kids to read Mark 10:13-16, Mark 11:1-11, and John 17:20-26 (or any others that you choose), and to pick a song from any that they know that would fit the story in the Scripture. If kids are in small groups, have the groups decide on the song, and then sing a verse of it after reading their assigned Scripture.

Next, in small groups, have the kids select a well-known song or hymn and then find Scripture that speaks to the message of the song in some way. Allow each group to share their song (either sing it or read the lyrics) and then read the passage of Scripture, explaining how the passage relates to the song. This exercise could be done instead of or in addition to the previous one.

Lastly, have the kids sing together a favorite song and close with prayer. *Brad Hirsch*

Music Messages

Try this game as a hook into a program on contemporary music messages. First think of as many tunes to current commercial jingles as possible. Have someone prepared either to hum the *tune* (not the words) or to pick out the tune on a musical instrument.

Divide the group into two teams. Have the "music person" begin to play or sing the tune. The object of the game is to be the first to name the product which is being advertised by the tune.

Score is 10 points a song. (You can choose whether or not to count off for wrong answers.) Team with the highest score at the end of a given time wins.

After the game you can point out how it demonstrates the power to communicate a message when a catchy tune is put together with lyrics. Even when we don't consciously pay attention to the lyrics of commercials, the message still gets through. Suggest that perhaps the same thing happen with the other music we listen to. You can then move into a discussion of the lyrics of several contemporary songs.

David Wright

Rewriting Rock

Instead of just condemning the immoral lyrics of so many popular rock songs, try having your group rewrite them with Christian themes. For example, the old classic "We Built This City on Rock-n-Roll" could be "We Built this Youth Group on Jesus Christ." It's fun and thought provoking, and you may find that when the song comes on the radio again, your kids will start singing along with the alternative lyrics. *Steve Gladen*

Patience Role Play

This program would work well for the topic of either patience or self-control. Prepare several scenarios from daily family life that would test any kid's (or parent's) patience. Here are suggestions for some scenarios:

- Your grandmother asks you to come over to help her set up the Christmas decorations. She ends up telling you exactly where to put every single light and strand of tinsel.

• (PARENT) You have just come home from a long day at the office and your son is glued to the television. You see that the dishwasher is not unloaded, which was something you asked him to do this morning. (CHILD) You have made your bed for the first time this summer, but you forgot to unload the dishwasher, which your mother asked you to do this morning.

• Your aunt comes to visit for three weeks and stays in your room. One day you find her going through your drawers because she says she's interested in "finding out more about young people today."

• You are the coach of an all-state team. The captain approaches you and says she can't come to pre-season practice because she's going to church camp.

• Your son has gone to the prom and has promised to be home by 2:00 a.m. Suddenly you wake up at 3:30 and he isn't home yet. He finally comes in at 4:00.

• You're nice to the class geek for a day, and he thinks you're in love with him.

• You've got a great idea about the theme of the novel you're reading in English class, but the teacher says you're wrong.

After all the situations have been acted out and reacted to by the rest of the group, divide into small groups for a discussion of patience, and how God works in us to bring about this specific fruit of the Holy Spirit.

Suggested questions for discussion:

- **What makes us feel frustrated? (feelings of helplessness, vulnerability, whatever)**
- **How should Christians handle impatience?**
- **Do you think God tests us? Why or why not?**
- **When and why do you get impatient with God?**
- **How can we become more patient?**
- **How does the Holy Spirit change us in this and other areas?**

Seeing family life scenes from the parents' as well as the kids' perspective helps make this exercise an effective reminder of the need to cultivate patience in daily life. *Laura D. Russell*

PRAYER SURVEY

The survey on page 114 should be printed up and passed out to the entire group. Each person simply marks an "X" on each line to show their relative position on the issues presented. Encourage kids to be as honest as possible. There are no correct answers in this test. The idea is to see just where you stand on the various questions that come up regarding prayer.

The survey can be followed up by having all those consistently on the positive side of the continuum get together in one group and the "negatives" into another group. Then have the two groups discuss the following statements as to their validity. One group tries to convince the other, offering examples, personal experience, Scripture, and other proof.

1. God does answer prayer.
2. God answers prayer in one of three ways—yes, no, or wait.
3. There are conditions to a yes answer.
4. A mature Christian needs to pray without ceasing.
5. Prayer shouldn't be governed by feelings.
6. The importance of public prayer.

Bob Gleason

SCREWTAPE LETTERS

This exercise is a good way to make the kids think about a topic by coming in through the back door. Divide them into groups of about five kids each and assign a recorder who is given pen and paper. Explain to the kids what *Screwtape Letters* is and, if you own the book (by C. S. Lewis), read a few excerpts so that they get the idea. Next have them write a Screwtape Letter on "How to Destroy a Christian's Prayer Life" or a similar topic. In the process, they must consider what makes a good prayer life before they can write down how to destroy it. If you want, you can have them first list five or 10 things necessary for a good prayer life and then work on those. Most kids love to show how devious they can be anyway, and in the process of being devious and creative, they have to consider what constitutes an effective prayer life.

PRAYER SURVEY

POSITIVE	1 2 3 4 5 6 7 8 9 10	NEGATIVE
• I believe beyond a shadow of a doubt that God answers prayer. I don't always know how God answers prayers but I always have faith he will.	— — — — — — — — — —	• I believe there is a God but I question whether he is personally interested in people. If I don't see an obvious answer, I begin to wonder if God answers at all.
• I often praise and thank God as well as ask things from him.	— — — — — — — — — —	• I treat God like a Santa Claus. Give me this, give me that.
• When God says "No," I feel it is for my own good.	— — — — — — — — — —	• I can hardly accept a no answer.
• When God answers a prayer, my faith is strengthened.	— — — — — — — — — —	• In my book answered prayer is just a coincidence.
• If God says "Wait awhile," I accept his timing without reservation.	— — — — — — — — — —	• I prayed once and God never answered, so I don't pray anymore.
• I find myself praying all during the day.	— — — — — — — — — —	• Days go by and I never pray.
• When I don't feel like praying, that's when I pray the hardest.	— — — — — — — — — —	• If I don't feel like praying, then I don't.
• I feel as comfortable praying in public as I do alone.	— — — — — — — — — —	• I won't pray in public.
• I feel my prayer life is really growing.	— — — — — — — — — —	• I've almost buried my prayer life.

Have each group read theirs and then discuss.
Len Carlson

Cliché Prayers

At the beginning of a unit or a discussion on prayer, have each member of your group compose a prayer using all of the cliches they have ever heard used in prayers (everything from flowery introductions of God to overworked catch-all phrases). Then read the prayers aloud. The results will not only be extremely entertaining but very effective in pointing out what prayer should not be. Then discuss the elements of effective prayer and give the young people a chance for personal and private prayer. *Philip Dougharty*

Prayer Bag

Supply the kids with magazines and brown paper bags. Ask each young person to search through the magazines for pictures or words that represent things they have prayed about. They can include things they have been thankful for as well as items they have asked for. After everyone has finished, divide into small groups and have each person share their prayer bags. End the sharing time by having the groups pray for each other. *Gary Odgon*

Please Answer My Prayer

The following dialogues are great for pointing out to kids how we must sound to God when we pray. The best way to do this is to pick out various members of your youth group and have them come forward while you use one of these dialogues on them (insert their names in place of the names that are printed). It doesn't take students too long to figure out the connection between what you are doing to them and what we often do to God when we pray, even though we don't say it out loud. God does know our hearts when we pray. Follow up with a discussion of each situation and relate it to Scripture, such as Isaiah 59:1-2, Matthew 6:33, and Matthew 21:22. It's a good learning experience, and it's a lot of fun.

1. "I know I haven't talked to you lately, but you know how it is. I've been really busy. I've had school, friends, family, and other things that are really much more important to me than you are, Marcy. But I wonder if you could help me with this homework assignment?"

2. "Hey, I know you don't know me, but could you give me $300?"

3. (The phrases in the parentheses should be said "under your breath," just loud enough to be heard) "Can you help me out, Louis? (You've never helped me out before!) I need you to do this for me. (I'm not even sure you're for real.) I think a lot of you. (When I'm not thinking of something else.) I know you can help me. (You probably can't do it.) You're the only one left to turn to. (If you don't help me, I'll find somebody else that can.) Would you wash the dishes for me tonight?

4. "Melanie, are you John's friend? You are? Really? Ha-ha-ha." (really start laughing: you'll find the whole group will join in the laughing) "You must be some kind of weirdo to be John's friend, ha-ha-ha, etc. I can't believe that you would really admit that you're his friend, ha-ha-ha, etc." (then turn very seriously to John) Say: "Will you wash my car?"

5. (To the group as you're going over to put your arm around her) "You know, Trish is really the greatest. I'd do anything for her. She asked me not to tell anybody she liked this guy, but I was sure that she didn't mean it, so I told a few (20) people. She asked me to help her with some chores, but I was sure she could find somebody else to do it. She is so nice. I'd just do anything for her." (to Trish) "Would you come clean my house for me tomorrow?"

6. "You know, Shelley, I'm really sorry I called you a Fig Newton in front of all those people. I know you don't like to be called Fig Newton, but listen, Fig Newton, I know you understand. I mean, none of us is perfect, right, Fig Newton? I would never do anything to go against your wishes. Are you listening, Fig Newton? By the way, could you help me learn this new song?"

7. "Robin, I really don't need your help, but Brandie told me I should ask you. I mean, I have always been able to take care of myself. I've gotten this far by myself, why should I need your help? But this problem is a little tougher than usual. Maybe if you gave me a little help, then I could do it a little better, and everybody will see how great I really am. Will you help me write my term paper?"

8. "Paul, I know you don't like me stomping on the daisies in your garden, but I really like stomping on daisies—it's my absolute favorite thing to do. I get such a high stomping on

daisies that nothing else compares to it. I don't know if I could make it through the day if I didn't have some daisies to stomp on. And it really doesn't hurt anybody else around. I'll do anything else you ask me to do, but don't ask me to stay off your daisies. Could you feed my dog while I'm on vacation?"

9. "I really like you, Mike. You are one of my best friends, and I'm so proud that I can call you a friend. I know that if every one of my other friends deserted me, you'd still be here. Just one thing, don't tell anybody that I like you, okay? Would you go to the store for me?"

Pam Bates

PRAYER CANDLES

This idea will help your youth group pray together more effectively, and pray for each other. Have the entire group sit in a circle (in a darkened room or outdoors at night) with everyone holding a candle. One candle is lit, then the person holding that candle silently or aloud prays for one other member of the group in the circle (preferably someone across the circle). After completing the prayer that person goes over to the person he or she just prayed for and lights that person's candle, then returns to his or her seat with the lighted candle. The one whose candle was just lit then prays for another in the circle and does the same thing. This continues until all the candles are lit and the leader closes in prayer. All the candles can then be blown out simultaneously. The symbolism involved can be very meaningful. *Rod Rummel*

PRAYERS IN THE WIND

Here's a meeting idea that takes the expression "go fly a kite" literally.

Begin by discussing the Greek word *pneuma*, which means "wind" or "spirit." Using John 3:8 as a text, discuss how God's Spirit is a lot like the wind—you can't limit God in how he works and reveals himself to us any more than you can control the wind.

Next, have the group write down prayers on small, thin pieces of cloth, about eight inches long and two inches wide. Then connect them all together to make the tail of a kite. Have the group assemble a kite and "launch" their prayers into the wind (pneuma), symbolizing the spirit. Run the kite out as far as it will go to the end of the string. When the end of the line is reached, let go, and the prayers will be "taken up" to God. Watch it disappear. Remind the kids that in a similar way, the ancient Israelites burned their offerings and incense so the smoke would rise to heaven with their prayers.

In Old Testament times many believed that if God didn't answer prayers, it was because he didn't hear them—which, of course, is not true. If the kite doesn't go up (for lack of wind or whatever), let the kids know that it's not because God didn't hear their prayers. Rather, it's because he chose to return their gift (kite) back to them. God always hears their prayers.

Use your own judgement in how you use this. Do it on a windy day. Make sure it will be okay to release the kite. (Don't violate any existing litter laws—the kite will eventually come down somewhere.) If you prefer you could use this same idea with a large helium balloon. *Dave Washburn*

PRAYER LAB

Prayer is a hot topic for discussion, yet it is often misunderstood. To help your students understand more about it, set up a prayer lab. Simply prepare four posters (copy pages 118 and 119) and place them in four separate areas or rooms of the church. Divide your kids into four groups and have them rotate from one lab to another at 10 or 15 minute intervals. If the lab idea works well with your group, try it with various subjects. *Daniel Van Loon*

PRAYEROBICS

Invest an hour of prayer via interval training of the Spirit. Divide your teenagers into small groups, and clock them for six minutes at a prayer station before moving to the next one. At each station kids receive the appropriate sheet that directs their praying. See our samples on pages 120 and 121. *Sid Huston*

RELATIONSHIPS

LOVE LISTS

Spend some time as a group reading and relating to various Scripture texts that deal with the subject of love. Possible choices might be the Cain and Abel story (Genesis 4), the words of Jesus concerning "the least of these" (Matthew 25), or numerous other passages that deal with relationships between people.

Then divide into small groups and supply each person with pencil and paper. Each person should make four columns on the paper with the following headings: Intimate, Close, Acquaintances, and Distant. Under each column, names of people are listed according to how intimate or distant they might be. Maximum for any column should be five (or so) names. The names can be friends and acquaintances at church, school, work, family, or elsewhere.

After each person has listed names under each column, have a time for sharing in the small groups. Teens should explain why certain people were listed under the various column headings and whether or not they are satisfied with their lists as they stand. Here they may share feelings, experiences, school or living situations that contributed to the list choices. In addition, have the students examine their lists again and pick out one name from the acquaintances or distant columns, and think specifically about ways to become closer to that person so that they might move up one column. Close with a chance for people in the group to share feelings of closeness or distance that they feel with other members of the group.

Jim Thompson

MAKE WAY FOR THE QUEEN

Here's a role-playing simulation that helps open up meaningful discussions about relationships, cooperation, and community. It's also a lot of fun.

Divide into teams of five to six kids each. Each team consists of a Queen, a Grand Duke, a Priest, a Cripple, a Rebel, and a Slave. If there are only five on the team, there is no slave.

Each person on the team should receive a card, like those pictured on page 122, which identifies his or her role and gives instructions on how to carry it out. The rules are:

1. You can't change roles.
2. You must do what your role requires, carefully obeying what is written on your instruction card.
3. You can only hold one leg of the chair.

Each Queen is seated in a chair along a starting line, with the Queens from the other teams. The subjects gather around their Queen and wait for the signal to start. The object is to lift the Queen by cooperatively lifting the legs of the chair, and then to carry her to a designated spot. For best results the distance should be far enough to make the task fairly difficult (perhaps 100 yards). The first team to complete the task has their Queen crowned as the Ruling Monarch. The roles of the Rebel and the Cripple complicate the task and can cause some real trouble if the Duke and the Priest don't do their jobs. But because of those roles, there is good potential for discussion after the game. Here are some questions:

- **What problems or obstacles did your team face?**
- **How were they handled?**
- **How did you feel about the others on your team?**

David Farnum

SCRIPTURE MEMORY

HIDDEN TREASURE

To help motivate your kids to memorize God's Word—while at the same time making them feel capable of doing it—try this. First, distribute pencils and paper to everyone and ask them to write down the following:

Their name

Their address and phone number

Their social security number

Their school locker combination

Their birth date, and the birth dates of immediate family members

Zip codes of five local towns

Phone numbers of five friends

Addresses of five friends

First verse of a favorite song

Five Bible verses

Supplication

Supplication is asking for something specific from God.

1. What changes or improvements does God want to make in your life? Ask God to accomplish these changes in your life and to help you accept them.
2. Make a list of 10 people you know well. List one spiritual need each person has. Pray through your list.
3. Pray for your leaders, such as those in government, parents, youth leaders, and teachers.
4. Pray that God will have a greater influence on the people in your school.

Submission

Submission is consciously putting your will under the authority of God. Those who submit humbly will want what God wants for them.

1. Ask God to take control of these areas of your life:

Friends	Studies	Job
Relationships with parents	Dating	Finances
Emotions	Spiritual journey	Attitudes
Pride		

CONFESSION

Confession is agreeing with God that your sin is in fact sin and then making plans to avoid repeating that sin. Sin involves not doing what we know is right and doing what is contrary to God's Word.

1. Make a list of the actions God may want you to take and the attitudes God may want you to develop that are not present in your life.
2. Confess these as sin.
3. Make a plan between you and God for how not to repeat them.
4. Destroy your list.

Adoration and Thanksgiving

Adoration is telling God how much you love him because of who he is. Thanksgiving is telling God how much you love him because of what he has done.

1. Pray through Psalm 103. Then pray it again, adding your name.
2. Adore God for each of his attributes. Then thank him for the way these affect your life. Thank you God that you are:

Loving	Wise	Holy Sovereign
Kind	Merciful	Creator
Righteous	Gracious	Self-Existent
Unchanging	Truth	Unified
All-Powerful	All-Knowing	Always Present

Station 1—Praise!
Praise God because he is—

Able
Acceptable
Creator
Complete
Compassionate
Exalted
Fair
Forgiving
Generous
Gracious
Healing
Infinite
Just
Kind
Loving
Majestic
Pure
Present
Powerful
Reliable
Responsive
Secure
Strong
Sufficient
Timeless
Unique
Wise
Wonderful

Awesome
Beautiful
Creative
Changeless
Eternal
Excellent
Faithful
Great
Glorious
Holy
Honorable
Invincible
Joyful
Knowing
Limitless
Merciful
Patient
Peaceful

Station 2—Focus on Jesus!
Meditate on the names of Jesus and thank him for being—

Advocate
Alpha and Omega
Author of Salvation
Chief Shepherd
Counselor
Deliverer
Chosen of God
Everlasting Father
Son of the Most High
Head of the Church
Jehovah or Yahweh
Light of the World
Only-Begotten Son
Savior
Truth
Prophet
Mighty God
Lamb of God

Almighty
Beloved Son
Bread of Life
Christ of God
Creator
Gate
Faithful Witness
Glory of the Lord
Good Shepherd
Prince of Peace
Shepherd
Rock
Word
Son of Man
Son of God
Mighty One
Mediator
King

Station 9—Special concerns

How about a "Friday-Night Thing" for the junior highers? Pray it up!
New time for High School Esprit—7:30
Things to work out with the facility
Staff schedules
Good attitudes
Good group-building time
Fellowship
Your school—teache[rs] administrators
For God to raise up Christi[ans] to be
[P]arental
[...]ry Tea[m]

Station 8—Pray for each other

Pray through the name list; pray for the growth of your friends—mentally, physically, spiritually, and socially.
Pray for us to be full of grace and truth.

Station 10—Just pray!

Ask the Lord to put something on your heart and pray for it!

Station 3—Thanksgiving

"Give thanks in all circumstances, for this is God's will for you in Christ Jesus." (1 Thess. 5:18)

Thank God for your—

Life
Faith
Family
Friends
Church
Youth group
Youth staff
What you have learned
The good times and the bad
Spiritual gifts and your ministry
Jesus at work in your life

Station 4—
Pray for our youth staff

Pray for them to be faithful, available, teachable, enthusiastic, responsible.

Pastor John
Randy and Nancy
Dee Dee Brestin
Margareta Karlsson
Russ Hansen
Peder and Katarina
Casey
Cindy
Kendra
Carol
Sid and Karen
Mark and Lynn
Wendy
Rich
Heather
Reo
Melissa
Susie
Deb

Station 5—
Pray for our youth program

Junior high group
Senior high group
Sunday school
Vine & Branches
Teens on the fringe
Positive attitudes
Spiritual maturity
For teens to use the new Scripture memory program
Unity

Station 7—
Pray for your student leaders

Pray for these students to be—
Without guile (not deceitful)
Totally committed
Excellent examples at school, church, everywhere
Loving, faithful, available, teachable, enthusiastic, responsible

Emil
Steve
Carmin
Crystal
Rafaela
Starlite
Danielle
Nikki
Taran
Ryan
Noah
Amanda
Vanessa
Kayly
Shawon
Sam

Station 6—Pray for the future

"Commit your way to the Lord; trust in him, and he will do this: he will make your righteousness shine like the dawn, the justice of your cause like the noonday sun." (Ps. 37:5,6)

Sunday evenings as we focus on how to say no to sexual pressure
Esprit Ski—for parents and teens
Festival of Praise—April 7-9
Esprit Summer Project
Challenge '98 in Indiana
Chicago work/service project

MAKE WAY FOR THE QUEEN

You are the **QUEEN.** (Congratulations!)

You must sit in the chair while your subjects carry you across the room. When you touch the wall, they are to bring you back and let you down.

You are the **SLAVE.**

DO NOT TELL ANYONE WHAT YOUR ROLE IS!

Your job is simply to do whatever the Queen or Grand Duke or the Priest tells you to do.

You are the **REBEL.**

DO NOT TELL ANYONE WHAT YOUR ROLE IS!

You are to be as uncooperative as you can.

Say things like, "This is stupid. She's not a queen. I'm not carrying her."

You can give in and carry her, but try to let someone else be Ruling Monarch by making your team lose.

The only thing you can NOT do is drop the Queen when you are carrying her.

You are the **GRAND DUKE.**

You function as the team captain, and your job is to get your Queen to the finish line so she can be crowned.

You are a Duke for life, which means you are not allowed to give up. If you do, the rival Queen will make sure you're not Duke much longer. (Get the hint?)

You are the **PRIEST.**

You are to see that your Queen wins, and you are to make sure that your team plays by the rules.

If you have any uncooperative members or people aren't getting along, you are to act as a peacemaker and try to get everyone to cooperate so your Queen can be crowned.

You are the **CRIPPLE.**

DO NOT TELL ANYONE WHAT YOUR ROLE IS!

The only thing you can tell them is that you have a broken arm and you cannot carry the chair.

Your job is to walk in front of the chair and shout "Make way for the Queen!"

After you have fun sharing answers to the first nine questions, emphasize how Scripture memory takes a backseat to relatively trivial details. Then use the following questions to generate a discussion about Scripture memory.

• How were you able to remember phone numbers, locker combinations, and the rest?

• Have you ever used these same methods to memorize Scripture?

• Why do we need to memorize God's Word? Perhaps these verses will help answer this question:

Joshua 1:8	**Psalm 119:9,11**
Matthew 4:1-11	**Romans 10:17**
Romans 12:2	**Ephesians 6:11-13,17**
Philippians 4:8	**2 Timothy 3:16-17**
Hebrews 4:12	

Remember this! After 24 hours we remember five percent of what we hear (Rom. 10:17), 15 percent of what we read (Rev. 1:3), 35 percent of what we study (Acts 17:11), and 100 percent of what we memorize (Ps. 119:11).

Now share some of the following hints for memorizing Scripture—and ask your teens for suggestions and methods of memorizing, too.

• Choose a verse that's special to you. Read and study the verse until you know what it means.

• Meditate on the verse. Think it over again and again until it becomes part of you.

• Write out the verse and reference a number of times.

• Categorize verses. 1 John 5:11-13, for example, would be under the "assurance of salvation" heading.

• When memorizing quote the topic, the reference, and the verse.

• Break the verse down into smaller phrases and work on memorizing one phrase at a time until you finish the entire verse.

• Start working on a new verse before you go to bed at night. You tend to remember what you are thinking about just before you fall asleep.

• Write out the verses on spiral-bound 3x5 index cards so you can carry them with you and work on them wherever you go.

• Use time that's often wasted, such as traveling to and from school, during meals, while exercising or jogging. This is an especially good way to memorize the books of the Bible. Rather than counting push-ups, recite the Bible books. You just may be able to increase your push-up maximum because you'll have no mental block as you often do when you approach a certain number.

• Accountability! Work with a partner to whom you can be accountable. Check up on each other and quiz each other.

• Set a goal (one or two verses a week, for example), then reward yourself or your partner when either or both of you consistently accomplish your goals over a one- or two-month period.

• Review, review, review. If you don't use your verses regularly, you will lose them.

Vaughn Van Skiver

COMMERCIALS FOR BIBLE MEMORY

Pair Bible verses with marketing slogans to encourage kids to recall the verses, and to invest the slogans with spiritual meanings.

Introduce the activity by reproducing and distributing the sheet entitled "How Is Your Memory?" (page 125). Ask students to match each slogan to the company or product it advertises. Here are the answers:

1. i	8. k	15. c
2. o	9. e	16. a
3. n	10. p	17. m
4. q	11. f	18. s
5. q	12. r	19. d
6. b	13. g	20. j
7. h	14. t	21. l

Now explore these questions:

1. How do we know and remember these phrases and products? *It's the job of advertisers to make up catchy phrases, tunes, and situations that are easily repeated and/or associated with the business or product.*

2. Why do we memorize things? *God made us with a memory that sometimes functions independently; memorizing makes life easier because we do not have to relearn everything; and memorizing provides a foundation for future experiences.*

3. What are some examples of things we memorize? *Tying shoelaces, multiplication tables, phone*

numbers, names, things that interest us like information about our hobbies.

4. How do we memorize? *Repetition, association, mnemonics, and patterns. For example, the following table can easily be memorized when the pattern is recognized:*

1
2 3
4 5 6
7 8 9 10
11 12 13 14 15

5. Ask several teens to explain how they do specific activities they have thoroughly memorized (e.g., the multiplication table or subtracting decimals). Ask them how they knew this. *Often math is memorized by repetition; names by association, repetition, or mnemonics; commercials by repetition or association.*

6. Why is it important to memorize God's Word? *Look up Joshua 1:8, Psalm 119:11; Ephesians 6:17, John 15:7, and 2 Timothy 3:16-17.*

To benefit from the association principle, match Scripture verses to the same slogans using the "How Is Your Scripture Memory?" sheet (page 126). Have students pick a favorite combination so that when they hear the slogan, the verse will be brought to mind. You might also point out that the pairs are a contrast between what God values and what the world values. Here are the answers:

1. i	8. s	15. d
2. u	9. a	16. h
3. r	10. b	17. c
4. a	11. j	18. l
5. g	12. o	19. n
6. m	13. e	20. p
7. f	14. t	21. k

Derek Chinn

SELF-IMAGE

FIRST IMPRESSION COLLAGE

This is a good game to use in a group where the kids know each other only slightly. Gather a mass of old magazines, paper, scissors, and glue. The kids go through the magazines cutting or tearing out pictures, ads, or phrases that remind them of another person in the room. They present each other with the cut-outs. Next, have each person make a collage using the pictures he or she has received. Break up into small groups and have each person discuss or explain the collage.

IMAGINARY ME

Here's a mixer that can be fun and also very enlightening for discussion purposes. Begin by having everyone choose a new name. It should be totally new; that is, not the name of a famous person or someone they know. Make name tags for everyone with these new names. Then tell each person to forget (for now) their "real" homes, jobs, families, past, etc., and to create for themselves whole new identities. Then have the group mingle around and "get acquainted" with each other. They will be like strangers, and they can talk about anything they want, just as long as they do it as under their new identities. Follow up with a discussion of the experience. You can get a lot of mileage out of this, and it really helps young people to learn some surprising things about themselves.

THE INDIVIDUALITY GAME

This game helps a person realize just how unique and special to God he or she really is. Give each group member one chocolate chip cookie. This is their special cookie. Ask them to remember the cookie size, the amount of chips, the location of the chips, any special pattern of chips, and any other unique features. Then break into small groups. Each group combines and mixes up their cookies. After this, each person has to find his or her own cookie. No one can take anyone else's. If a person disagrees with someone regarding certain cookies, have both state reasons why they think the cookie in question is theirs. The application is that if all these cookies can be differentiated by their uniqueness, how much more unique we must be to God.

Match the phrase with the company or product.

______ 1. You've got the right one baby.

______ 2. Membership has its privileges.

______ 3. We run the tightest ship in the shipping business.

______ 4. Ya gotta have it.

______ 5. The choice of a new generation.

______ 6. Button your fly.

______ 7. You're in good hands.

______ 8. Quality is job one.

______ 9. Life's short. Play hard.

______ 10. We bring good things to light

______ 11. From sharp minds come sharp products.

______ 12. Reach out and touch someone.

______ 13. Food, folks, and fun.

______ 14. Just do it.

______ 15. Built for the human race.

______ 16. If you don't look good, we don't look good.

______ 17. The power to be your best.

______ 18. I love what you do for me.

______ 19. Build your future on the rock.

______ 20. When you care enough to send the very best.

______ 21. Run for the border.

a. Vidal Sassoon
b. Levis
c. Nissan
d. Prudential
e. Reebok
f. Sharp Electronics
g. McDonald's
h. Allstate
i. Diet Pepsi
j. Hallmark
k. Ford
l. Taco Bell
m. Apple
n. UPS
o. American Express
p. General Electric
q. Pepsi
r. AT&T
s. Toyota
t. Nike

How Is Your Scripture Memory?

Match the phrase with the Scripture verse.

______ 1. You got the right one baby. (Diet Pepsi)
______ 2. Membership has its privileges. (American Express)
______ 3. We run the tightest ship in the shipping business. (UPS)
______ 4. Ya gotta have it. (Pepsi)
______ 5. The choice of a new generation. (Pepsi)
______ 6. Button your fly. (Levis)
______ 7. You're in good hands. (Allstate)
______ 8. Quality is job one. (Ford)
______ 9. Life's short. Play hard. (Reebok)
______ 10. We bring good things to light. (General Electric)
______ 11. From sharp minds come sharp products. (Sharp Electronics)
______ 12. Reach out and touch someone. (AT&T)
______ 13. Food, folks, and fun. (McDonald's)
______ 14. Just do it. (Nike)
______ 15. Build for the human race. (Nissan)
______ 16. If you don't look good, we don't look good. (Vidal Sassoon)
______ 17. The power to be your best. (Apple)
______ 18. I love what you do for me. (Toyota)
______ 19. Build your future on the rock. (Prudential)
______ 20. When you care enough to send the very best. (Hallmark)
______ 21. Run for the border. (Taco Bell)

a. Hebrews 11:6
b. Matthew 5:16
c. 2 Peter 1:3, 4
d. Romans 5:8
e. Hebrews 10:24, 25
f. Proverbs 3:5,6
g. Joshua 24:15
h. 1 Corinthians 12:26
i. 1 Corinthians 15:57
j. Proverbs 16:23
k. 1 Corinthians 9:24, 25
l. John 13:35
m. 1 Corinthians 6:18-20
n. Isaiah 26:4
o. Matthew 28:18-20
p. John 3:16
q. Ephesians 5:15, 16
r. Colossians 1:28, 29
s. Philippians 2:9-11
t. Matthew 9:37, 38
u. John 15:5

WHAT OTHERS THINK OF ME

The following exercise is designed to give young people the opportunity to discover what their peer group thinks of them, thus helping each young person to develop a better self-image and to see where changes should be made.

Give each person a 3x8-inch slip of paper. Have them write their name at the bottom and a one-word self-description at the top. They are then instructed to fold the paper down from the top twice to conceal the word they wrote. The paper should look like this:

The kids then exchange papers twice, so that no one knows for sure who was their paper. Each person then writes at the top of the page a one-word description of the person named at the bottom. Kids should be instructed to be honest, kind, constructive, and as helpful as possible to the person they are describing.

(If they don't know the person at all, they should leave it blank.) The papers are folded down to conceal the word they wrote, and then exchanged again and the process is repeated until the papers are full of one-word descriptions of the person named at the bottom.

The completed papers are returned back to the person whose name is at the bottom, and the kids are given a few minutes to look them over. Each person can then compare their own self-image with how others think of them. Discussion can follow, with young people sharing their feelings about the exercise, and what their response to it will be.

This exercise is best when groups know each other pretty well ahead of time. As the leader, you will need to help kids to not take the experience too personally and give them guidance in evaluating it as well. It can be pointed out that although what others say about us may be valid, our own self-image is also valid. Maturity is the ability to accept criticism or praise without being threatened or thinking too highly of ourselves. We can instead use such information as a source of renewal in our own personal lives. Tie this in with related Scripture and instruction from the Word of God.

WHAT'S NUMBER ONE?

The questions below are to be answered by each individual on a sheet of paper, then followed up by discussion.

1. What's your favorite magazine?
2. If you could be anyone else, who would you be?
3. When you daydream, what are you doing?
4. If you could buy anything, what would you buy?
5. When you picture yourself doing something "cool and neat" (mental act of heroism), what are you doing?
6. When you see a person of the opposite sex, how do you picture this person in relationship to yourself?
7. When you see a person of the same sex, how do you picture this person in relationship to yourself?
8. What would you like to do for your life's work?
9. What's good about you? (Don't be humble!)
10. If you could change anything about you, what would you change?

Points to make during a wrap-up of the discussion:

- **These questions show fairly clearly what the most important thing in a person's life is.**
- **Complete involvement of an individual in one specific area of life is abnormal. The activity becomes distorted. It is not that important.**
- **Read Matthew 6:33 and discuss what this means for us today.**
- **Questions 9 and 10 show a person's "self-concept." God loves each one of us as we are, and he can use us as we are (physical build, etc.). We don't need to be heroes to be useful in his sight.**

APPLES AND YOU

After kids are in the room, dump a pile of apples on the floor. The kids are to look over the apples and choose one that reminds them of themselves or "appeals" to them in some way. Then for the next five minutes, they are to analyze their apple. Really get to know it, every spot, bruise, color, etc. All apples then go back into one big pile and after some mixing up, the kids are told to find their apple. And they nearly always do. As they find their apple, they are to pair off and share with their partner by completing the following four sentences:

1. I picked this apple from all the others because...

2. The thing about this apple that reminds me of myself is...

3. The area in my life in which I naturally shine is...

4. The area in my life that needs a little polishing is...

After this sharing, each one closes his eyes and feeds his apple to his partner. After the apples are eaten, close with a short time of prayer for each other. *Jim Hudson*

MAP OF ME

Give each person a large sheet of paper and a marking pen or crayons. Have each person think of himself as a place and draw a map which would describe that place. For example, what would you look like if you were a city, or an island in the middle of the ocean? What kinds of buildings, hills, valleys, roads (some under construction), areas of interest, etc.? Allow each person to describe what he or she has drawn to the entire group. This is great as a way of getting kids to open up about their lives and their individuality. *Andrea Sutton*

HOW GOD SEES ME

Each person is asked to take a sheet of newsprint and on one side draw pictures, cartoons, or sayings expressing "How I See God." The other side is to be filled with symbols expressing "How I Think God Sees Me." Allow 20 to 25 minutes to complete. After everyone is finished, each person should explain her drawing to the entire group. This exercise opens a group up to sharing where each one stands with God at present and demonstrates the varying facets of an individual's experience with God. *David Markle*

SHOES OF CHRIST

Here's an idea that can be used to illustrate the meaning behind Paul's concept of the uniqueness of each member within the body of Christ. Have the kids sit in a circle, remove their shoes, and place them in the middle of the circle. Talk about the features that shoes have in common and then discuss what makes each pair unique. Then have the kids take a pair of someone else's shoes and attempt to put them on. They will soon discover how difficult it is to wear someone else's shoes. Return everyone's shoes and discuss what it means to be unique in the body of Christ. *Van Edington*

SHOW AND TELL

Invite each person in your group to bring a personal object that represents something about their feelings about life. They could bring anything including trophies, books, pictures, mementoes, etc. After each person shares what he or she brought with the group, then others in the group may ask questions. When everyone has shared, the leader then asks: (1) What new things did you learn about the people who shared? (2) What did you each learn about yourselves? *Don Highlander*

THE TATOR FAMILY

Here is an idea that can (and has) been used in a number of ways—from bulletin inserts to sermons, plays, and skits. However it is used, it is a clever and rather entertaining way to illustrate both the positive and negative aspects of common traits found in people.

Here are the members of the Tator family:

- **Speck Tator.** He likes to watch everyone else rather than get involved in anything personally. He is always on the outside looking in. He is usually expert at evaluating and helps those who are participating by cheering them on. But because Speck has the advantage of watching from the stands, he can also make unrealistic assessments from a distance and be quite fickle with his support.
- **Dick Tator.** Dick doesn't consult anyone. He makes all his decisions by himself and sees others only as means to accomplish his will. Dick usually gets high marks for getting things done, but low marks for working with others.
- **Agi Tator.** Whenever things get dull, Agi is always

there to stir things up. She is often a nuisance, but many times keeps everyone on their toes by disturbing the comfortable status quo.

- **Hesi Tator.** It is very difficult for Hesi to make decisions. She always needs just a little bit more information before making a decision. If and when Hesi does make a decision, however, it has usually been thought through carefully.
- **Emmy Tator.** Emmy is a follower and can easily become a hero worshiper. Heavily influenced by those around her, Emmy's future is determined by the kinds of people she patterns her life after.
- **Common Tator.** Common always has advice or criticism on any subject. Always talking and always very authoritative sounding, he often sounds like he knows what he is talking about, but usually doesn't.
- **Irri Tator.** Irri is a twin of Agi with a mean streak in her. She likes to stir things up just for the sake of causing confusion and disarray. She is abrasive and even when she takes the correct position on a subject, still winds up alienating those around her.
- **Vegi Tator.** Some call Vegi lazy because she just sits around doing nothing. She doesn't take any risks and tends to take what's given without giving anything in return. But at least Vegi is predictable and somewhat stable.
- **Devis Tator.** Devis is a revolutionary. He believes in confrontation and radical change. It is his philosophy that the only way to change something is to destroy it and start all over. Devis is weak on alternatives or ideas for rebuilding, and considers that someone else's job.
- **Facili Tator.** Facili is warm and personable. She is almost selfless. She works hard at enabling others to become better. She is a good listener and asks the kinds of questions that allow people to speak about things that matter to them. But Facili can sometimes be a nuisance because she sees every gathering as an opportunity to use her gifts and sometimes she just needs to let her abilities remain dormant.
- **Cogi Tator.** Cogi is a thinker. She is different from her brother Medi, in that Cogi thinks about matters that will affect the way she acts. She weighs everything carefully before acting and attempts to make sure she has considered all the alternatives.
- **Medi Tator.** Medi thinks deeply and finds satisfaction in the act itself. His thinking never really leads to any constructive action, however. It is the act of pondering that matters to Medi and not the content.
- **Roe Tator.** Roe is a systems man. He believes that everyone should have their turn regardless of qualification. He is task oriented and is only involved as long as the task is his responsibility. He believes in change for change's sake and doesn't like to remain in one spot too long.

Kenneth Jacobsen

REFLECTIONS IN A ROCK

Sometime prior to your youth service, collect some rocks, enough rocks so each person in your group receives one. Collecting these rocks may take some time depending on the number that will be participating; but time well spent because each rock should, if possible, be quite different in shape, color, roughness, size, etc.

The next step is to form a circle with your group as close together as possible. Before handing out the rocks explain in detail the object of this, which would be your introduction for your lesson.

You should explain that each person will receive a rock and that they will be given time to study, to examine in great detail, their own rock; they should know its complete detail. Then they should ask God what he can show them in their rock that reflects their own life. (Example: the sharp edge on one side of the rock might represent sin in one's life that needs to be smoothed out and that like the water of a swift stream smooths the stone, so might people, parents, youth leaders, etc.) You the leader will be pleased as you see youth participate like never before. You'll learn things in kid's lives you'd never discover in a counseling discussion or even by being close to them. They'll reflect the past, present, and even future process they feel will have to occur so that God can use them daily. *John B. Warren, Jr.*

EGO TALK

This activity can be done at any meeting and would make a great lead-in to a discussion on selfishness, self-esteem, or a similar topic.

Give each person in your group an equal amount of play money (about $10 is sufficient—print your own, find some from a board game, or buy some at a store). At some point during the activity, announce that during the next 10 or 15 minutes, you're absolutely not allowed to talk about yourself. In other words, you must not say any of the following words: I, me, my, mine, etc. If someone catches you saying those words, they may ask you for $1, and you must give it to them. If you run out of money, then you are not permitted to talk until the time is up.

Of course, the object is to try to accumulate as much money as you can. You might want to have an auction afterward, so they can use the money they accumulated. The experience can be very enlightening, as it is almost impossible to carry on a conversation without making reference to yourself. *Bob Ingrem*

How Many F's?

Here's a fun little experiment that can be tied in quite nicely with a lesson on awareness. Print up the sheet on page 131, allow one card for each person. At your meeting pass them out, face down. At a signal everyone turns the page over and begins at the same time. Each person should work alone—give them 30 seconds. (Try it yourself before you read the answer below.)

Most people will count three. Others will see four or five. Only a few will count all six F's that are in the box. After the 30 seconds are up, ask the group how many F's they counted, and you will get a variety of answers. Those who counted only three, four, or five will be quite surprised when you tell them the answer. But after they find all six F's, they will feel rather silly that they didn't see them in the first place. Most people tend to overlook the word *of* when they are counting. This is because they are looking only at the bigger words.

This test is often given to people in driving classes to demonstrate how we often fail to see motorcycles on the road because they are so small, and because we aren't looking for them. After they are pointed out, they become obvious. This lesson can also be applied to people. We often miss the good qualities in other people because we aren't looking for them. We tend to look instead for the things that we want to see—the bad things. This is to make ourselves look good by comparison.

Follow up on this idea with an exercise in which youths look for the good in each other, and affirm each other's gifts and abilities. It's amazing how when these things are pointed out, they then become more obvious. It also does a lot for everyone's self-esteem.

Sexual Purity

(See also Values)

The C.O.N.D.O.M.

To assist your kids to take action against the lure of becoming sexually active, try this brand of C.O.N.D.O.M.

Reproduce the cards on page 132. Bring them to a meeting in a small, unlabeled box. At the meeting explain the following to the group:

> **Since many schools have decided that the best method to assure safe sex is to distribute condoms, it's time for the church to take action and engage in the battle for the lives of America's youths. After much prayer I have decided that I will distribute condoms to this youth group.**
>
> **Unlike the condoms that schools distribute, however, my brand of condom has unique features. It is 100 percent effective, it's reusable, it has no clumsy wrapper to mess with, it doesn't need a government-paid social worker to demonstrate how it is used, it doesn't need to be hidden from nosy parents (in fact, I encourage you to give one to your parents), it fits easily in a wallet or a purse, and it's the only condom that promotes truly safe sex. It's even endorsed by God. With features like these, it just makes good sense that every teenager use the C.O.N.D.O.M. every day.**

Mark Lehman

Speech

Personal Speech Inventory

The questionnaire on page 133 can be used as a good lead-in to a discussion on the importance of what we say and how we say it. Have teens circle the response that they feel best describes themselves.

The statements on the survey and corresponding Scripture verses can then be used as a basis for further discussion. Some questions that the students should think about:

1. **What does the Bible say about the described behavior?**
2. **What can be the result of using your speech in the way described?**
3. **What can a person with this problem do to overcome it?**

Read the following sentence in the enclosed block. After reading the sentence, go back and count the F's. You have one minute.

FINISHED FILES ARE THE RESULT OF YEARS OF SCIENTIFIC STUDY COMBINED WITH THE EXPERIENCE OF YEARS.

Number of F's in the block ______________

Read the following sentence in the enclosed block. After reading the sentence, go back and count the F's. You have one minute.

FINISHED FILES ARE THE RESULT OF YEARS OF SCIENTIFIC STUDY COMBINED WITH THE EXPERIENCE OF YEARS.

Number of F's in the block ______________

Read the following sentence in the enclosed block. After reading the sentence, go back and count the F's. You have one minute.

FINISHED FILES ARE THE RESULT OF YEARS OF SCIENTIFIC STUDY COMBINED WITH THE EXPERIENCE OF YEARS.

Number of F's in the block ______________

Read the following sentence in the enclosed block. After reading the sentence, go back and count the F's. You have one minute.

FINISHED FILES ARE THE RESULT OF YEARS OF SCIENTIFIC STUDY COMBINED WITH THE EXPERIENCE OF YEARS.

Number of F's in the block ______________

Read the following sentence in the enclosed block. After reading the sentence, go back and count the F's. You have one minute.

FINISHED FILES ARE THE RESULT OF YEARS OF SCIENTIFIC STUDY COMBINED WITH THE EXPERIENCE OF YEARS.

Number of F's in the block ______________

Read the following sentence in the enclosed block. After reading the sentence, go back and count the F's. You have one minute.

FINISHED FILES ARE THE RESULT OF YEARS OF SCIENTIFIC STUDY COMBINED WITH THE EXPERIENCE OF YEARS.

Number of F's in the block ______________

Read the following sentence in the enclosed block. After reading the sentence, go back and count the F's. You have one minute.

FINISHED FILES ARE THE RESULT OF YEARS OF SCIENTIFIC STUDY COMBINED WITH THE EXPERIENCE OF YEARS.

Number of F's in the block ______________

Read the following sentence in the enclosed block. After reading the sentence, go back and count the F's. You have one minute.

FINISHED FILES ARE THE RESULT OF YEARS OF SCIENTIFIC STUDY COMBINED WITH THE EXPERIENCE OF YEARS.

Number of F's in the block ______________

Safe Sex C.O.N.D.O.M.

CONTROLLING OUR NATURAL DESIRES BY OBEYING THE MASTER

"It is God's will that you should be sanctified: that you should avoid sexual immorality; that you all should learn to control your own bodies in a way that is holy and honorable, not in passionate lust."
1 Thessalonians 4:3-5

Safe Sex C.O.N.D.O.M.

CONTROLLING OUR NATURAL DESIRES BY OBEYING THE MASTER

"It is God's will that you should be sanctified: that you should avoid sexual immorality; that you all should learn to control your own bodies in a way that is holy and honorable, not in passionate lust."
1 Thessalonians 4:3-5

Safe Sex C.O.N.D.O.M.

CONTROLLING OUR NATURAL DESIRES BY OBEYING THE MASTER

"It is God's will that you should be sanctified: that you should avoid sexual immorality; that you all should learn to control your own bodies in a way that is holy and honorable, not in passionate lust."
1 Thessalonians 4:3-5

Safe Sex C.O.N.D.O.M.

CONTROLLING OUR NATURAL DESIRES BY OBEYING THE MASTER

"It is God's will that you should be sanctified: that you should avoid sexual immorality; that you all should learn to control your own bodies in a way that is holy and honorable, not in passionate lust."
1 Thessalonians 4:3-5

Safe Sex C.O.N.D.O.M.

CONTROLLING OUR NATURAL DESIRES BY OBEYING THE MASTER

"It is God's will that you should be sanctified: that you should avoid sexual immorality; that you all should learn to control your own bodies in a way that is holy and honorable, not in passionate lust."
1 Thessalonians 4:3-5

Safe Sex C.O.N.D.O.M.

CONTROLLING OUR NATURAL DESIRES BY OBEYING THE MASTER

"It is God's will that you should be sanctified: that you should avoid sexual immorality; that you all should learn to control your own bodies in a way that is holy and honorable, not in passionate lust."
1 Thessalonians 4:3-5

Safe Sex C.O.N.D.O.M.

CONTROLLING OUR NATURAL DESIRES BY OBEYING THE MASTER

"It is God's will that you should be sanctified: that you should avoid sexual immorality; that you all should learn to control your own bodies in a way that is holy and honorable, not in passionate lust."
1 Thessalonians 4:3-5

Safe Sex C.O.N.D.O.M.

CONTROLLING OUR NATURAL DESIRES BY OBEYING THE MASTER

"It is God's will that you should be sanctified: that you should avoid sexual immorality; that you all should learn to control your own bodies in a way that is holy and honorable, not in passionate lust."
1 Thessalonians 4:3-5

Safe Sex C.O.N.D.O.M.

CONTROLLING OUR NATURAL DESIRES BY OBEYING THE MASTER

"It is God's will that you should be sanctified: that you should avoid sexual immorality; that you all should learn to control your own bodies in a way that is holy and honorable, not in passionate lust."
1 Thessalonians 4:3-5

PERSONAL SPEECH INVENTORY

Circle the response that you feel best describes yourself

R—rarely S—sometimes F—frequently

R—S—F **When I am angry with someone, I tell him off. (Prov. 15:1)**

R—S—F **I help my friends to get back at others. (Prov. 17:9)**

R—S—F **I respond quickly when provoked. (Prov. 29:20)**

R—S—F **I talk about other people. (Prov. 11:13)**

R—S—F **I talk a lot. (Prov. 10:19)**

R—S—F **I talk in ways which dishonor God. (2 Tim. 2:16)**

R—S—F **I speak before I think. (Prov. 13:3)**

R—S—F **I say things that hurt others. (Eph. 4:29)**

R—S—F **I listen to or tell dirty jokes. (Eph. 4:29)**

R—S—F **I stir up trouble by the things I say. (James 3:5-10)**

R—S—F **I tell untrue things about other people. (Lev. 19:16)**

R—S—F **My speech is inconsistent with my faith. (James 1:26, Col. 3:8)**

Conclude the session with a brief interpretation of James 3:3-4. *Stan Taylor*

SPIRITUAL GROWTH

SPIRITUAL PILGRIMAGE

One effective way to help a group share their spiritual lives with one another is to have them visualize it. Ask them to think back to the first memories they have of God. Then ask them to think through all the highs and lows, ups and downs they have been through up to the present time. Invite them to draw a picture or a graph or some type of drawing that represents their spiritual life through history. Another way is to give them a piece of wire and have them mold and bend it to represent their pilgrimage. Divide into small groups and let each person share the meaning of his or her drawing or molding.
William C. Moore

WHERE ARE YOU LETTER

This can be effective following a service of commitment. Pass out plain paper and instruct the youths to write a letter to themselves, in all seriousness and honesty, telling where they would like to be in a year's time (or six months). This letter should reflect goals for Christian growth. The students determine how they would like to grow spiritually in a year and/or what they would like to accomplish. After writing the letters, each person self-addresses an envelope, places the letter inside, seals it, and passes it on to you for safekeeping. Mail them out at the appropriate time (in a year) and kids can see how they progressed, in contrast to their hopes. This makes for good discussion and follow-up. *David Parke*

GRAB-BAG TESTIMONIES

Here's a good way to get your kids to reflect on their present spiritual condition and to share their thoughts with others. Prepare several slips of paper each containing a verse of Scripture and a sentence instructing them to read the statement and relate how they have or have not applied this verse to their own life in the past weeks or months. The following are several examples.

Read this verse and tell how it has or has not been applied to your life this school year.

"Do not be anxious about anything, but in everything by prayer and petition, with thanksgiving, present your requests to God. And the peace of God, which transcends all understanding, will guard your hearts and your minds in Christ Jesus."—Philippians 4:6-7, NIV

Read this verse aloud and tell us how you have or have not put this into practice this month.

"Seek first his kingdom and his righteousness, and all these things will be given to you as well."—Matthew 6:33, NIV

Looking at yourself objectively, in what ways are you growing to be like Jesus? In what ways are you not? What are some characteristics that Jesus had that you would like in your own life?

"A student is not above his teacher, nor a servant above his master. It is enough for the student to be like his teacher, and the servant like his master..." —Matthew 10:24-25, NIV

After reading this verse aloud, explain what this verse means to you now and how you have applied it, hope to apply it, or have failed to apply it.

"Flee the evil desires of youth, and pursue righteousness, faith, love and peace, along with those who call on the Lord out of a pure heart."—2 Timothy 2:22

At the beginning of your session, ask for volunteers—it is your choice whether or not to tell them what's going on. Have them reach into a paper bag to retrieve one slip of paper. Give volunteers enough time to collect their thoughts. Then ask them to respond to the verse and to the question. Be prepared to ask probing questions to help the volunteer communicate clearly and not to merely say "I think this verse means...." (Give volunteers an out if they are uncomfortable.) Keep the activity brief—two to three minutes per person. Allow others to give their feedback too. *Fred O. Pitts*

M.U.S.T.

The following is an idea to make the summer months more of a challenge for your youths. At the beginning of the summer, give the youth group the name Metamorphosis Union in the Summer Time (M.U.S.T.). Metamorphosis means "change," and as a key verse, you can use Paul's admonition about being "changed from within by the power of God" rather than being changed by how the world squeezes us into its mold (Romans 12:2).

To begin with have the kids write letters to themselves about how they would like to change as a person during the summer (and beyond if they care to). These are sealed in self-addressed envelopes. During the summer, the kids attempt to expose themselves to as much as possible in the way of activities, projects, study, and each other to help bring about personal metamorphosis. The emphasis is focused on personal development and maturity, with special individual projects and activities designed by the youth minister. At the end of the summer, mail the letters back to the kids and have them discuss any metamorphosis that took place during the summer. *Glenn Jolley*

Hello God, Where Are You?

Here is an idea to help your youth group get in touch with God in a personal way, enabling them to see how God works in their own lives.

Begin by having each person write down a few ways they have actually experienced God's active involvement in their lives during the last week or two. These can then be shared with the entire group. You might also ask the students to write down some barriers in their lives that have kept them from experiencing God's involvement in their lives. These can also be shared and discussed.

After this discussion, introduce the idea of keeping a journal as a way of helping us overcome some of these barriers. It also enables us to see God's activity in our lives. A journal is a type of diary in which the youth write down (everyday or whenever possible) their insights, observations, questions, discoveries, and so on.

You can provide inexpensive spiral notebooks for use as a journal or the students can come up with their own. Have each person choose one or more of the following journal formats which would be most appropriate to his or her own personal needs. Also decide on a time span for this journal keeping period. It could be a week, a month, or even longer. Each person should include the date on each entry, although they do not have to be done every day. However, in order for it to be effective, it should be written in at least twice a week. Hand out the list on page 136 of possible sections to include in their journals.

You may want to keep in touch with the kids personally during this journal-keeping period to encourage them and to see how they are doing. At the end of the time period, get together with the group so that you can share and reflect on some of the things that they've learned, struggled with, or become more aware of while keeping their journals. Some students may want to continue keeping their journals long after this experience. Those who are unable to follow through with the journal can share why it was difficult for them. *Anna Hobbs*

Spiritual Growth Chart

Here's a creative way to get your kids to think about spiritual growth and to evaluate their own walk with God. Distribute paper. Have kids draw a straight line on their papers to represent the last two years of their lives, labeling the months and years on the time line. Next, ask them to draw a flexible line charting their spiritual ups and downs. Anything above the time line represents a time of growth, anything below indicates decline and anything along the line represents no change in their spiritual progress.

Have kids circle major high, low, or no-change periods and briefly note why that condition existed. Discuss these findings together. Some questions to consider are: What causes growth in our spiritual lives? Is there anything wrong with a chart that looks like a roller coaster? What have we learned about ourselves from these charts?

After the discussion, you might want to chart the spiritual progress of some colorful characters in the Bible (David or Peter, for example) and compare their struggles. *Phil Print*

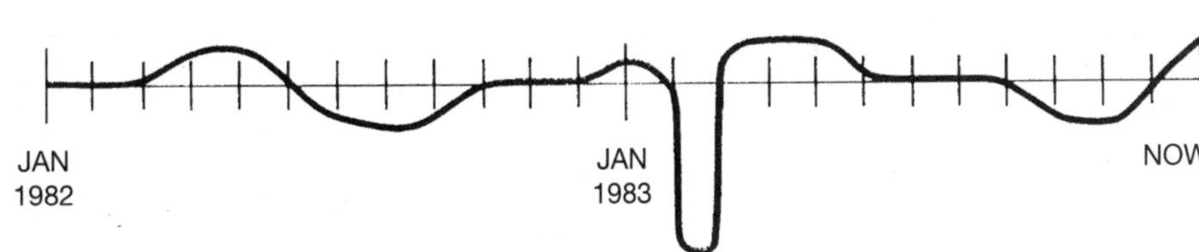

HELLO GOD, WHERE ARE YOU?

Here are some possible sections that you could include in your journal:

INSIGHTS. The focus here is on being aware of the relationship between our faith, things around us, and the experiences we have. Whenever something happens that makes you aware of your relationship to God, or if you see him at work in your life, you should write it down as it comes to you.

QUESTIONS AND SEARCHINGS. Write down questions that you have each day or week—the things that bothered you, challenged you, that seemed to cause conflicts, that made you wonder. Look for these things that you would like to understand better, and write them down as you review your day or week.

THANKSGIVINGS. Each day write down two or three things that give you reason to celebrate, to be happy, or that you are thankful for.

MEDITATIONS. The focus here is on making Scripture real and practical. Read a passage of Scripture each day and write down the verse that sticks in your mind from that day. Write below it three or four ways you could apply it that day or week.

SELF-MOTIVATION. Write down a goal for the week at the top of the page. You might want to look for a verse in Scripture that would help encourage or support you in accomplishing this goal. Write down three or four ways you could work on your goal during the coming week. A self-evaluation blank at the bottom of the page could be included so that you can keep a record of how you are doing toward attaining that goal. Make the goals simple, specific, and attainable.

PRAYERS. Write out prayer requests, leaving a space below or beside the request. When the prayer is answered, you can write the date in the space.

STEREOTYPES

STEREOTYPES

Go through several magazines and newspapers and find a number of pictures of people—some who are recognizable, others who are not. Careful searching will turn up some good ones for this game, in which you judge others strictly on the basis of their appearance.

Post all the pictures and ask the kids to identify them, using these labels: millionaire, bank robber, prince, minister, rapist, author.

After you reveal the true identities of each person, lead a discussion or a Bible study on passages like James 2:1-13 or Matthew 7:1-2. *Marti Lambert*

THANKFULNESS

COUNTING BIBLICAL BLESSINGS

This Bible study is effective at any time of the year, especially at Thanksgiving. Have the group look up the following Scripture passages and discover in each what the different writers or biblical characters were thankful for.

Psalm 30:4-5	**Psalm 97:10-12**
1 Chronicles 29:6-13	**Daniel 2:23**
Acts 27:34-35	**Romans 1:8**
Romans 6:17-18	**1 Corinthians 15:55-57**
2 Corinthians 2:14	**2 Corinthians 9:15**
Philippians 1:3-5	**2 Thessalonians 1:2-3**
1 Timothy 4:3-5	**Revelation 11:16-17**

Have students choose one or two items from the list that they also are thankful for and explain their choices. Spend time thanking God for these things. *Richard Starcher*

THANKSGIVING EXCHANGE

This activity starts a good discussion near Thanksgiving or anytime you want to teach a lesson on gratitude. It works best with students who know each other fairly well. Begin by having students share one or two things that they are thankful for. These will usually be the kind of things that are most obvious to them.

Then give everyone a piece of paper and have kids write their names at the top. Collect the sheets and redistribute them so that everyone has a sheet with someone else's name on it. Now have kids write down on those sheets what they would be thankful for if they were the person whose name is at the top. They can list as many things as they want. Sheets go back to their originators and you can begin the discussion. Ask:

- **What is written on your sheet that you haven't thanked God for lately?**
- **What is written on your sheet that you had never even thought about thanking God for?**
- **Is anything written on your sheet that you disagree with? That you didn't think you should be thankful for?**

This exercise helps young people realize that they take a lot for granted. *Randy Wheeler*

TRUST IN OTHERS

TRUST TEST

Here's a good exercise to build trust within the group. Break into groups of six to eight. Each group forms a close circle with one person in the center. The person stands stiff, keeps feet together, and doesn't bend his knees. He falls (keeping his body in this fixed position) toward the people in the circle. He must trust each member of the circle to keep him from falling as they push him around from person to person, back and forth across the circle. Follow with a discussion of the experience.

OBSTACLE ILLUSION

Here is an activity that is not only fun but has great discussion potential. It is a combination trust walk and obstacle course. First you will need a large area with a lot of minor obstacles such as light poles, trees, playground equipment, etc. (One group used the church boiler room after they had shut down all of the heating and cooling equipment.) Then pick a starting point and run some heavy cord to the nearest obstacle. At that point string out two or more lines to other nearby obstacles. Only one line will continue beyond one of the obstacles, the others will dead end. Continue the main line to the next obstacle with more dead ends, etc. Mark the end of the line by hanging a coffee can full of marbles from the last obstacle.

Divide into small groups of eight to 12 kids. Have each group choose a leader and two or three assistants. Line the kids up in a hand-on-shoulder single file line and blindfold each one (unless you are in a room and can make it absolutely dark). Lead each group separately by a confusing path to the starting point and let each group follow the course alone.

Explain to the groups that the object is to follow the main line together without separating. (The leader can stop the group and send out assistants to check when they come to more than one line.)

Be sure to vary the heights of the line. For example, if the main line leads to an obstacle at shoulder level, it could go out from the obstacle at knee or ankle level, while a dead end continues from shoulder level. Also plan obstacles that require the kids to stoop under. Make sure the course is long enough so that it takes 20 to 25 minutes to finish!

Bob Kerstetter

VALUES

WHAT WOULD YOU DO?

Sometimes it's easier to get into Scripture when it can be looked at in light of some everyday situations. The following six situations are designed to help kids to think through various passages of Scripture and how they might apply to them personally. One good way to use them would be to divide the entire group into six small groups and give one situation to each group and give them enough time to work through the discussion questions. When they are finished, each group can then share their conclusions with the other groups. *Marva L. Mehaffey and Jane O. Kimberly*

Jeremiah 17:9-10

Cheating

In an English exam you need an A or B to pass the course for the semester. You studied long and hard. Your friend didn't study at all. While the teacher is busy checking papers, you notice that your friend is copying answers from another student who always does well. You get a C while your friend gets an A.

1. How do you feel?
2. What would you do as a Christian?
3. Does this experience change your relationship with your friend?
4. Would you discuss the issue with your friend? Other friends? Your parents? The teacher?
5. How would you feel if you were the cheater with an A knowing your friend studied and received only a C when he needed at least a B?

Proverbs 1:29-31

Instant Gratification

The group is going to an amusement park and you need $20. Your parents agree to help you earn it by allowing you to keep money from the recycling of aluminum cans and the return deposits on glass bottles. Normally the money is put into the family entertainment budget. On the way home with the money, you discover a new CD by your favorite group and decide you can get the money for the trip from the next returns, so you buy it. When you get home your parents are very upset and tell you that they will not help you earn any more money and, because you broke the agreement, you cannot go on the trip even if you have the money.

1. How do you feel?
2. How do you think your parents might feel?
3. Who was cheated?
4. Has an impulsive act such as the above ever cost too high a price?
5. If you were the parent would you have handled this differently? If so, how?

Proverbs 3:1-6

Trust

You are not allowed to go on any type of dates. You've agreed to meet your girl/boy friend at the movies. You tell your parents you are going to the movies with your best friend. Your parents discover what you did. Now you can go nowhere unless taken and picked up by your parents. Over the last few weeks you feel they are beginning to trust you again.

1. Did you "fess up" or try to "fake it?"

2. Will you go sneak again now that they are beginning to trust you again?

3. How do you think your parents felt when you betrayed their trust in you?

4. Would a Christian react differently?

Proverbs 16:6

Loyalty

You are at your friend's house. Your friend "sneaks" a cookie for you. You say nothing even though you think it is not quite right not to ask. On the way home from school, you and your friend stop at the store to pick up an item for your mom. When you leave the store, your friend gives you a candy bar. After you've eaten it, your friend tells you he "sneaked" it for you from the store.

1. How does the candy taste now?

2. How do you feel about your friend?

3. Should you tell someone? Who?

4. Should you have discussed it earlier when you noticed that the friend was "sneaking" the cookie at home?

5. Would you discuss this with your parents? Why or why not?

6. If this pattern continues, does your friend deserve your loyalty?

7. Can you get into trouble for being loyal? How or why not?

8. Does loyalty overlook anything and everything?

Deuteronomy 5:16, 1 Samuel 19:1-3

Obedience

You are not allowed by your parents to call guys on the telephone. You feel times have changed and your parents are old-fashioned. You go to a neighbor's house "to use the phone." The neighbor discovers you are using the phone to call guys and also knows that your parents do not approve or allow it.

1. In what position do you place the neighbor?

2. Do you know why your parents do not want you to phone guys?

3. Do you open discussions with your parents, or just complain to your friends?

4. Do you expect parents to automatically know how you feel? Why or why not?

5. Will your parents trust you if they find out?

6. Did you consider the consequences of being found out?

Matthew 25:34-40

Respect for Others

Your youth group goes on a retreat. You find yourself the only person from your group in a discussion group. You are not being included so you speak up but the others ignore you. You ask a question or make a suggestion. They pour cold water on your idea. You attempt to sit closer to the nucleus of the group and someone pulls the chair out from under you just as you sit down.

1. How did you feel?

2. Could you have done anything to improve your situation?

3. What should the group have done?

4. Did it upset you differently coming from a church group rather than a school group?

5. If you had been part of the antagonizing group, what would or could you have done to improve the situation?

6. Have you ever been part of a group that excluded someone? How did you feel? What were your thoughts? Your actions?

7. Would a Christian react differently?

WAR GAMES

This is a good way to lead into a discussion on the morality of war. The group is divided in half, and a leader is chosen for each group. The two groups represent nations. One nation is told that it is a Christian nation and the other is not told whether it is or not.

The Christian nation is told that it has just been attacked by the other nation. The attacking nation then leaves the room and decides just how much destruction has occurred in the initial attack. They return and announce that to the Christian nation. The Christian nation must then meet and decide what it will do to retaliate or to respond to the attack. After they announce what they have done to the other nation, that nation then meets and the process continues. Once any nation declares that it has wiped out the entire enemy nation (like with a huge nuclear attack), then the game is over. Killing the other country's leader also ends the game.

After this, discuss the decision-making process that was used during the game. Was the Christian nation trying to use Christian principles, and if so,

what were those principles? What about the other nation; not knowing whether you were Christian or not, what principles did you adopt to guide you in your actions? Are there any Christian nations today? Is it possible to run a country on Christian principles?
Sidney Forsyth

THE FOOD STORE ROBBERY

This is an excellent situational story centered around the issue of stealing. There are many subtopics that can be discussed, such as the corporate structure, family stress, justice, and law and order.

To use with your group, simply tell the story as it is presented on page 141, and discuss the questions that are provided (or any other questions that may arise). You might find it useful to distribute copies to each person. As you will discover, the circumstances of the story present some very difficult problems not unlike those that we have to deal with every day of our lives. The answers are not as clear as we would often like for them to be, which is the beauty of an exercise such as this. It is through struggles with the hard questions that we grow and learn.

The story involves seven people:

The husband, Ed

The injured child

The teenage driver

The wife, Hilda

The plant manager

The banker

The food store owner

Questions for discussion:

- **Which person was most responsible for the robbery of the food store? Rank the characters from most responsible to least responsible. Give reasons for the order that you chose.**
- **Was Ed wrong to rob the food store? Why or why not?**
- **Hilda was certainly a nagging wife, but didn't she have something to nag about? Do you feel any compassion for Hilda?**
- **Do you agree with Hilda's refusal to accept welfare?**
- **What do you think Hilda did after Ed was arrested? What should she have done?**
- **If you were the food store operator, would you press charges?**
- **If you were the judge at the trial and Ed confessed to the crime, what sentence would you hand down?**
- **Which person was the worst? Which was the best? Why?**
- **What is your concept of "justice?"**

Jody Kerr

MONITORING YOUR MORALS

The true-false questions on page 142 are to be answered individually by the members of the group, then discussed collectively by the entire group. Explain that the answers given should be honest opinions, not answers which might be considered correct by the church or youth director. Be prepared to work through each question thoroughly in the discussion period. *Bob Gleason*

PAUL'S DILEMMA

You will find a contrived situation involving a teenage boy named Paul on page 143. He faces a problem for which he receives advice from friends and relatives holding various points of view. This situation can be either read to the group by the leader or acted out in a sort of role-play. After presenting the situation to the group, including all the advice which Paul receives, discuss the questions provided with the entire group.

Questions for discussion:

- **Evaluate each of the arguments given to Paul. What are the strengths, if any, and what are the weaknesses, if any?**
- **Which person do you most agree with? Why? Least agree with? Why?**
- **What answer would you have given Paul? What would you do in Paul's situation?**
- **Is there a right answer to Paul's dilemma?**
- **What were Paul's alternatives?**
- **If Paul had weighed all the alternatives and made what you considered to be a wrong choice, what would you say to Paul if you were:**

  a. a close friend

  b. a girlfriend

FOOD STORE ROBBERY

The automobile factory where Ed has worked for the past 10 years is experiencing hard times because of a recession and is forced to lay off a number of employees. Management has left the responsibility to each of the plant managers. Ed's plant manager has been protecting his job for a long time and has always been worried that Ed might get his job. He lays Ed off to remove this threat.

Ed cannot find a job anywhere. After 18 months of unsuccessful job hunting, his unemployment runs out and Ed is forced to sell his insurance so his family can have food and make the house payments. When that money runs out, Ed and Hilda discuss the possibility of applying for welfare. Hilda will not hear of it. She considers it degrading and a sign of failure. In fact, Hilda considers Ed a failure and constantly nags him to do something about their situation. She threatens to leave him.

One evening one of Ed's children is playing in the street. (The child had been warned many times to stay out of the street.) A stolen car driven by a 19-year-old runaway runs into Ed's child, seriously injuring him. The child requires hospitalization and the bills will be enormous. Of course the runaway does not have any insurance or money.

In desperation Ed goes to the bank to apply for a loan. Ed does have good credit, but the banker refuses the loan. (The banker has involved the bank's money in a number of questionable investments and has overextended the bank's loan limit.)

Ed explains the situation to Hilda. She explodes into a rage, hysterically threatens to leave, and calls Ed a failure and a no-good who doesn't care about his child and his wife. She gives him an ultimatum to be gone when she returns and stomps out of the house. Distraught and confused, Ed robs the local food store. When his wife returns he shows her the money and explains that a close friend loaned it to them. They use the money to purchase food and clothing for the children, but within a day Ed is arrested by the police. He explains, "All I wanted to do was feed my family."

After discussions with the city officials, the prosecutor decides to drop the case if Ed will pay back the money and seek counseling with the welfare department. But the store owner is a strong law and order advocate and refuses to drop the charges. He believes that Ed is a thief and ought to be punished. Ed is forced to go to trial where he pleads guilty and is sentenced by the judge.

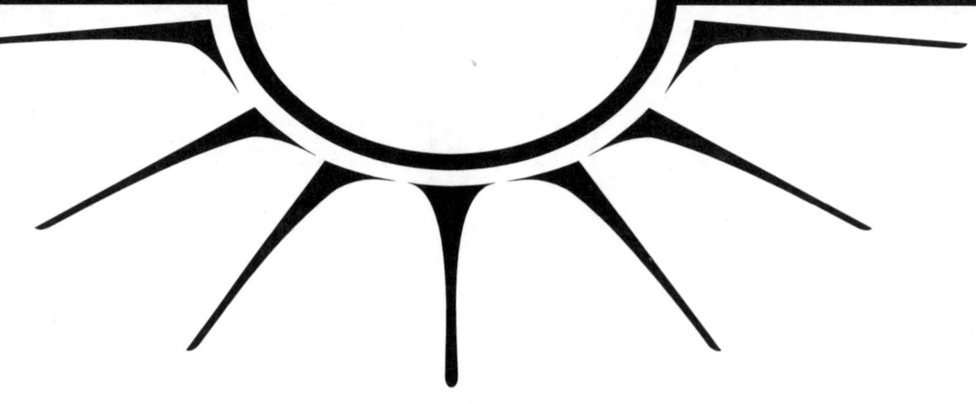

MONITORING YOUR MORALS

1. Overeating is as wrong as smoking or drinking. _____

2. While your father was walking home from work one night, a robber came from the shadows and demanded all his money. Your father gave his wallet to the robber. He looked in the wallet and asked "Is this all the money you have?" Your father said, "Yes." The thief crept away satisfied, but your father had lied to the thief: he had a 20 tucked away in his shirt pocket. This was wrong. _____

3. To goof off on your job is as wrong as if you stole money from your boss. _____

4. There are degrees of sin with God and he won't punish us for the little ones. _____

5. Killing a man is justified when a person is called by his government to defend his country. _____

6. As Christians we are to obey all people who are in a position of authority over us. This means police officers, parents, teachers, youth directors, etc. _____

7. You are late for church so instead of driving at the 45 mile per hour speed limit, you drive at 50. Because you are going to church this is not wrong. _____

8. Going into your history final, you are just squeezing by with a C. Passing or failing this test could mean the difference between passing or failing this course. There are several questions you don't know, so you look on your neighbor's paper, an A student, and copy from him. When you get your paper back you found that you would have flunked without the correct answers from your neighbor's paper. Cheating was justified in this case. _____

9. You are very much in love with your girlfriend and plan to get married. On a date you get carried away and she gets pregnant. Because you love her as your wife-to-be, the act was not wrong. _____

10. There is a guy at school that really gets on your nerves. If there was ever a person who you hated, it would be this guy. The feeling you have for this guy is as wrong as if you killed him. _____

PAUL'S DILEMMA

Paul is a junior in high school. He is relatively well accepted by his friends. He makes average grades and is a member of several school organizations: choir, the basketball team, and student council. He has been friends with one group of five guys through most of his junior high and high school years. His parents are respectable members of the community. His father is a lawyer and his mother the secretary of a popular civic organization. The whole family is active in a local church where his father and mother hold leadership positions.

Paul's problem is this: he has been close with this group of five guys for a long time and their values have always been quite similar. But lately the guys have been experimenting with drugs and alcohol. Although Paul has participated until now, he is beginning to feel more and more uncomfortable. He has discussed the problem with his buddies and they do not feel uncomfortable. If Paul decides to stop going along with the group, it may cost him his relationship with the guys. He approaches a number of acquaintances seeking advice:

Youth Group Sponsor: He is concerned that Paul may get sucked into the habits of his buddies. His advice is to break the relationship pointing out that Jesus never allowed relationships to get in the way of his convictions. He refers to others, such as Martin Luther, who did what they knew was right regardless of the circumstances.

Paul's Uncle: His favorite uncle, who is also a lawyer, listens nervously as Paul confides that he really doesn't see what is so wrong with all of these things. It's just that he doesn't feel right. Paul's uncle immediately attempts to point out through statistics the dangers of marijuana and alcohol. He attempts to rationally investigate all of the phony justifications for using grass and alcohol and makes a case for abstinence, the only really logical and safe conclusion.

Sunday School Teacher: He points out that you are either "with" Christ or "against" him. You either are committed or not committed. What is at stake is behaving like a Christian should and renouncing every appearance of evil or capitulating and being worldly and "sold out" to sin.

Youth Director: He relates to Paul a true story of a close friend who was bothered by the direction his friends were going, but didn't have enough courage to stand for his conviction. The result was that he became heavily involved in drugs, disgraced his family and friends, and eventually committed suicide. He suggests that Paul has great potential to influence hundreds of young people and he could blow his chances of potential greatness. In fact, the youth director confides, he was just going to ask Paul to take a leadership position in the group.

A Neighbor (who is also a policeman): He confronts Paul with the fact that he saw a report on some of Paul's friends who are on the brink of getting into trouble with drugs, etc. The neighbor is concerned that Paul understands the legal implications of his friends' behavior and counsels him to stay away lest he and his friends get busted. He then goes on to explain that he personally does not see what's wrong with a kid experimenting with marijuana, but that we must all obey the laws or there would be total chaos. Laws are there for our protection and we must follow them.

The Pastor: He points out that the church has always spoken out against non-Christian behavior and that ever since the church was founded such things were not acceptable for church members. The purity of the church, whether it's a local body of believers or the church universal, has always been a focal point for "our doctrine."

His Girlfriend: She points out that she does not care what anyone else says, he must do what's right. If he made the wrong choice, he would never be able to live with himself. She reminds him that if his parents knew he was experimenting with marijuana and alcohol, "his mother would be crushed" and "his father would be humiliated." "Besides," she says, "What about me and our relationship? You know what I think of yourgroup of friends and what they are doing, and if I meant very much to you, you would think carefully about what you're doing."

Paul's Older Brother: He thinks Paul is too narrow and making an issue out of nothing. He feels Paul is experiencing false guilt produced by the unenlightened views of their parents. He points out that he regularly smokes pot and drinks and still maintains a high grade point average and also holds down a good job. He counsels Paul not to get involved in heavy drugs or excessive drinking but warns him not to sacrifice his good friendships for a nonissue.

c. a parent

d. a brother/sister

e. a youth director

f. a minister

g. a school counselor

Al Simons

EUTHANASIA ON TRIAL

This mock trial idea not only raises a very timely and difficult issue but allows the entire youth group to participate in the decision-making process.

The setting is a trial or hearing on the issue of euthanasia (this could also work with any other sticky issue). Part of the youth group is designated the jury, the rest are court room observers. Youth sponsors can be used as the lawyers to present the pro and con sides of the issue to the jury. Youth group members can be chosen to represent family members in the three cases described. The youth minister or another sponsor plays the part of the judge. (It is important that the judge be acquainted thoroughly with the issue along with portions of Scripture that are applicable.)

The job of the lawyers is to present a convincing case for either the pro or con side of the issue using whatever sources they can find to prove their argument. They can also call witnesses (youth group members who represent family members in the cases described) to bolster their case. Of course, there should be opportunity for cross examination. After both cases have been presented and summary statements made, the jury adjourns for a matter of minutes to vote on the issues. The jury is not deciding on the pro and con of euthanasia, rather on Case A, B, and C. The jury should then vote on each case and give the results to the judge who will read the results to the courtroom. (There should be little or no discussion by the jury while deliberating. Save that for the discussion with the whole group later.)

The entire group then discusses the decisions. The judge can then wrap up the discussion with some biblical insights without telling the group the conclusions they should have reached. Let the young people go home and struggle with their decision themselves.

Cases for the jury to consider:

1. Hortense is a severely retarded, 19-year-old girl. She has control of her motor (muscular) faculties but seems to be around the age of one or two mentally. Through nearly eight years of therapy, doctors and aides have taught her to button the buttons on her clothes. The method they used was much like the method a dog trainer would use to teach a dog tricks: stimulus-response. She might be able to be trained to hold down some extremely simple job on a factory production line, but it would take years to train her. Those years would take large amounts of money both from taxpayers and family, and in addition, it would take precious time from a doctor or psychiatrist who could be spending his time on someone who was more promising. The family of this patient has asked that they be released from any legal holdings on Hortense or, if that is not possible, that she be mercifully put to death. The jury must decide.

2. Alex is a successful 47-year-old business man. He went in to the doctor for a routine check-up and the doctor found a large lump in the middle of Alex's back. X-rays showed cancer of some sort. A biopsy was done and the cancer was determined to be malignant. It was too far along to take out, so radiation therapy was performed. That was unsuccessful and a month later Alex was in the hospital in a coma. Doctors believe that he won't live beyond six months, but he could be given medication (morphine) to lessen the pain. He would have to remain in the intensive care ward till death ($120/day), plus the family would have to bear the cost of doctor bills and medication totaling thousands of dollars. This family could bear the expense but they cannot bear to see the pain that Alex is in, and so they ask the doctors to either (a) give Alex a lethal dose of morphine, or (b) discontinue all medications and care and let him die naturally and, hopefully, quickly. The jury must decide.

3. A baby is born to John and Jane Doe. They have waited so long for a child and both eagerly await the time when they can go on home with their new arrival. The shape of the baby's head bothered a couple of the doctors and routine tests were run to test the baby's brain waves. It was found that during delivery the baby's skull contracted too tightly around the brain and the child suffered severe brain damage to the point that it will be a vegetable. The baby

remained in intensive care while John and Jane went home to think the whole matter over. They are just a young couple, and have no way financially of putting the child in an institution. They decided to go to the doctor and ask if the child could be put out of its misery, and they would try to have another child. It was brought before the courts and the jury must decide.

Lawyer's case against euthanasia:

1. Euthanasia could easily be misconstrued as a mere recommendation of suicide or of wholesale murder of aged or infirmed people.

2. How could a weak and/or unbalanced mind, incapable of weighing aright the conditions which may be held to render death more desirable than life, make this momentous decision?

Case-in-point: One miraculous cure given a great deal of publicity was that of a clergyman's wife who, in a widely circulated letter, had begged for "scientific kindness" by her physicians to terminate her suffering and give her painless death. Many laymen supported her arguments, but the physicians ignored them and succeeded in restoring her health. She rejoiced that her pleas were disregarded.

3. What about the obstacles concerning practical applications in our modern society—who will determine who is to die and how?

4. If infants born with retardation or complete body disfigurement are put to death under a Euthanasia Law, this would lead to a degrading of morality, a new form of infanticide. In other words, belated abortion.

5. One alternative is segregation and special training instead of euthanasia. For example, the feeble-minded can be made actually useful, as many of them have considerable physical skill, and they seem to be happy under such conditions.

6. We should hold on to the value of the individual and the value of life at any cost.

7. Wouldn't a pro-euthanasia morality have a hard time dealing with incidences of mistakes and/or abuse?

8. What about the danger that legal machinery initially designed to kill those who are a pain to themselves may some day engulf those who are a pain to others?

Lawyer's case for euthanasia:

1. What type of life would a baby have who was born a complete vegetable—the issue is quality of life, rather than quantity.

2. Special segregation and training involves heavy expense of all sorts: emotional and economic.

3. A carefully controlled system of euthanasia would eliminate the most hopeless cases at once.

4. The quality of life of those around the incapacitated individual will be adversely affected if the individual is left to linger in pain.

5. There are those who are afflicted with incurable and painful diseases who want to die quickly. A law which tries to prevent such sufferers from achieving this quick death, and thereby forces other people who care for them to watch their pointless pain helplessly, is a very cruel law! In such cases the sufferer may be reduced to an obscene image of a human being, a lump of suffering flesh eased only by intervals of drugged stupor.

6. There should be a concern for human dignity, an unwillingness to let the animal pain disintegrate a person.

7. Suffering is evil. If it were not, why then do we expend so much energy in trying to relieve it?

8. The goal of the Euthanasia society, "would permit an adult person of sound mind, whose life is ending with much suffering, to choose between an easy death and a hard one, and to obtain medical aid in implementing that choice."

Stephen Wing

FREE ASSOCIATION GAME

This game can help your youth group get in touch with differing world views. For a warm-up, have each person write down the first word that comes to their mind after each of the following words is said:

Fish	Pastor	Neck
Brother	God	Acne
Car	Pit	

After the list has been given, have the group share their free-association responses. Then divide the group into three small groups and give them the following instructions:

You have been divided into three groups each with a different identity. The game we're playing depends on your individual responses as a member of your group. It is very important that you do not discuss your responses with any member of your group or with the members of other groups.

Now give each group the following descriptions and give them time to read and think about the character they are to be:

- **Group One.** For a moment, forget your past and present life. Place yourself in the position of a person who has never known any life beyond that of the ghetto. With this in mind respond in one-word associations to the list of words you are about to hear.
- **Group Two.** Think of yourself as being a parent. Consider the responsibilities entailed in making decisions that may affect your child for the rest of his/her life. How would you respond to the following list? (Use one-word association answers.)
- **Group Three.** Put yourself in the position of being a drug pusher. Your survival depends upon your contact with street people. What would be your responses to the following words? (Use one-word association answers.)

Then have them free-associate the following words:

Sex	Religion	Crime
Future	Dollar	Doctor
Law	Cheat	Black
Death	Health	Home

After everyone has responded to the complete list of words, compare each other's responses, first as individuals within each group and then as groups. This should lead to a very lively discussion. *John Boller, Jr.*

DECISION

Kids have 10 minutes to decide which of the following things they consider to be the most harmful. Their job is to rank order each one using the number one by the one they think is the most harmful; number two by the second most harmful, etc. Afterward, discuss the results. Define "harmful" as it relates to all areas of life.

- Getting drunk
- Moderate drinking (alcohol)
- Lack of exercise
- Cigarette smoking
- Guilt feelings
- Poor eating habits (types of food, how eaten, etc.)
- Marijuana
- Drugs (amphetamines, pot, etc.)
- Overwork
- Lack of medical attention when necessary
- Premarital sex
- Nervous anxiety and tension
- Fatigue, caused by never getting enough sleep
- Overeating

You can add others. *Bobbie Yagel*

IF SURVEY

Surveys are excellent ways of getting your audience involved. The following survey is very successful when used either as a written survey, or presented as discussion questions. Everyone has feelings and opinions for each question. This survey can be followed up with a short talk by you or a lesson on self-acceptance, happiness, God's will, and the like.

- If you could live in any period of history, when would it be?
- If you could go anywhere in the world, where would you go?
- If I gave you $3000, what would you spend it on?
- If you could change anything about yourself, what would you change?
- If you could be someone else, who would you be?
- If you could have any question answered, what would it be?

VALUE TRADING GAME

Print up play money from pages 148 and 149. You might have 100 stars, 100 light bulbs, 100 keys, etc. The total number of bills you print should be about 15 times the number of kids participating.

To begin the game distribute the money to your group any way you want. One way is to divide it up, put it into envelopes, and pass out the envelopes. Another good way is to just throw the whole works out and let the kids catch it or pick it up off the floor. It is not important that it be distributed evenly.

The first thing the kids must do is to decide which bills are of value and which are not. This is left completely up to them (for the time being). They must attach value to the symbols on a scale of "minus 100" to "plus 100" points. In other words, some of the symbols are "good" (1 to 100) and some are "bad" (-1 to -100). The best bill (in their opinion) might be worth 100 while the worst would be -100. Anyway, the kids are given one minute to decide (individually) what each bill is worth.

The second step is to try to accumulate as much value as possible within the time limit. The kids can trade or give away bills to do so. They are encouraged to try to convince each other why a trade would be beneficial. They need a strategy to obtain as many valuable bills as possible and get rid of bad bills that would be minus points. The kids are free to circulate around the room gaining value any way they can, except by mugging and stealing. (Also, no one can throw away bad bills.)

They may also trade with the bank, which is you, the leader. You will give them one of anything for five of anything else. In other words, if a kid is trying to collect stars, he might first get five of some other symbol and trade them to you for a star.

At the end of the time limit (usually around 10 minutes), all the action stops. All the trading ends and you then announce the correct value for each bill and tell the kids to add up their score, depending on what money they have in their possession.

For example:
Star = 25 points
Flag = Minus 50 points
Flower = Zero
Key = 50 points
Cup = 100 points
Heart = 75 points

The values which you announce are final, regardless of what each person thought the values would or should be. (The values you announce are left up to you, incidentally.) The kids add up their scores and the highest score wins a prize.

You will notice that you, the leader, are in complete control of the game. You arbitrarily choose when the game is over and the value of each of the symbols on the play money. However, because the kids don't really know what you are going to do, they are in a sense playing your game by their rules. They have to.

The discussion:

- **Ask several kids for their interpretations of the symbols and why they placed values on them as they did.**
- **Do you think the final standard was fair?**
- **What kind of strategy did you use to come out ahead?**
- **Did you play by the values you really believed to be right, or by the values you thought should be or probably would be right?**

The wrap-up:

The wrap-up is the most important part of this simulation, as you attempt to tie together the loose ends. Although the form of the presentation is left somewhat up to you, the following points are offered as a guide:

- As in the game, people in real life place values on many different things. Things that are truly valuable are often considered unimportant and vice versa. Archbishop William Temple has said that prevailing values of modern society can be likened to a jewelry store that has been broken into by vandals. Instead of stealing anything, the vandals simply switched around the price tags so that things that were of value were regarded as cheap and things that were really worthless were put on premium. (Give some examples of this.)
- In the game you just played, you played by your own rules. You had no choice. But there *was* a standard. You either won or lost depending on whether or not you were in agreement with that standard. In life, people usually play by their own rules, too. And like in the game, there is a standard. God has given us a guidebook for living in his Word, the Bible. The game was a dictatorship, and you had no control over the outcome, but God has given us complete control over our own lives. It is in this sense that God created us in his image. He has shown us the "standard," but given us a choice. We can play by God's rules or by our own.
- A common tendency among Christians is not being able to determine when a standard is God's and when it is ours. In other words, we often (through tradition, etc.) make our standards God's standards. (Such as the issue of whether or not a Christian should go to a dance.) Have your group make a list of commonly accepted Christian "standards" and other traditional Christian beliefs and have them categorize these as a "God standard" (detailed instruction provided in the Bible) or a "man standard" (no direct reference to it in the Bible). The question is not whether or not the standard is "right" or "wrong," but "what is its origin?"
- God not only gave us a guide for living in his Word, but he also sent an example in his son, Jesus Christ. We can invite Christ into our lives and then begin to live with his direction. Christ can begin to control your life if you let him and then his values begin to be your values. Discuss the life of Christ; where he placed value, what his priorities were, etc.

Earthling Collage

Divide the group into smaller groups of three or four people. Hand each group a stack of magazines and newspapers (magazines heavy on advertisements are best). Ask each group to pretend that they are Martians who have spent several days observing earthlings' habits. To illustrate what earthlings are like, they have brought back to Mars photographic evidence (pictorial advertisements devoid of words). Each group then tears out a collage of advertisements and, from first-time observation, labels each picture in terms of what they see. A first impression of what one sees in a pictorial advertisement without the attached brand names and flowery phrases can provide quite a social and often hilarious commentary on our priorities and style of living. *Glen Miller*

Managing Your Time

Young people are no different than adults when it comes to the proper management of their time (high school and collegians, especially). A survey is on page 151 which could be given each student to fill out and then follow up with discussion and helps by you, the leader, on time management. Related Scripture: Romans 12:2, Colossians 4:5 (Phillips). *Bob Griffin*

No Other Gods

Read the second commandment given to Moses to your group or study together the story of the golden calf which followed the receiving of the Ten Commandments. Then give each youth the necessary materials to sculpture a modern day image out of balsa wood or clay. The sculptured images can be realistic or symbolic but should represent things that young people often put before God. A discussion can follow, with each person sharing his image. The images can further be dedicated to God by their destruction. For example, the wooden ones could be burned or the clay ones could be heaped together and remolded into a symbol of the faith. *Rose Tozer*

Life Skills

Copy page 152 and give each person 10 cards. On each card the person fills in a word or two that describes who or what he or she is. (Example: "I am a student," or "I am an American," etc.) After each of the cards has been filled out (allow five minutes for this) each person stacks the cards in the order of the characteristics he would most easily give up in his life, to those he would least be willing to give up. In other words the card on the bottom would be something about him that he would find most difficult to give up (such as "I am a Christian").

Next, divide up into small groups no larger than eight per group. Each person then shares their top card with the others in the group. This is done by going around the circle, with each person laying their first card on a table in the center and commenting on it if they want to. Then they go around the circle again, this time laying down their second card, and so on until all 10 cards have been revealed.

The value of this game is dependent on the attitudes of the individual players. Some people find it difficult to even write down the things that describe them. But this can be a very effective means to helping people open up to each other in a new way, thus deepening relationship on a human level. A game such as this can be followed up by a discussion on the whole person—the idea that all of us are made up of many characteristics, all of which are important to God. There is often agony in having to give up even one-tenth of your personal identity. Some people may have written down things that they would like very much to give up in their lives. Allow them to share their thoughts with others and perhaps discuss ways to accomplish this. *Paul Loewen*

The Moral of the Story

Read a story (proverb, fable, biblical, or make-believe) and leave out the moral at the end, if there is one. Challenge each person to write down what they think the moral of the story could be. They can then share them and discuss. It's amazing how many different things you can learn from one simple story. *Nido Qubein*

Picture That

Hang various pictures on the wall. Have each youth pick a picture and think of a one-word description for

MANAGING YOUR TIME

The Survey

1. List everything that you have to do in an average week.

2. List everything that you would like to do in an average week.

3. List all that you would like to be personally.

4. List all you could do each week to help develop the above.

5. Having thought through the above carefully, now review all your lists and assign each a priority; for example, number the most important No. 1 and so on.

6. Again, return to your lists and decide how much time would be necessary each week (more or less) to accomplish each item listed.

7. On a separate sheet, make a time chart (Note to leader: you can print these up ahead of time and provide them) which shows each day and the hours available in each. Beginning with your top priorities, pencil in the time you would like to give each area of importance. As you begin to eliminate the less important, you will find it necessary to make changes. For example, you may have to cut back time allotted to a "top priority" so that you can squeeze in something important enough not to be entirely left out of your schedule.

LIFE SKILLS

I am a

____

I am a

____

I am a

____

I am a

____

I am a

____

I am a

____

I am a

____

I am a

____

I am a

____

I am a

____

that picture. In turn have each youth present his word and let the youths guess which picture the word describes. With a good imagination interesting discussions can be generated by asking the youths why they chose their word. *James Brown*

PRIORITY AUCTION

The following is a delightful way of enabling a youth group to set priorities in their plans for future programs, without having to first overcome the usual resistance to the work that this task entails. This procedure could also be used for any process of ranking or priority setting.

1. Distribute fake money in equal proportions to the group members.

2. Distribute a list of the tasks, programs, or whatever is to be ranked according to priorities to the group members.

3. Explain that the list is like a catalog issued before an art auction, and that the members are going to bid on each item listed. The members can bid individually or pool their money and bid as small groups, but they can spend during the auction only as much money as they have been given. This will mean that each member must rank in his own mind which items are most valuable to him, and bid accordingly.

4. Make sure that each member understands each item listed, and then proceed with the auction, item by item. Make sure to collect the money from the top bidder as each item is sold, and list the selling price. This list, giving relative amounts in dollar value, can then be a means of ranking the items according to the group's sense of priorities. *John Bristow*

FACE TO FACE

This game is great for giving people a nonthreatening way to communicate what they believe. It's also great for helping people discover how well they know each other. The game is played by two, three, or four people with a regular deck of playing cards. Each player receives cards of the same suit, except the jack. Jacks and jokers are not used. The players sit face-to-face and the first player says a sentence expressing an attitude about something. These statements may describe emotions ("I feel fine when I am alone"), opinions ("I am against capital punishment"), reactions ("I blush when someone praises me"), tastes or preferences ("I like working outside"), values ("I feel it's more important to have a good reputation than to be rich"), or beliefs ("I believe in reincarnation"). Each player indicates his position on the statement made by choosing a card between 1 (the ace serves as 1) and 10. He chooses the card from 1 through 10 on this basis:

1 indicates total disagreement

2 or 3 indicates strong disagreement

4 or 5 indicates slight disagreement

6 or 7 indicates slight agreement

8 or 9 indicates strong agreement

10 indicates total agreement

The players then place the cards they have chosen down to their left. For the same statement, each player chooses a card which corresponds to the position taken by the other person, that is, the card she thinks the other player chose. The player places this second card face down to her right. The other player does the same thing: he places the "me" card to the left and the "you" card to the right. The players then turn over the cards, taking care not to reverse their positions.

Each player counts his points by noting the difference between the value of the right hand card (the one by which he describes his partner's position and the card his partner has placed before this card, namely his partner's left hand card. For example, let's say John and Louise are playing face-to-face. John

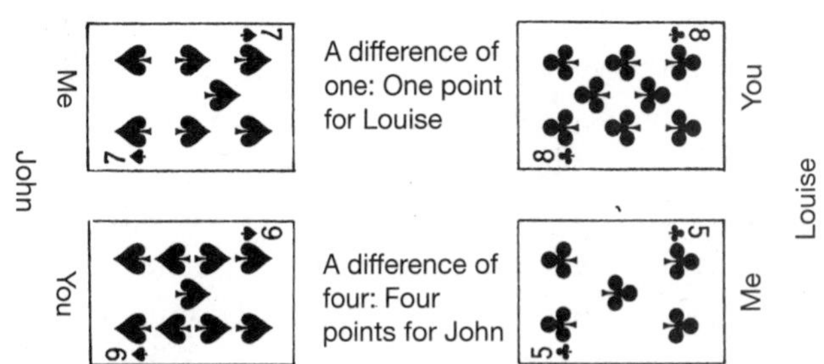

places a 9 to his right, thinking that Louise strongly agrees with the statement just said. Louise, however, has rated her own position with a 5. John's score is 4. Meanwhile, Louise has placed an 8 on her right to indicate what, in her estimation, is John's position on the statement. John has rated himself with a 7. So, the score for Louise is 1.

The players note their scores, take back their cards, and the next player makes a statement. Once again, each player lays down two cards as described above. Points are counted again and the first person or pair to obtain a score of 50 or 100 points loses the game.

If a player does not want to reveal her position on the statement given or to guess the position of her partner, she puts down a king or queen. The score for that player is then the highest of all other scores on the table for that particular round.

If there are three players, one person makes a statement and the two others play face-to-face, placing their cards and noting their scores. Then the next person makes a statement and the other two play face-to-face, etc. If there are four players, the two people playing face-to-face add up their points. This pair plays against the other pair. *John Boller*

Problem Letter

One way to present a case study to your group is in the form of a letter. Copy page 154 and present it to the youth group for their answers. If you create your own and the case is an actual one, take care to fictionalize it enough to hide the identity of the person seeking help. You don't want kids playing a guessing game as to who the mystery person is. That kind of thing could be disastrous. You should make every effort to keep from revealing the identity of any actual person who might be involved.

After the letter is presented to the group, it can be read aloud and the problems discussed, seeking some answers to resolve the issues presented. One approach might be to break into small groups to work on answers. The leader must take care to ensure the answers that arise apply to the problems and also that the group is not just swapping ignorance—a lot of head knowledge or advice-giving. The key is the type of questions the leader may ask. For example, "Why do you think that?" or "How would Christ respond?" Also emphasize the practical by asking, "What things have you found to work in such situations?" Be careful to stimulate up-to-date and down-to-earth, meaningful responses.

The letter on page 154 is a sample of one used before. It should appear to be as real as possible. That way kids are more serious about helping out with some good advice. You might even want to give some background information on the person the letter is from, again without revealing anything that would tip off kids as to who it is. *Alvie Robbins*

Foto-Match

Hang up 20 or so photos of people (all kinds...old, young, attractive, ugly, fat, slim, wealthy, poor, etc.). The first week the pictures are displayed, have the kids write descriptions of each person based on what they see in the picture. Collect them all and during the following week, combine all the individual descriptions into a concise paragraph that accurately reflects the group consensus. Attach the descriptions to each picture for the next meeting. Have the students look at the photos with descriptions carefully (make sure they are numbered) and then answer the following questions:

- **Choose five people you would want to travel with for one year. Why?**
- **Is there any one person you would not want anything to do with? Why?**
- **Who, if any, would you be willing to marry?**
- **Who, if any, would you worship with?**
- **Which person do you think you could really like? Why?**
- **If only five others and yourself were allowed to live and the others executed, which five would stay with you? Why?**

You could have your group go through the questions again and decide how their parents would respond. And, of course, you can easily come up with other questions equally as good as these. *Pat Cox*

Gospel According to Dear Abby

Select letters from "Dear Abby" and "Ann Landers" columns, which reflect problems relevant to your youth group. Then read one of the letters to your group without the columnist's reply. (If you have a large group, give one letter to each small group.) Then discuss how they think Jesus would have answered the letter. After sufficient discussion, read the columnist's reply and compare her answer with Jesus' hypothetical answer. Discuss the differences, if any.

Read as many letters as time allows, skipping the ones that don't generate any interest. Another

Problem Letter

Dear Alvie,

How are you doing? You know I have been having problems at home and I value your opinion more than anyone else's that I know. I know that if I give you a problem to solve or whatever, you can take it and look at it objectively. I think that is real good.

Well first of all, my parents tend to put their beliefs, convictions, or whatever on me. Now I realize that they have experienced some things that I haven't and that I never may, but I feel that they are sheltering me too much. For example, no guy is allowed over here if they aren't at home. This right here insults me and also hurts me (let alone annoys me). It insults me because it infers they don't have faith in the type of people I choose for friends. Whenever I ask them about it, they always say, "What will people say," or "What will the neighbors think," or else "We are only trying to protect you from a bad situation." Those are exact quotes.

Now, I understand I am their daughter and that they are responsible for me, but why do they have to carry it so far? I'd like to know what they are going to do in a year when I have my own apartment and I can do whatever I please (to a certain extent).

People tell me to grin and bear it a year longer but I live right now, not in the future, and I don't care to live under such tight circumstances. I'm not saying I don't have freedom because I have some—like I drive the car to school every day, but Dad uses that as a string to get me to do what he wants. It's like a threat every time I don't comply with what he wants.

I guess what I am asking for is advice on how I can think for myself and not have to be protected. One of the latest things that happened was this Sunday. I told them that they didn't have to worry about trusting me, because I didn't ever try to cover up anything from them. I told them that I have smoked and drank and smoked dope. Then they thought I was some sinner and that I needed to become closer to God. They kept me up 'till midnight preaching at me and telling me how bad and how wrong I was.

First of all, I'll tell you my feeling on smoking, etc. I think smoking cigarettes is bad for a person and it is a habit I hope I never have and, no, I don't smoke. I've tried it and I didn't think it was too cool.

I drink every now and then and I don't feel it is wrong for me. What I think would be wrong is for me to get drunk. That is one thing I just don't dig and I can't see it—having a hangover and everything else that goes along with it.

I guess you could call me a social drinker. I'll have a beer or whatever if I am out with kids but I very seldom do—like maybe one or two times a month. In essence, I feel drinking is fine with moderation. But what about reputation?

Smoking dope is a constant front to me. Kids are always doing it and I say no. I've smoked it more than once but it didn't affect me. It was just like smoking hot air. The last time I did was last summer and I haven't since. I don't know if grass is right or wrong. That is just one thing I can't decide on. I don't really care, because if I want to smoke it I can and if I don't want to, then I won't. I'm not planning on it. It doesn't turn me on—neither does it turn me off.

Alvie, what I wish you would do is give me your views on the three previous things and also give me some advice on how I can get along better with my parents.

You are probably wondering about my Christian life. Well, I know God is there and if I want him I can get him. I try to read my Bible in the morning and at night. Sometimes I fail because I am tired or hurried. Praying is a struggle for me, because I have not found any effective way to communicate with God and Christ. Sometimes I wonder if I love God. I know the Bible says, "If you love me, you will keep my commandments," but what are they? I really would like to have a personal relationship with God but I am not sure how. If I did know how, I don't know if I would be willing to put out the effort. Maybe you could advise on this also. I would appreciate it greatly.

Well, I guess the last topic of discussion is Steve. He comes and sees me every Saturday. This weekend he is taking me down to Junction City to meet his parents. I really like him a lot, possibly love him more than just a friend. I don't want to end this relationship ever and neither does he. It's a type of agreement between Steve and me. I someday want to marry him if things work out the way they have been. Both of us feel the same way about it, and we are willing to wait for things to work out the way that is best, which wouldn't be until after we both graduate this year. If you would, please pray that I can be open-minded about this and will do what is best from God's point of view.

I hope this letter hasn't been too exhausting. If you could, please answer me promptly. I realize you have other things to do besides answer letters, but I would be happy if you could just show this some special thought and consideration. However, I will understand if you can't because you are so busy. Thanks for your time and trouble. Hope to hear from you soon.

Your friend,

Jan

twist to this would be to have each individual write his/her response to the Dear Abby letter and then compare each other's responses. Then using each person's letter as a resource, have the group compile a group letter combining the best elements of each individual letter. *Craig Boldman*

VULNERABILITY

BROKEN BANANA

In order for people to really know us, we must "peel off" our outer skin.

To make the point get three bananas. Ahead of time, take one and bruise it badly so that the insides are brown, but the outside doesn't show it. Take another banana and slice it in several places without peeling it. Here's how to do it:

NEEDLE AND THREAD

BANANA CROSS SECTION

Take the needle and thread and "sew" the banana as shown in the diagram. Then grab both ends of the thread and pull. This will slice the banana inside without damaging the skin. Do this in several places.

Now ask the kids to describe the three bananas: How do they look the same and how do they look different? Take the banana which has not been tampered with and peel it. Describe how good it looks, how pure, fresh, and wholesome it is. Now take the smashed up, rotten banana. Peel it and the kids will describe it for you. The inside will be mushy, dark, and rotten. Take the third banana and peel it. As you peel it, the sliced sections will fall off. The kids will be amazed at how you were able to slice it without slicing the skin.

Some questions for discussion:

- **How were the bananas like people?**
- **How can we really get to know people?**
- **What must you do for people to know the real you?**
- **How can you help a person who is hurting on the inside?**
- **How is being vulnerable important for good relationships?**

Matt Boyers

WILL OF GOD

WILL OF GOD

Give a copy of page 157 to each person. Participants should circle yes or no. Then discuss their answers.

THE ENVELOPE, PLEASE

The following idea is designed to stimulate discussion and insight into the subject of God's will. To begin, have the kids write down a question or problem that requires knowledge of the will of God. For example: "Should I go to college next year or should I join the Marines?" If the group feels comfortable doing so, have the kids share these questions with each other.

Next, give each person a sealed envelope with her name on it. Label it "Enclosed: The Will of God." Instruct kids to keep the envelopes sealed for now.

Discuss the following questions:

- **If your envelope truly contained the will of God for your life, what do you think it would say?**
- **What would you like it to say?**
- **Why is it important to seek God's will for questions such as those we expressed? Isn't our own judgement good enough?**
- **Does God always have a will for us in every situation?**

After the discussion, tell kids that, believe it or not, the envelope does contain God's will for them. They can now open up the envelopes. Inside is a piece of paper that reads (in big block letters):

PRAYER **CIRCUMSTANCES**

THE WORD **ADVICE**

THE WILL OF GOD

YES NO 1. Has God ever communicated with you directly?

YES NO 2. Does God have an absolute moral standard for humanity?

YES NO 3. Is humanity responsible to God for its actions?

YES NO 4. Can two people in the same situation be led by God to make opposing decisions?

YES NO 5. Has God already chosen a wife or husband for you?

YES NO 6. If you make a major mistake or a wrong choice, are you forever outside of God's will?

YES NO 7. Have you ever consulted the Bible when making a decision and found help?

YES NO 8. Should God be consulted when you select a career?

YES NO 9. Should God be consulted when you buy clothes?

YES NO 10. Should God be consulted when you choose a deodorant?

Help the kids to see that those four words do indeed represent God's will for their particular situations. Through prayer we make our needs known to God, and God speaks to us when we pray as well. Through the Word we learn basic principles that we know to be the revealed will of God. Through circumstances we see God leading us. This is the "open door, closed door" idea. Through the advice of parents, pastors, and Christian friends, God speaks to us as well. You can elaborate on these.

You can adapt this basic idea any way you wish. You might want to save the envelopes until last—delivered by a mailman of some kind, direct from heaven. The point of the envelopes is to emphasize that God's will is not just an abstract thought but something that God wants us to receive and to understand. *Steven Clouser*

HOW GOD WORKS IN MY LIFE

Have kids write these three column titles across the tops of their papers: MY RESPONSIBILITY; GOD'S RESPONSIBILITY; TOO CLOSE TO CALL.

Then read the following list of responsibilities (or a similar list) asking each person to classify the items by placing them in one of the columns.

Making the decision whether I marry or remain single

Protecting me from drunken drivers

My doing well when I perform a solo

My decision to become a Christian

Keeping me from illness

Keeping me encouraged about the Christian life

Choosing my vocation

My understanding Scripture

My understanding geometry

Keeping me from doubt

My financial condition

My health

Discuss each item and why kids classified these items as they did and why they agree or disagree on the classifications. Discuss how God performs those functions that we feel he is responsible for. This discussion works very well with high school, college age, or adults. Follow up by reading and discussing Psalm 121. *Dan Mutschler*

YOUTH SPECIALTIES TITLES

Professional Resources

Administration, Publicity, & Fundraising (Ideas Library)

Developing Student Leaders

Equipped to Serve: Volunteer Youth Worker Training Course

Help! I'm a Junior High Youth Worker!

Help! I'm a Sunday School Teacher!

Help! I'm a Volunteer Youth Worker!

How to Expand Your Youth Ministry

How to Speak to Youth...and Keep Them Awake at the Same Time

One Kid at a Time: Reaching Youth through Mentoring

A Youth Ministry Crash Course

The Youth Worker's Handbook to Family Ministry

Youth Ministry Programming

Camps, Retreats, Missions, & Service Ideas (Ideas Library)

Compassionate Kids: Practical Ways to Involve Your Students in Mission and Service

Creative Bible Lessons in John: Encounters with Jesus

Creative Bible Lessons in Romans: Faith on Fire!

Creative Bible Lessons on the Life of Christ

Creative Junior High Programs from A to Z, Vol. 1 (A-M)

Creative Meetings, Bible Lessons, & Worship Ideas (Ideas Library)

Crowd Breakers & Mixers (Ideas Library)

Drama, Skits, & Sketches (Ideas Library)

Dramatic Pauses

Facing Your Future: Graduating Youth Group with a Faith That Lasts

Games (Ideas Library)

Games 2 (Ideas Library)

Great Fundraising Ideas for Youth Groups

Great Retreats for Youth Groups

Greatest Skits on Earth

Greatest Skits on Earth, Vol. 2

Holiday Ideas (Ideas Library)

Hot Illustrations for Youth Talks

Incredible Questionnaires for Youth Ministry

Junior High Game Nights

Kickstarters: 101 Ingenious Intros to Just about Any Bible Lesson

Memory Makers

More Great Fundraising Ideas for Youth Groups

More Hot Illustrations for Youth Talks

More Junior High Game Nights

Play It Again! More Great Games for Groups

Play It! Great Games for Groups

Special Events (Ideas Library)

Spontaneous Melodramas

Super Sketches for Youth Ministry

Teaching the Bible Creatively

Up Close and Personal: How to Build Community in Your Youth Group

Wild Truth Bible Lessons

Worship Services for Youth Groups

Discussion Starter Resources

Discussion & Lesson Starters (Ideas Library)

Discussion & Lesson Starters 2 (Ideas Library)

4th-6th Grade TalkSheets

Get 'Em Talking

High School TalkSheets

High School TalkSheets: Psalms and Proverbs

Junior High TalkSheets

Junior High TalkSheets: Psalms and Proverbs

Keep 'Em Talking!

More High School TalkSheets

More Junior High TalkSheets

Parent Ministry TalkSheets

What If...? 450 Thought-Provoking Questions to Get Teenagers Talking, Laughing, and Thinking

Would You Rather...? 465 Provocative Questions to Get Teenagers Talking

Clip Art

ArtSource Vol. 1—Fantastic Activities

ArtSource Vol. 2—Borders, Symbols, Holidays, and Attention Getters

ArtSource Vol. 3—Sports

ArtSource Vol. 4—Phrases and Verses

ArtSource Vol. 5—Amazing Oddities and Appalling Images

ArtSource Vol. 6—Spiritual Topics

ArtSource Vol. 7—Variety Pack

ArtSource Vol. 8—Stark Raving Clip Art

ArtSource CD-ROM (contains Vols. 1-7)

Videos

EdgeTV

The Heart of Youth Ministry: A Morning with Mike Yaconelli

Next Time I Fall in Love Video Curriculum

Understanding Your Teenager Video Curriculum

Student Books

Grow For It Journal

Grow For It Journal through the Scriptures

Wild Truth Journal for Junior Highers